THE
ORAL
HISTORY
COLLECTIONS
of the
MINNESOTA
HISTORICAL
SOCIETY

THE ORAL HISTORY COLLECTIONS of the MINNESOTA HISTORICAL SOCIETY

Compiled by
Lila Johnson Goff
James E. Fogerty

MINNESOTA HISTORICAL SOCIETY PRESS
St. Paul • 1984

Minnesota Historical Society Press, St. Paul 55101

© 1984 by Minnesota Historical Society. All rights reserved

Manufactured in the United States of America

10 9 8 7 6 5 4 3 2 1

Library of Congress Cataloging in Publication Data

Minnesota Historical Society.
    The oral history collections of the Minnesota
Historical Society.

    Includes indexes.
    1. Minnesota--History--Sources--Phonotape catalogs.
2. Minnesota Historical Society--Phonotape catalogs.
3. Oral history--Phonotape catalogs. I. Goff, Lila
Johnson. II. Fogerty, James E., 1945-   . III. Title.
F606.M6635 1984   977.6   84-651

International Standard Book Number 0-87351-170-0

Contents

Foreword

The Oral History Collections of the Minnesota Historical Society describes the tape recorded, oral history interviews that are in the Minnesota Historical Society and the Regional Research Centers. The project to describe some of the society's oral history collections began when James E. Fogerty compiled the 1975 publication, Preliminary Guide to the Holdings of the Minnesota Regional Research Centers. The second such guide, issued by the society in 1980, excluded oral history because the compilation of the present publication was under way. The Oral History Collections, however, includes both the entries from the Preliminary Guide and all interviews that were added to the centers' holdings between 1975 and 1982. It also contains all taped interviews housed at the society in St. Paul.

The term "oral history" has created difficulties for those who have sought to define it. Louis M. Starr of the Columbia University Oral History Office explained it as "primary source material obtained by recording the spoken words -- generally by means of planned,

tape-recorded interviews -- of persons deemed to harbor hitherto unavailable information worth preserving." The term, Starr observed, originated in the 1940s and became so "firmly embedded in the language" that "alternatives like oral documentation and living history have not survived the hour." The commendable flexibility of Starr's definition has served the profession well. Practitioners realized that preservation of oral tradition and personal testimony began in the ancient world centuries before the invention of the tape recorder, that the tape recorder was not the earliest device used to capture sound, and that sound recordings, which are important as primary sources, are not limited to interviews.[1]

Minnesotans first undertook oral history projects in the last century. J. Fletcher Williams, the society's secretary, issued circulars in the 1870s asking pioneers to give "an account of their own personal adventures and experiences in the early settlement of Minnesota." The outcome "was most gratifying," he boasted. "Nearly all kindly responded, some very full and complete, others more meagerly, but all giving valuable information, nowhere else on record, and placing in the archives of this Society a large mass of materials for the early history of the State." Williams himself conducted interviews, but he often converted the gathered data into biographical sketches instead of preserving the original form. He also enlisted others in the cause, urging them to record the reminiscences of the "fast-shortening roll" of pioneers before it was too late.[2]

Williams felt that documentation of the Indian peoples' history was a particularly urgent task. "In a few years more," he wrote in 1879, "when the tremendous wave of immigration now filling the prairie and mining states

---

[1] Louis M. Starr, "Oral History," in Allen Kent, Harold Lancour, and Jay Elwood Daily, eds., Encyclopedia of Library and Information Science, 20:440, 444 (New York, 1977).

[2] Minnesota Historical Society, Annual Report, 1872, 17, 18 (St. Paul, 1873). Many of the biographical sketches appeared in J. Fletcher Williams, A History of the City of Saint Paul to 1875 (Reprint ed., St. Paul, 1983). For an example of a response by a pioneer, see Thomas Henry Armstrong, "Answers to Questionnaire," April 26, 1872, in Biographies File, Division of Archives and Manuscripts, Minnesota Historical Society (DAM-MHS).

shall have surrounded the few remaining tribes, and largely obliterated or destroyed their identity, even more interest and curiosity will be felt regarding them than now." The concern for preserving information about Indian culture led to notable efforts in oral history before and after Williams sounded the alarm. The earliest systematic investigator to enter the field may have been William W. Warren, a Minnesotan of Ojibway-Euro-American heritage. In 1853 he finished a work published as History of the Ojibways. It was, the author stated, "an account of the principal events which have occurred to the Ojibways within the past five centuries, as obtained from the lips of their old men and chiefs who are the repositories of the traditions of the tribe."[3]

Another trail blazer in oral history who chose Indian culture as a field for investigation was Frances Densmore of Red Wing. Early in the twentieth century, she became aware of the culture of Dakota Indians at Prairie Island near her home and began collecting data through observation and from informants. Assisted by a grant made in 1907 by the Bureau of American Ethnology, she bought an Edison Home Phonograph. She then proceeded with her study of the Ojibway, recording their music, taking photographs, and making voluminous notes.[4]

While Densmore expanded her investigations by traveling to many parts of the United States in pursuit of information about several Indian tribes, oral historian Gilbert L. Wilson concentrated largely on Hidatsa and Mandan informants living on the Fort Berthold Reservation in North Dakota. A Presbyterian minister serving churches in Minnesota and North Dakota before becoming professor of anthropology at Macalester College in St. Paul, Wilson entered the field as early as 1905 and later worked under the auspices of the American Museum of Natural History in New York City. On a machine furnished by the museum, he recorded songs on wax cylinders. He also meticulously preserved data on Indian culture in notebooks, reports prepared for the museum, photographs, and drawings made by his artist brother, Frederick.[5]

Other Minnesotans joined the small corps of people amassing documentation through interviews. Among them were Lucy Wilder Morris and other members of the Daughters of the American Revolution who, in the early twentieth century, interviewed dozens of pioneers. Morris then compiled accounts of their experiences into Old Rail Fence Corners, first published in 1914. Included, too, was William W. Folwell, who interviewed extensively while preparing A History of Minnesota, published in four volumes from 1921 to 1930 by the Minneso-

ta Historical Society; his notes are preserved in his papers. Another such researcher was Marjorie Edgar, who from the 1920s collected Finnish folk songs, charms, and proverbs and folk tales about "imaginary animals" of the north woods. Her work in assembling proverbs was done under the auspices of the Writers Project of the Work Projects Administration, a New Deal agency that deployed inquirers to interview members of ethnic groups. Grace Lee Nute, head of the society's Manuscripts Division from 1921 to 1946 and later research associate, was also keenly interested in documentation through interviews. In 1949 she urged the Manuscripts Division to establish an oral history program and ushered in a new era by acquiring a wire recorder for the society.[6]

The society soon switched from wire to tape, and successive generations of tape re-

[3] J. Fletcher Williams, "Proposed Paper on Minnesota Indians," May 5, 1879 -- a memorandum in the John Fletcher Williams Papers, DAM-MHS; William W. Warren, History of the Ojibway People (Reprint ed., St. Paul, 1984).

[4] Nina Marchetti Archabal, "Introduction to the Reprint Edition," in Frances Densmore, Chippewa Customs, i–iv, ix (Reprint ed., St. Paul, 1979). Materials Densmore collected, which include artifacts as well as recordings, notebooks, and other papers, are in the Bureau of American Ethnology, Library of Congress, Minnesota Historical Society, Goodhue County Historical Society, and Museum of the American Indian.

[5] The materials, including copies of reports to the museum, are in the Gilbert Livingstone Wilson Papers, DAM-MHS. See also accessions data in the files of Museum Collections, MHS.

[6] Lucy L. M. Morris, Old Rail Fence Corners (Reprint ed., St. Paul, 1976). For an example of Folwell's notes, see "Mem. of Conversation with Capt. John Tapper, September 25, 1903," in volume 82, William W. Folwell Papers, DAM-MHS. See also Marjorie Edgar, "Finnish Charms and Folk Songs in Minnesota," "Imaginary Animals of Northern Minnesota," "Finnish Proverbs in Minnesota," -- all in Minnesota History, 17:406-410 (December, 1936), 21:353-356 (December, 1940), 24:226-228 (September, 1943); William C. Edgar and Family Papers, DAM-MHS; Writers Project, United States Work Projects Administration, Minnesota, Records, DAM-MHS. Information on the wire recorder is in Manuscripts Division, Quarterly Report, October-December, 1949, Minnesota Historical Society Archives, DAM-MHS.

corders were an advance over the heavy, awkward early models. The oral history program also improved. Most of the few interviews recorded during the 1950s were done without serious preliminary planning and without placement in a context of documentation. In 1955 Helen McCann White conducted a project to collect data on St. Croix Valley lumbering for the Forest History Foundation, Inc., a national organization then housed at the society; the project demonstrated that a major change was taking place. The subject-matter concept, extensive preparation for interviews, and careful selection of informants that characterized the St. Croix Valley project became a standard for the society's program after the establishment of the Oral History Office in 1967. Within a year, Lila Johnson, head of the undertaking, commented that the emphasis had "changed from interviewing elderly individuals on their reminiscences to interviewing several people on specific projects."7

Although the Oral History Office, which soon merged with the Picture Department into the Audio-Visual Library, still conducted single-session interviews, it emphasized subject-matter projects and in-depth, often multisession, interviews with individuals. It continued the "Voices of the Governors" series begun in the early 1960s and initiated others that appear in this guide. To expand the program beyond the capability of the small staff, it contracted with interviewers and collected tapes made by persons engaged in projects not sponsored by the society.

Within the society, too, oral history efforts, although never intensive, were widespread. For example, in the 1970s Robert C. Wheeler, then associate director, and others created the series "Forest History/Lumbering" while collecting information needed to develop the society's Forest History Center in Grand Rapids, and White in 1968-69 contributed "North Shore Fishermen" while amassing papers on Lake Superior fishing as a member of the Manuscript Division's staff. The program's scope broadened still more when the Regional Research Center network, established in 1967 and co-ordinated by the Manuscripts Division, expanded its activities during the 1970s. The

centers conducted oral history projects as well as individual interviews.

The interviews described in this guide span the years from 1948 to 1982. The entries reflect not only the growing project orientation of the program, but also its acceleration after the late 1960s. Furthermore, they show a wide variety of interviewers and informants -- a diversity that produced source material on many facets of economic, political, social, religious, and cultural history. Represented in the collection is testimony from the lips of "old men" and of "chiefs," in the broad sense, but present, too, is evidence contributed by men and women of many ages, ethnic backgrounds, experiences, and interests who lived on farms, in small towns, and in cities throughout the state.

The compilers' backgrounds attest to their long interest in oral history. Lila Johnson Goff is now the society's assistant director for libraries and museum collections, a division that includes the Audio-Visual Library. She has conducted interviews, initially trained Regional Research Center personnel in oral history techniques, and is a long-standing member of the Oral History Association -- an organization that has been important in developing standards and sharing experiences on a national scale. James E. Fogerty, now deputy state archivist, began his experiences in oral history as co-ordinator of the Regional Research Centers. As co-ordinator and from 1979 as deputy state archivist, he has held training workshops in many parts of the state, directed projects, and expressed a sustained commitment to oral history documentation by conducting interviews.

Lucile M. Kane
Senior Research Fellow

7 Helen M. White, "Thoughts on Oral History," in American Archivist, 20:19-21 (January, 1957); Oral History Office, Annual Report, 1968, Minnesota Historical Society Archives. Transcripts of White's interviews are in DAM-MHS.

Note to Readers

The Oral History Collections of the Minnesota Historical Society is divided into two parts. The first covers tapes housed in the Audio-Visual Library of the Minnesota Historical Society, 690 Cedar Street, St. Paul. These tapes, if not restricted, may be listened to there. Although appointments are not required to use this collection, it is sometimes necessary to schedule the use of a tape deck. None of the tapes may be checked out, but researchers may purchase duplicate copies of unrestricted tapes. The typed transcripts of these interviews are located in the Audio-Visual Library and also in the Division of Archives and Manuscripts in the Minnesota Historical Society Research Center, 1500 Mississippi Street, St. Paul. At this time not all transcripts are in both places and an advance inquiry may eliminate unnecessary traveling between the two repositories.

The second part of this guide contains a consolidated listing of the oral history holdings of the Minnesota Regional Research Centers. These centers were formerly a part of a network established by the society to collect and preserve documentary sources on areas other than Minneapolis and St. Paul. The manuscript collections in these centers are listed separately in two guides, the first of which includes oral history interviews.* The collections housed in the regional centers are owned by the society but are administered by the various institutions that house them. The following letter abbreviations are used in this guide to indicate the regional center in which the interview is located:

(B)   North Central Minnesota Historical Center, Bemidji State University, Bemidji, Minnesota 56601

(C)   Central Minnesota Historical Center, St. Cloud State University, St. Cloud, Minnesota 56301

(D)   Northeast Minnesota Historical Center, University of Minnesota-Duluth, Duluth, Minnesota 55812

(M)   Northwest Minnesota Historical Center, Moorhead State University, Moorhead, Minnesota 56560

(O)   Southern Minnesota Historical Center, Mankato State University, Mankato, Minnesota 56001

(R)   West Central Minnesota Historical Center, University of Minnesota-Morris, Morris, Minnesota 56267

(S)   Southwest Minnesota Historical Center, Southwest State University, Marshall, Minnesota 56258

(W)   Southeast Minnesota Historical Center, St. Mary's College, Winona, Minnesota 55987

Each of the two parts of this guide is subdivided into sections beginning with "Individual Interviews and Reminiscences," which includes interviews ranging from very short, single tapes to extensive, multitape sessions

*James E. Fogerty, comp., Preliminary Guide to the Holdings of the Minnesota Regional Research Centers (St. Paul, 1975) and Manuscripts Collections of the Minnesota Regional Research Centers, Guide Number 2 (St. Paul, 1982).

with individual narrators. This section is followed by the "Public Affairs Center" interviews with individuals in politics and government and special Public Affairs Center projects. The remaining sections are arranged alphabetically by project title and include a description of the project and the major subjects discussed by each person interviewed on that topic.

The entries are numbered sequentially to simplify use of the guide and indexes. Within each project the names of people interviewed are arranged alphabetically, followed by their birth and death dates, if known. Each entry also lists the date of the interview, length of the interview in minutes (or hours if more than 120 minutes), number of pages of typed transcript if one has been completed, and any restrictions. The notation "Restricted" indicates that the tape cannot be used nor the transcript read before a specified date without the written permission of the donor. The notation "Open for research only" indicates that the interview cannot be quoted or reproduced but may be listened to (or the transcript read) for general research purposes. Information on specific restrictions may be obtained from the appropriate repository.

Each interview includes a brief description giving the highlights and topics discussed and in some cases the background of the person interviewed. All place names are in Minnesota unless otherwise noted. In Part 1 the name of the interviewer follows the description, but in some instances the interviewer is listed in the project description.

Not included in this guide are audio tapes of television interviews, produced programs, celebratory or political speeches, and other recordings. Such tapes, however, are collected by the society's Audio-Visual Library and are available for use there.

Users of this guide are urged to consult the index of interviewers and the index of names, places, and subjects. Individuals may be listed in more than one part and in more than one section.

The compilers wish to acknowledge the assistance of those who helped with this publication. Elizabeth Knight diligently prepared much of the preliminary data and verified many details in Part 1; her work was essential to the compilation process. In addition Cheryl N. Thies checked and arranged information for Part 2. The directors of the regional research centers co-operated fully in this project's development. The staff of the Minnesota Historical Society Press deserves credit for its support during the final phases of production; the patience and editorial skills of Sarah P. Rubinstein are especially appreciated.

Lila Johnson Goff
James E. Fogerty

PART 1

Minnesota Historical Society Collections

INDIVIDUAL INTERVIEWS AND REMINISCENCES

This section lists the taped personal recollections of a cross-section of Minnesotans. Many of the interviews deal with the immigrant experience, homesteading, and pioneer life. In others the respondent may describe his or her life as a nurse, artist, prison warden, banker, railroad worker, member of the clergy, or author. Some people recall prominent relatives and friends, saying little about their own, more ordinary lives.

1. ABEL, WALTER C. (1898-1977). 1963. 60 min.
   An American actor recalls his grandparents, Swiss and German immigrants in the Lake Minnetonka area, his early life in Minnesota, and his experiences and stage successes in New York in the 1920s.
   Interviewers: Thomas Deahl, Russell Fridley, Robert Wheeler

2. BAILEY, FRANK (1886-). 1969. 30 min. Open for research only.
   A logger who arrived in Clearwater County in 1894 with his homesteading parents recalls his early life and describes his career working for lumberman Sumner C. Bagley.
   Interviewer: Dale LaRogue

3. BAKER, HARRY (1874-). 1968. 60 min. Open for research only.
   A resident of St. Croix Falls, Wis., discusses the settlement of the St. Croix Falls area, establishment of Interstate Park in Minnesota and Wisconsin, development along the St. Croix River, his family (including his brother, author Ray Stannard Baker), and publisher DeWitt Wallace.
   Interviewer: Lila Johnson

4. BEKKEN, HELEN VAN MOORLEGHEM (1913-). 1978. 35 min.
   At a Van Moorleghem family reunion, Bekken discusses Belgians in the U.S. and Canada, the migration of the Van Moorleghems to South Dakota, and the Minneota, Lyon County, area in the 1930s.
   Interviewer: Louis deGryse

5. BELL, WILLIAM J. (1888-). 1968. 2 hrs., 30 min. 57 p. Open for research only.
   Born in Otter Tail County and educated at Macalester College, St. Paul, Rev. William J. Bell discusses his missionary work on the "Range Parish" in northern Minnesota for the Board of Home Missions of the National Presbyterian Church (1913-32) and with the Board of Christian Education in the Midwest.
   Interviewer: Lila Johnson

6. BERG, OLGA OTTOLINA LARSEN (1899-). 1976. 90 min. Restricted.
   Mrs. Palmer Berg, of Swedish descent, has lived on a farm in the Lake Park, Becker County, area most of her life. She recalls her childhood (she was an orphan) and domestic and farm life.
   Interviewer: Viki Sand

7. BERG, PALMER (1892-1980). 1976. 20 min. Restricted.
   A farmer of Norwegian descent from Clay and Becker counties discusses family life, orphans, and farming.
   Interviewer: Viki Sand

8. BERGUM, ELLEN (1903-). 1975. 30 min. Open for research only.
   A daughter of Swedish immigrant parents, Bergum grew up in Upsala, Morrison County. She discusses family life, Swedish Christmas

customs, music, and the 1930s Depression in Minneapolis.

Interviewer: Susan Bostrom

9. BESTER, CONNIE POPPENBERG (1904-   ). 1969. 110 min. Open for research only.

Mrs. Earl Bester discusses family background and the career of her husband, a labor organizer of steelworkers on Minnesota's iron ranges. Her daughter Charlene also comments.

Interviewer: Helen White

10. BÍLÝ, JAN (JOHN F.) (1881?-   ). 1968. 80 min. Open for research only.

A violinist from Spillville, Iowa, whose cousin was secretary to Antonín Dvořák when the composer visited America in 1893 reminisces about Dvořák's visit to Spillville and St. Paul, the Kovařík family, and various musicians. He also plays his violin.

Interviewers: Kenneth Carley, Lionel Davis

11. BLEGEN, THEODORE C. (1891-1969). 1967. 30 min. Open for research only.

A director of the Minnesota Historical Society (1931-39) and professor of history and dean of the graduate school at the University of Minnesota (1940-60) discusses his life and experiences at the university.

Interviewer: Robert Boyle

12. BLUESTONE, ROSE WHIPPLE (1910-   ). 1976. 60 min. 18 p.

A Dakota Indian born at Prairie Island and raised in Santee, Neb., recalls her childhood and her education at boarding schools for Indians. She discusses the Dakota War of 1862 and Christianity, particularly her Episcopal upbringing.

Interviewers: Nanette Graves, Tori Graves

13. BOWEN, KATHERINE GILTINAN. 1966. 90 min. 31 p. Open for research only.

The granddaughter of Ignatius Donnelly (1831-1901) reminisces about the Donnelly family and life at Nininger, Dakota County, and recalls her experiences in China during World War II.

Interviewers: Russell Fridley, Lucile Kane, Helen White

14. BROBIN, KENNETH (1916-   ). 1977. 2 hrs., 30 min.

The son of an English railroad worker who arrived in the Ely, St. Louis County, area in 1910 discusses family history and the friction between English-speaking bosses and immigrant laborers. Brobin, who worked on the railroads and in the mines of northern Minnesota (1940-67), describes the work of underground miners and discusses conservation controversies in that region during the 1970s.

Interviewer: Lynn Laitala

15. BUTLER, PIERCE, III (1918-   ). 1968. 90 min. 30 p. Restricted.

The grandson of U.S. Supreme Court Justice Pierce Butler (1866-1939) discusses family history since the Butlers' emigration from Ireland in the 1840s, particularly his memories of his grandfather.

Interviewers: Robert Goff, Lila Johnson

16. CANNON, RAYMOND WINFORD (1892-   ). 1977. 3 hrs.

The grandson of early black settlers in Minnesota recalls family history. Cannon discusses his work as a pharmacist, his World War I military service, and his law education and practice. A member of the Minneapolis Fair Employment Practices Commission (1947-59) and active in the Urban League until he retired in 1959, Cannon talks about the black community in the Twin Cities, particularly the problems of discrimination and the work for civil rights.

Interviewer: Steve Trimble

17. CAPSER, HENRY CASPER (1865-1963). 1950. 90 min. 51 p. Open for research only.

A pioneer resident of Sauk Centre, Stearns County, recalls the career of his father, Joseph, as the owner of a general store and a legislator in the 1870s and 1880s, the Red River ox carts, Father D. J. Cogan's Grove Lake Academy (later St. Paul's Select School, near Sauk Centre) in the 1870s and 1880s, Ignatius Donnelly, and August Lindbergh.

Interviewers: Lucile Kane, Grace Lee Nute

18. CARNES, NORRIS K. (1895-   ). 1974. 60 min. Restricted.

The general manager of the Central Livestock Assn., South St. Paul, Dakota County (1930-73), discusses that organization and his education and teaching years (1919-23) at the University of Minnesota School of Agriculture.

Interviewer: Warren Gardner

19. CARSON, ANNA JOSEPHINE GRAN (1886-   ). 1973. 4 hrs., 30 min. Open for research only.

Mrs. Paul Carson was born on her Swedish immigrant parents' farm near Kensington, Douglas County. She discusses family history and vividly depicts pioneer life and the Finnish population near Kensington. She

recalls her nursing career, her marriage, and family life.
Interviewer: Cary Carson

20. CERNY, GEORGE (1912?-   ). 1967. 100 min. Open for research only.
A former employee of the Midland Cooperative Wholesale and of the Cooperative League discusses co-operatives in Minnesota.
Interviewer: Helen White

21. CLARK, HOMER PIERCE (1868-1970). 1964. 60 min. 27 p. Open for research only.
A pioneer resident comments on life in St. Paul since the 1870s, giving details about the Ramsey House (where the interview took place), the Ramsey and Furness families, the James J. Hill family, Ignatius Donnelly, and St. Paul buildings, including the James J. Hill Reference Library and the Capitol Approach area.
Interviewers: John Dougherty, Russell Fridley, Mrs. James Holman, and Robert Wheeler

22. COOVER, OSCAR, JR. (1920-   ). 1977. 3 hrs. Restricted.
Active in radical politics and union organizing, Coover was a member of the Communist party national committee until 1974. He discusses his family, particularly his father, Oscar Coover, Sr., a leader in the 1934 truckers' strike in Minneapolis. He also describes the Hennepin County Home School for Boys, a juvenile detention home at Glen Lake.
Interviewer: Steve Trimble

23. COVEY, WES (1890-   ). 1977. 60 min.
Covey began working for the Burlington railroad in 1907 and was active in labor unions. He recalls riding the rails during the 1930s Depression, railroad accidents, hobos, and Hoovervilles.
Interviewer: Martin Duffy

24. DAVIDOV, MARVIN (1931-   ). 1971. 18 hrs. Restricted.
A long-time political activist discusses the Honeywell Project, a program directed toward bringing public pressure on the Honeywell Corporation of Minneapolis to stop the manufacture of certain bombs used in the war in Vietnam and Indochina.
Interviewer: Lee Anderson

25. DECKER, EDWARD WILLIAMS (1869-1956). 1954, 1955. 30 min. 29 p. Open for research only.
A Minneapolis banker discusses banking in the 1920s and 1930s, development of the Northwest Bancorporation, Thomas Lowry and the Minneapolis streetcar system, development of the Lynnhurst area, and Wilbur Foshay.
Interviewers: Clarence Chaney, Lucile Kane

26. DEGERSTROM, JOHN AND MRS. JOHN DEGERSTROM. 1956. 30 min. Open for research only.
Immigrants from Sweden in 1907 describe pioneer life, including threshing in North Dakota and farming in Minnesota in the 1920s.
Interviewer: Robert Weber

27. DOBBS, FARRELL (1907-83) AND MARVEL S. DOBBS. 1977. 4 hrs. Open for research only.
The Dobbses, who grew up in Minneapolis, discuss personal history, the development of their political philosophy, Carl Skoglund, and their membership in the Communist and Socialist Workers' parties. They also talk about radical unionism and describe in detail the 1934 truckers' strike in Minneapolis and their involvement in organizing it.
Interviewers: Tim O'Connell, Steve Trimble

28. DuBOIS, BENJAMIN F., SR. (1885-1981). 1967. 2 hrs., 15 min.
A banker from Sauk Centre, Stearns County, talks about life there in the 1880s and 1890s and about his family, particularly his father, Julian DuBois. He reminisces about political and economic affairs, including the Nonpartisan League, the Communist party in the 1930s and 1940s, the Independent Bankers Assn., U.S. foreign policy, and Minnesota politics. He also comments on a number of political figures and author Sinclair Lewis.
Interviewers: Russell Fridley, Robert Goff, Lila Johnson

29. DUNNE, VINCENT RAYMOND (1889-1970). 1969. 105 min. 45 p. Restricted.
A major organizer of the 1934 truckers' strike in Minneapolis describes his boyhood in Kansas and on a Minnesota farm, migrant work on the West Coast, and his experiences in the Industrial Workers of the World and the Communist party in the 1920s. He discusses ideological differences within the Communist party and the Socialist Workers' party, organizing labor groups, and the 1934 strike.
Interviewer: Lila Johnson

30. FISK, WILBUR (1890-   ). 1972. 60 min. 14 p.
A former newspaperman in South St. Paul, Dakota County, discusses personal history, Macalester College, St. Paul, his fellow

student Elmer Smith, and lumbering along the St. Croix and Mississippi rivers.
Interviewer: Tom Copeland

31. FRIDLEY, RUSSELL W. (1928-   ). 1978. 70 min.
A director (1955-   ) of the Minnesota Historical Society discusses the institution's history, the role of the director and other officers, the development of the historic sites program, and highlights of his career.
Interviewers: Mark Haidet, Mary O'Keefe

32. FURNESS, ANITA EARL RAMSEY (1876-1964). 1962. 10 min. Open for research only.
Alexander Ramsey's granddaughter recalls social life in St. Paul in the early 1900s, describing events at the James J. Hill house and the St. Paul winter carnivals.
Interviewer: Lillian Smiley

33. GAMMONS, EARL H. (1893?-1974). 1964. 2 hrs., 30 min. Open for research only.
A former manager of WCCO Radio in Minneapolis discusses the history of that station. Included is information about its predecessor station WLAG, ownership by the Washburn-Crosby Co., affiliation with CBS, and early programs, performers, commercial broadcasts, and employees.
Interviewer: Lawrence Haeg

34. GELDMAN, MAX (1905-   ). 1977. 4 hrs. Restricted.
An immigrant from Poland in 1914 who settled in Minnesota in 1929 recalls family background and his childhood in New York and describes his introduction to radical politics, the Young Communist League, and his involvement in the Communist party. He discusses unions and strikes, including his activities in the 1939 Works Progress Administration strike, and his subsequent arrest and imprisonment in Sandstone Prison.
Interviewer: Steve Trimble

35. GODFREY, CHARLES (1890-   ). 1971. 75 min. Open for research only.
An Itasca County land commissioner discusses the Godfrey Boat Co.; his family's steamboat building business in Wabasha, Wabasha County; his education as an engineer; his work in logging and as a land commissioner; and forest conservation.
Interviewers: Lee Anderson, Newell Searle

36. GOODHUE, HORACE (1904-   ). 1974. 2 hrs. Open for research only.
A high-school teacher and psychologist who was educated at Carleton College, Northfield, recalls his early life on a farm, his

education, and family members, including James M. Goodhue, who established the first newspaper in Minnesota Territory in 1849. He also discusses American Indian culture, particularly beadwork, a craft in which he is skilled.
Interviewer: Glen Krueger

37. GRAN, FRANK WALTER (1894-1973). 1970. 75 min. Open for research only.
A farmer from the Kensington, Douglas County, area where the rune stone was discovered in 1898 discusses the Olof Ohman family, discoverers of the stone, and expresses his opinion of it as a hoax.
Interviewers: Paul Carson, Russell Fridley

38. GRAN FAMILY. 1967. 60 min.
Frank Walter Gran and his sister, Anna Josephine Gran Carson, who knew the Olof Ohman family, discoverers of the Kensington rune stone, discuss the stone as a hoax. Also included are Gran family reminiscences.
Interviewer: Paul Carson

39. GRAVES, PETER (1872-1957). 1950. 30 min. Open for research only.
A leader of the Red Lake band of Ojibway Indians comments on family history, the Leech Lake Indian uprising (1898), Chief Bugonaygeshig, and the fish and lumber industries and law enforcement on the reservation.
Interviewer: Arch Grahn

40. GREENMAN, FRANCES CRANMER (1890-1981). 1974. 30 min.
A portrait painter born in South Dakota recalls her early life as an artist and designer in New York and discusses two of her works: "Woman Riding the Wind," a painting of an Ojibway woman, and a portrait of Governor Karl F. Rolvaag, which hangs in the Minnesota State Capitol.
Interviewer: Lila Goff

41. GRENGS, ALOYSIUS (1909-   ). Narrations, 1976, 1977. 14 hrs. One of the 1977 tapes is restricted.
This autobiography of a retired St. Paul carpenter includes memories of riding trains during the 1930s Depression and working on a ranch in South Dakota. He also sings and yodels railroad and cowboy songs, some from the 1930s.

42. GUTHRIE, MIKE (1890-   ). 1962?. 17 min. Open for research only.
Raised near Bigfork, Itasca County, where his parents homesteaded, Guthrie discusses his work for the state forest service (1911-62).
Interviewer unknown

43. HAFEMAN, WILLIAM. 1972. 60 min. Open
    for research only.
    Hafeman describes in detail the construc-
tion of a birch-bark canoe -- including selection and preparation of materials -- an art he
learned in the early years of the 20th century.
    Interviewer: Robert Wheeler

44. HALVERSON, LEILA (1883-1976). 1967. 3
    hrs., 30 min. 47 p. Open for research only.
    A registered nurse in North Dakota and
Minnesota recalls family and personal history.
She describes her education at Luther Hospital
Training School in St. Paul, work as a private
and school nurse, service with the American
Red Cross in France, Palestine, and Poland
during and after World War I, and her career
as secretary-treasurer of the Minnesota State
Board of Examiners of Nurses (1927-48).
    Interviewers: Leonora Collatz, Lila
Johnson

45. HARJU, WALTER (1900-   ). 1977. 4
    hrs. Restricted.
    Born on a South Dakota homestead, Harju
discusses his family background, his work as a
harvest hand, and his developing political
consciousness and activities. He had an interest in the Industrial Workers of the World
and joined the Future Leaders and the Young
Workers League, both associated with the Communist party. He was active in the Nonpartisan League, the Farmer-Labor party, the Writers' Union, and labor organizing efforts on
the West Coast in the mid-1920s. He ran for
lieutenant-governor of Wisconsin in the 1930s
on the Communist party ticket, managed the
Farmers' National Weekly, and worked in the
co-operative movement with various farmer and
labor organizations.
    Interviewer: Steve Trimble

46. HEMMINGSEN, CLARENCE (1895-   ). 1977.
    2 hrs., 30 min.
    This son of Norwegian immigrant parents
recalls his family background, childhood, and
apprenticeship as a pipefitter. He discusses
his political and labor union activities, including membership in the Socialist party and
the Proletarian Party of America, attempts to
organize a national Farmer-Labor party, and
being expelled from the Pipefitters Union in
the early 1930s. Hemmingsen also talks about
moving to the north shore of Lake Superior and
operating a small resort.
    Interviewer: James Youngdale

47. HESS, ROBERT E. (1918-   ). 1969,
    1970. 105 min. 29 p.
    The president of the Minnesota CIO (1951-
56) and executive vice-president of the Minne-

sota AFL-CIO (1956-66) discusses family background, his childhood in St. Paul, early union
activities including organizing the Minnesota
Mining and Manufacturing Co., St. Paul, for
the CIO in the late 1940s, the merger of the
AFL and the CIO, the Democratic-Farmer-Labor
party, legislation affecting organized labor,
and the 1959 packinghouse-workers' strike of
the Wilson Co. in Albert Lea, Freeborn County.
He talks about his responsibilities as a member of the University of Minnesota Board of
Regents (1959-66) and comments on various political figures including Orville L. Freeman
and Karl F. Rolvaag.
    Interviewer: Lila Johnson

48. HOKANSON, NELS (1889?-   ). 1977. 60
    min.
    A Swedish immigrant recalls family back-
ground and his childhood in St. Paul's Swede
Hollow, including the history of the area and
the occupations of the residents.
    Interviewer: Steve Trimble

49. HOLT, OTTO (1880-   ). 1973. 65 min.
    Open for research only.
    A Norwegian immigrant describes his fami-
ly's crossing of the Atlantic during a storm
in 1883. He recalls picnics at Lake Minnetonka, his father's janitorial duties in the old
courthouse in Minneapolis, and his own career
as a deputy sheriff and jailer beginning in
1914.
    Interviewer: Peggy Korsmo

50. HOMESTEADER (Anonymous). 1956. 30 min.
    The woman interviewed was born in Norway
and emigrated in 1905 to North Dakota where
she filed a homestead claim in 1906. She describes homestead life, her work as a waitress
and cook for a threshing crew, her education,
and her nursing career.
    Interviewer: Robert Weber

51. HOWARD, HAROLD PALMER (1866-1951).
    1950. 2 hrs. Open for research only.
    The son of Sauk Centre, Stearns County,
pioneers recalls community life in the 1870s
and 1880s, including descriptions of his father's hardware and machinery store, schools,
and bands and music. He reminisces about
Edwin Whitefield, Joseph Capser, Solomon
Pendergast, Dr. Benjamin Palmer, Max Gruber,
and Josiah Briggs and describes fur traders in
the Sauk Centre area.
    Interviewer: Lucile Kane

52. HUNTER, JOE. 1961. 45 min. Open for
    research only.
    An Ojibway Indian, named for his great
hunting ability, discusses hunting and trapping, tells stories, and speaks of the need to

preserve traditional Indian ways. He speaks Ojibway, which is translated.
Interviewer: Evan Hart

53. JACKSON, NORRIS D. (1895-   ) AND ELIZABETH AMES JACKSON (1895?-   ). 1978. 30 min. Restricted.
Lifelong residents of Summit Avenue, St. Paul, recall their acquaintance with F. Scott Fitzgerald.
Interviewers: Russell Fridley, Lloyd Hackl, Lawrence Haeg, John Koblas, Virginia Martin

54. KALMAN, ALEXANDRA. 1975. 90 min.
Mrs. C. O. Kalman and her husband were close friends of the F. Scott Fitzgeralds during the 1920s and remained in contact throughout their lives. Mrs. Kalman reminisces about Scott and Zelda Fitzgerald and comments on other acquaintances, including Sinclair Lewis.
Interviewer: Lloyd Hackl

55. KAUKOLA, EINO (1900-   ). 1978. 40 min.
A Finn who emigrated with his family to northern Minnesota in 1903 recalls personal history and describes in detail his primary occupation of trapping.
Interviewers: Slavko Nowytski, Peter Trygg, Robert Wheeler

56. KIDDER, WILLIAM (1887?-1974). 1968. 15 min. Open for research only.
A pioneer aviator discusses the beginnings of Northwest Airways, a forerunner of Northwest Airlines, in 1926, including financing and the types of aircraft flown.
Interviewer: James Williams

57. KILTY, REGINALD. Narration, 1975?. 45 min. Open for research only.
A World War I veteran gives details of his army experiences from his enlistment at Fort Snelling through his service in France.

58. KOSKI, LEO A. (1912-   ). 1977. 60 min.
The son of Finnish immigrants in northern Minnesota discusses family history, his activities as a Young Communist League organizer in Michigan and on the Mesabi Range in the 1930s, the Finnish cultural movement, and later developments in Marxist ideology.
Interviewers: Tim O'Connell, Steve Trimble

59. KOVAŘÍK, ANNE M. (1892?-   ). 1968. 2 hrs. Open for research only.
The sister of Josef J. Kovařík, secretary to Antonín Dvořák during the composer's stay in America, recalls Dvořák's visit to Spillville, Iowa, and St. Paul (1893) and offers information about the Dvořák and Kovařík families.
Interviewers: Kenneth Carley, Lionel Davis

60. LAMPI, HERMAN. 1951. 30 min. Open for research only.
A Finn recalls his emigration in 1881 with his parents and various early travels. Lampi was employed by the St. Croix Lumber Co. at Winton, St. Louis County, and Stillwater, Washington County, and he describes logging methods and life in the lumber camps and communities.
Interviewer: Lucile Kane

61. LA PLANTE, ED (1900-   ). 1959, 1961. 60 min. Open for research only.
An Ojibway Indian offers his recollections of Grand Portage Reservation, Cook County. He plays and comments on some of Frances Densmore's recordings of Ojibway songs.
Interviewer: Evan Hart

62. LAW, VICTORIA BOWLER (1863-   ). 1967. 60 min. Open for research only.
The daughter of James Madison Bowler (1838-1916), a Civil War major who served as state dairy and livestock commissioner, reminisces about her early life at Nininger, Dakota County, and about Ignatius Donnelly.
Interviewer: Lila Johnson

63. LAWRENCE, ELIZABETH (1877-1966). 1965. 25 min. Open for research only.
Mrs. Harry Lawrence, whose Dakota Indian name is Morning Star, is the niece of Chief Little Crow. She sings six songs in her native language: a love song; three Christian hymns; "God's Creation," learned from her father, White Spider; and the song the morning star sang to her father at her birth.
Interviewers: Lucile Kane, Mary Proal Lindeke

64. LAWRENCE, HARRY. Narration, 1958?. 60 min. Open for research only.
A Dakota Indian gives information about the history of the Dakota in Minnesota, particularly their settlements on the Minnesota and Mississippi rivers. He recalls the Dakota War of 1862 and Chief Little Crow's part in it. His wife, Elizabeth, also comments.

65. LEIMER, LOUIS. 1950. 15 min. Open for research only.
The operator of a boardinghouse for lumbermen during the 1890s and early 1900s talks

about lumbermen and the contract work he did for lumber companies.
Interviewer: Lucile Kane

66. LEMBERG, SIGRID (1897-   ). 1969. 90 min. Open for research only.
The wife of Lauri Lemberg (1887-1965) discusses her emigration from Finland, the life of Finnish immigrants in the Duluth area, the work of her husband (a playwright, theater director, journalist, and cultural promotor), and the nationwide booking service for Finnish-language plays they managed in Duluth.
Interviewer: Helen White

67. LINDBERGH FAMILY. Discussion, 1976. 60 min. 50 p. Restricted.
Anne Morrow Lindbergh, Reeve Lindbergh Brown, Land Lindbergh, and Eva Lindbergh Christie Spaeth discuss with Minnesota Historical Society staff members ideas about an appropriate way to observe the 50th anniversary of Charles Lindbergh's 1927 transatlantic solo flight.

68. LUMBERJACK (Anonymous). 1952? 65 min. Open for research only.
A lumberjack born in 1880 in Wisconsin went to work for the Davis Lumber Co. in 1896. He details many aspects of logging and logging camps, including descriptions of the different jobs, equipment, work techniques, camp life, and the amusements of music and dancing.
Interviewer unknown

69. MARTIN, JERRY AND KATHERINE MARTIN (1890-   ). 1962. 45 min. Open for research only.
Mrs. Martin is the granddaughter of Misquadace, the last leader of the Sandy Lake band of Ojibway Indians. Mr. Martin sings and discusses several Ojibway and Dakota songs. They describe various aspects of tribal life. Mrs. Martin speaks of her family and tells the Waba-Bosho story, "Becomes a Wolf," in English to complement her husband's Ojibway version.
Interviewer: Evan Hart

70. MASNARI, BEATRICE MASSARI (1910-   ). 1975. 40 min. 20 p.
An Italian who immigrated to the U.S. in 1931 to join her husband recalls his motives for immigrating and her sea voyage and train trip to Ely, St. Louis County. She describes her difficulties during the 1930s Depression and discusses the importance of maintaining ties with relatives in Italy.
Interviewer: Lynn Laitala

71. MATTALA, EMMA. 1956. 30 min. Open for research only.
An immigrant who arrived with her parents from Finland in 1880 describes her family's homestead in 1887 at New York Mills, Otter Tail County, and her parents' impressions of America.
Interviewer: Robert Weber

72. McCANN, EDWARD (1876-1965). 1964. 4 hrs., 30 min.
A Methodist minister discusses his family background and early life in Shieldsville, Rice County, and Minneapolis in the 1880s and 1890s, including his education, the recreation of attending theaters, and his work as a telegraph operator. He recalls his conversion to Methodism and his early ministries in Koochiching County and at Onamia, Mille Lacs County, where he occasionally preached to Ojibway Indian congregations.
Interviewer: Helen White

73. McEVOY, JAMES. 1968. 80 min. Open for research only.
An employee of Midland Cooperative Wholesale discusses various types of co-operatives (including the first co-op grocery store in the Twin Cities) and their successes, failures, and future.
Interviewer: Helen White

74. McGINN, GEORGE (1869-   ). 1956. 60 min. Open for research only.
A Canadian who immigrated to the U.S. in 1887 and arrived in Minnesota in 1895 describes his family's pioneer life in Canada; Walker, Cass County, in 1895; and his life and work as a lumberman and summertime harvester.
Interviewer: Robert Weber

75. McGOUGH, MARY. 1968. 30 min. Open for research only.
A retired teacher and former member of the board of directors of the St. Paul Teachers Federation and the Minnesota Education Assn. discusses lobbying for legislation for teachers (1920s-1940s) and her attempts to involve other teachers in Minnesota politics.
Interviewer: Frithjof Wannebo

76. MERRILL, JOSEPH (1878-   ). 1956. 30 min. Open for research only.
Merrill describes homesteading in Montana in the 1910s and his return in the 1920s to farm in northern Minnesota and to work in logging camps in the winters.
Interviewer: Robert Weber

77. MIHELCIC, FRANK (1892-   ). 1977. 60 min. 24 p.
A Yugoslav who emigrated to the U.S. in 1910 to escape military conscription recalls Slovene history, his emigration, and his edu-

cation at St. Paul Seminary. Ordained in 1917, he discusses his parish in Ely, St. Louis County, and his parishioners, many of whom were miners.
Interviewer: Lynn Laitala

78. MITAU, G. THEODORE (1920-79). 1976. 2 hrs., 30 min. 84 p.
The chancellor (1968-76) of the Minnesota state university system discusses its growth and development including the beginning of Metropolitan State University and the issues involved in securing a bargaining unit for faculty members.
Interviewer: Joanne Poehlman

79. MURRAY, FRANCIS HENRY (1873-1963). 1959? 30 min. Open for research only.
Murray discusses his activities in settling the area near Perham and New York Mills in Otter Tail County, Catholic colonization societies, the American Immigration Co., and other land and colonization companies in the 1910s.
Interviewer: Lucile Kane

80. NELSON, GEORGE U. (1899-). 1977. 60 min.
The son of Swedish immigrants recalls family history, life on the north shore of Lake Superior in the early part of the century, and work as owner and operator of the Lutsen Resort, Cook County.
Interviewer: James Youngdale

81. NEUMAIER, JOHN (1921-). 1968. 90 min. Restricted.
An immigrant from Germany (1940) who became a teacher of philosophy, dean of Hibbing Junior College, and president of Moorhead State College (1958-67) discusses various aspects of higher education.
Interviewer: Viki Sand

82. NUTE, GRACE LEE (1895-). 1978. 90 min. Restricted.
A professor of history, curator of manuscripts (1921-46) and research associate (1947-57) at the Minnesota Historical Society, and author of many articles and books on the fur trade in North America recalls her family background, early life in New England, and her first impressions of Minnesota. She discusses her years at the MHS and sketches the characters of Warren Upham, William W. Folwell, and Solon J. Buck. She also talks about her writing.
Interviewers: Mark Haidet, Mary O'Keefe

83. OBERHOLTZER, ERNEST C. (1884-1977). 1948, 1960, 1963, 1964, 1968. 28 hrs. Open for research only.

A conservationist, explorer, and writer reminisces about the summers on an island in Rainy Lake and winters at Ranier, Koochiching County. He recalls his Harvard University days, his friends Conrad Aiken and Samuel Morison, and his travels in Europe. He describes canoe trips, including one to Hudson Bay (1912), and his Indian traveling companion, Billy McGee. He discusses efforts to preserve the Quetico-Superior wilderness and to establish the Boundary Waters Canoe Area and Voyageurs National Park in northern Minnesota. He reflects on the social customs, legends, and stories of the Ojibway Indians he knew at Rainy Lake and comments on Frances Densmore's work. He also discusses Eric Sevareid's book, Canoeing with the Cree.
In 1948 Oberholtzer recorded three tapes of stories and songs in Ojibway that are told and sung by Johnnie Whitefish, Maggie Jackpot, and Minta Boya of Rainy Lake.
Interviewers: G. M. and Frances Andrews, Russell Fridley, Evan Hart, Pete Heffelfinger, Lucile Kane, Gene and George Monahan, Mary Nagle

84. OHMAN, EDWARD (1888-1950). 1949. 20 min. 14 p. Open for research only.
The son of Olof Ohman, discoverer of the Kensington rune stone, gives information about the discovery in 1898 and the ensuing interest in the authenticity of the runes.
Interviewers: Lucile Kane, Bergmann Richards, Maugridge Robb, Ralph Thornton

85. OLSON, SIGURD F. (1899-1982). 1976. 4 hrs., 15 min. 46 p. Open for research only.
A conservationist, biologist, and author recalls his childhood and education in northern Wisconsin and discusses his lifetime concern with conservation, particularly of the Quetico-Superior wilderness. He also talks about his writing and about the commissioner of the Minnesota Department of Natural Resources.
Interviewers: Robert Herbst, John McKane, Newell Searle

86. ORENDAIN, JUAN C. (1894-). 1959. 90 min. 41 p. Open for research only.
A Filipino who arrived in Minnesota as a high school student in 1917 discusses the eight years he lived in the state, including his education at Bethel Academy, St. Paul, and the University of Minnesota, and various jobs he held. He also talks about his early life in the Philippines and the effects of the American conquest after 1900.
Interviewer: Helen White

87. PARKER, CHARLES ASA (1870-1957) AND GERMAIN QUINN (1865?-   ). 1950. 2 hrs. Open for research only.

Parker owned the Grand Opera House in Minneapolis in the 1880s and 1890s. Quinn worked as a prop boy at the Pence Opera House in Minneapolis in the 1870s and as a stagehand and property manager at several Minneapolis theaters until he retired in 1941. They reminisce about the theater, road shows and stock companies that performed in Minneapolis, and such performers as Edwin Booth, Sarah Bernhardt, and Oscar Wilde.
Interviewers: Lucile Kane, Robert Murphy, Donald Woods

88. PATTERSON, JAMES (1911-   ). 1974. 50 min.

An employee (1937-74) of Brown & Bigelow, St. Paul, discusses that advertising specialty firm.
Interviewer: Warren Gardner

89. PAULL, IRENE LEVINE (?-1981). 1977. 110 min. Restricted.

Born in Duluth, the daughter of Ukrainian Jews recalls her childhood and the origins of her socialist beliefs and interest in the Communist party. She discusses her and her attorney husband's activities in leftist politics and labor organizations in the 1930s and 1940s, as well as the nature and effectiveness of political literature, including her own writing. She comments on the Farmer-Labor party and various political figures.
Interviewer: Steve Trimble

90. PAVLICEK, JOSEPH (1890-   ). 1975. 60 min. Open for research only.

A Czech who immigrated to St. Paul in 1908 discusses Sokol, a Czech social and cultural club that he joined in 1923 and served as president of the northern district organization.
Interviewers: Theresa Brill, Kathy Wilson

91. PEDERSON, ANNIE BRADBURY (1884-   ). 1968. 30 min. Open for research only.

Mrs. Harry Pederson reminisces about pioneer life, including her father's experiences trading in Minnesota, her parents' and her own homesteads in North Dakota, and the Nonpartisan League.
Interviewer: Russell Fridley

92. PETERSEN, STEIN (1881-   ). 1977. 60 min.

A Dane who emigrated in 1900 and settled in Washington County discusses family history,

his work as a bricklayer and stonemason, and his move to California in 1942.
Interviewer: Joanne Baldwin

93. PILLSBURY, JOHN SARGENT (1878-1968). 1966. 60 min. 42 p. Open for research only.

A son of Charles A. Pillsbury discusses family history, the migration of the Pillsbury family to Minneapolis, and the establishment of the Pillsbury milling enterprise. He comments on prominent residents of the Twin Cities and on politics and social life in Minneapolis.
Interviewers: Welles Eastman, Russell Fridley, David Winton

94. PLANTE, MRS. GODFREY. 1961, 1962. 2 hrs. Open for research only.

Mrs. Plante, who is part Ojibway Indian, and some of her relatives, including Ed La Plante, recall many aspects of Ojibway tribal life at Grand Portage, Cook County.
Interviewer: Evan Hart

95. PRYATEL, JOSEPH (1915-   ). 1976. 60 min. 32 p.

The son of Slovene immigrants recalls family history, his education, his father's work as a miner, and Slovene community life in Ely, St. Louis County.
Interviewer: Lynn Laitala

96. QUINN, GERMAIN (1865?-   ). 1950. 90 min. Open for research only.

The author of Fifty Years Back Stage (1926) describes his work as a prop boy and stagehand in Minneapolis theaters in the 1880s to early 1900s. He also reminisces about his early life in Shieldsville, Rice County.
Interviewers: Lucile Kane, Donald Woods

97. REGNIER, A. MARGARET (1907-   ). 1978. 60 min.

A retired schoolteacher, born in Ghent, Lyon County, of Belgian and French-Canadian descent discusses her ethnicity, ethnic group relations, Belgian and French-Canadian attitudes toward farming, and pioneer homes in the Ghent area.
Interviewer: Louis deGryse

98. ROBERTSON, ALICE GOODRICH. 1962. 90 min. Open for research only.

A childhood playmate of the children of James J. Hill reminisces about the Hill family of St. Paul in the 1890s and early 1900s.
Interviewer: Lillian Smiley

99. ROINI, ANDREW (1885-   ). 1968. 30 min. 7 p. Open for research only.

A Finnish-born immigrant describes home-

steading near Angora, St. Louis County, and
life as a dairy farmer from 1907 to the 1960s.
Interviewer: Irene Paull

100. SANDBERG, FRANK (1902-   ). 1974.
3 hrs., 20 min. Open for research only.
An engineer for the Milwaukee Road (1920-71) discusses his work, job training, steam and diesel engines, and wrecks and accidents.
Interviewers: New City School (St. Paul)
students

101. SHERMAN, NETTIE HAYES (1900-   ).
1974. 75 min.
A black entertainer who worked for WLAG (later WCCO) Radio in soap operas and sang in various night clubs in Minneapolis, St. Paul, Chicago, and New York discusses her personal history and experiences in radio and the entertainment business.
Interviewer: Lila Goff

102. SHIELDS, JAMES M. 1968. 75 min. 32 p.
An employee of the National Labor Relations Board in Minneapolis (1936-47) recalls his family background and childhood and discusses working for the Federal Emergency Relief Administration and Works Progress Administration, the Farmer-Labor party in the 1930s, the merger of the Farmer-Labor and Democratic parties (1944), and Governor Elmer A. Benson.
Interviewers: Russell Fridley, Lila
Johnson

103. STODDARD, CHARLES H. (1912-   ).
1967. 75 min. 35 p.
The regional co-ordinator of the upper Mississippi-western Great Lakes area for the U.S. Department of the Interior discusses conservation and his role as consultant to the Democratic party and President John F. Kennedy.
Interviewer: Helen White

104. SUNDBERG, ARTHUR E. (1898-   ). Narration, 1970. 25 min. Open for research only.
A resident of St. Paul's Swede Hollow (1908-14) discusses Swedish immigration to St. Paul, particularly the Swede Hollow and Phalen neighborhoods.

105. SWINDEHEARST, A. G. (1873?-   ).
1965? 60 min. Open for research only.
Swindehearst describes the Cass Lake region of northern Minnesota, particularly during the period before 1900, and discusses exploration of the area, Ojibway Indians, fur traders, and missionaries.
Interviewer: Cedric Schluter

106. TAYLOR, JOHN S. 1962. 30 min. Open
for research only.
A retired carpenter discusses his father's role in the construction of the Alexander Ramsey house in St. Paul (1870s), architectural details of the house, and later repairs. He offers impressions of the Ramsey and Furness families from whom the Minnesota Historical Society acquired the house in 1964.
Interviewers: John Dougherty, Russell
Fridley

107. TORSTENSON, JOEL S. (1912-   ). 1967.
45 min. Open for research only.
The chairman of the sociology department at Augsburg College, Minneapolis, discusses many civil rights organizations in which he has served.
Interviewer: Stephen Batalden

108. TRYGG, J. WILLIAM (1905-1971). 1969.
90 min. Open for research only.
A forest ranger discusses forests and soils of Minnesota, forest regeneration, and early agricultural methods.
Interviewer: Newell Searle

109. UTECHT, LEO F. (1888-   ). 1968. 60
min. Open for research only.
The assistant deputy warden (1923-25), deputy warden (1925-36), acting warden (1937), and warden (1938-53) of the Minnesota State Prison at Stillwater discusses his career.
Interviewer: Lila Johnson

110. VAPAA, IVOR. 1968. 2 hrs., 15 min.
Open for research only.
A Finn who immigrated to the U.S. in 1908 discusses his labor background, the Industrial Workers of the World, and The Industrialisti (Duluth), an IWW newspaper he edited.
Interviewer: Helen White

111. VERMEERSCH, ARTHUR (1911-   ) AND
CHARLES LENS. 1978. 90 min.
Vermeersch and Lens, both of Belgian descent, discuss family history, Belgians' motives for emigrating, and the retention of Flemish language and customs in the Ghent area of Lyon County.
Interviewer: Louis deGryse

112. WALKER, ARCHIE D. (1882-1971). 1965.
60 min. 23 p. Open for research only.
The son of Thomas B. Walker (1840-1928) reminisces about family history and his father's lumber interests in Akeley, Hubbard County, and in Westwood, Calif. He also talks about the Minnesota Theater Company.
Interviewers: Lucile Kane, Russell
Fridley

113. WEST, MICHAEL. 1972. 60 min. Open for
     research only.
       A fur trapper and former dog trainer dis-
     cusses training dogs for military use and var-
     ious aspects of trapping and the fur trade.
       Interviewer: Gilbert White

114. WILLIAMSON, ARTHUR S. (1894-   ).
     1969. 2 hrs. Open for research only.
       Williamson discusses his experiences as
     a student (class of 1921) and teacher at Ham-
     line University, St. Paul, including changes
     in administration and curriculum.
       Interviewer: Helen White

115. WILSEY, LESTER A., SR. (1900-   ).
     1974. 3 hrs., 30 min.
       The founder of Indianhead Trucking Co.,
     St. Paul, discusses his childhood in Minneapo-
     lis and Wisconsin, early employment as a log-
     ger in northern Wisconsin and as a conductor
     for the Minneapolis Street Railway Co. (1923-
     29), and his early trucking work in Weyerhaeu-
     ser, Wis. He describes the history of Indian-
     head Trucking Co., which he moved to St. Paul
     in 1944, various state and federal trucking
     regulations, lobbying for the trucking indus-
     try in the Wisconsin and Minnesota legisla-
     tures in the 1930s and 1940s, and other as-
     pects of his career.
       Interviewer: Warren Gardner

116. WILSON, CHESTER S. (1886-   ). 1978.
     2 hrs., 15 min.
       A county attorney, state assistant attor-
     ney general, chief deputy attorney general,
     conservation commissioner (1943-55), water
     control commissioner, and national outdoor
     recreation resources commissioner (1958-62)
     recalls his personal history and offers an in-
     sider's view of the Minnesota Department of
     Conservation.
       Interviewer: Gloria Thompson

117. WOLTMAN, MARIAN HANSON DONNELLY (1877-
     1964). 1950. 30 min. Open for research
     only.
       The second wife of Ignatius Donnelly
     (1831-1901) recalls her family's emigration
     from Norway, her education and newspaper work
     before her marriage to Donnelly in 1898, and
     her life with Donnelly.
       Interviewer: Martin Ridge

118. WOOLSON, ALBERT (1847-1956). 1952.
     20 min. Open for research only.
       The last surviving Union Army veteran
     comments on the Civil War and its aftermath.
       Interviewer: Kathryn Johnson

119. WRIGHT, HELEN DIX. 1974. 50 min. Open
     for research only.

The wife of St. Paul photographer Kenneth
M. Wright (1895-1964) reminisces about his career, photograph collection, and interest in
the north shore of Lake Superior.
  Interviewer: Steven Quaal

120. YOUNGQUIST, WALTER R. (1893-   ).
     1973. 75 min. 42 p.
       The president of Minneapolis Savings and
     Loan Assn. (1936-63) entered the banking busi-
     ness in 1918. He discusses his term as a con-
     servative state representative (1935-37),
     Governor Floyd B. Olson, and the savings and
     loan business.
       Interviewer: Warren Gardner

121. ZECK, OTTO. 1965. 10 min. Restricted.
       Zeck discusses information supplied by
     John Anderson, a neighbor of the Olof Ohman
     family that discovered the Kensington rune
     stone in Douglas County in 1898.
       Interviewer: Birgitta Wallace

[[[[[[[[[[o]]]]]]]]]]

THE PUBLIC AFFAIRS CENTER COLLECTION

  The Minnesota Historical Society established the Public Affairs Center in 1967 to
stimulate acquisitions of politicians' and
government officials' papers and use of the
society's manuscripts collections relating to
politics and government. The interviews
grouped here document the careers of men and
women who held positions of national and
international importance or who were involved
in local and state governments and in both
major and minor political parties.
  The first section consists of individual
interviews of Minnesotans involved in public
affairs. These people reflect on their careers and experiences in politics and government. The second section includes special
oral history projects in which a number of
people were interviewed for each project.

122. ANDERSON, EUGENIE MOORE (1909-   ).
     1971. 15 hrs. 353 p. Restricted.
       The first woman U.S. ambassador attended
     Carleton College, Northfield, and married John
     Pierce Anderson of Red Wing, Goodhue County.
     She recalls her life from childhood through
     her political and governmental career. She
     became active in Democratic-Farmer-Labor party
     politics in 1944, was ambassador to Denmark
     (1949-53), chair of the Minnesota State Com-
     mission for Fair Employment Practices (1955-
     60), U.S. minister to Bulgaria (1962-65), and

a member of the U.S. delegation to the United Nations (1965-68).
Interviewers: Lila Johnson, Jan Musty

123. BENSON, LOUIS. 1977. 60 min.
The brother of Governor Elmer A. Benson recalls his family background and discusses the origins of the Farmer-Labor party, conflicts between farmers and laborers, radical politics, and a variety of other political topics.
Interviewer: Steve Trimble

124. BERNARD, JOHN TOUSSAINT (1893-1983). 1968?, 1969, 1977. 10 hrs. The 1968? interview is open for research only; the 1969 interview is open; the 1977 interview is restricted.
Born in Corsica, Bernard emigrated to the U.S. in 1907. He recalls personal history and describes working in the iron mines of northern Minnesota (1911-17). He discusses activities in the Farmer-Labor party, including his term as U.S. Congressman from the eighth district (1937-39), and his involvement in the labor movement, particularly in organizing miners. An accomplished raconteur, he tells many stories about labor union and political figures.
Interviewers: Irene Paull (1968?, 1969), Steve Trimble (1977)

125. BJORNSON, KRISTJAN VALDIMAR (VAL) (1906-   ). 1974. 3 hrs., 30 min. 90 p.
A Minnesota state treasurer (1951-55, 1957-75) recalls his family background and describes his involvement in newspaper publishing. In 1918 Bjornson joined his father's newspaper, the Minneota Mascot (Lyon County), and was editor in 1925-27 and 1931-35. He also worked for the Minneapolis Journal, the Minneapolis Tribune, and the St. Paul Pioneer Press and Dispatch. He discusses the beginning of the Farmer-Labor party, the Republican party in Minnesota in the 1920s-40s, his role as state treasurer, and his bid for the Republican gubernatorial nomination in 1960.
Interviewers: Warren Gardner, Bruce Larson

126. DAY, WALTER E. (1880-1969). 1967. 75 min. 33 p. Open for research only.
A state representative as a member of the Nonpartisan League (1918-33) and a member of the Farmer-Labor and Democratic-Farmer-Labor parties (1937-57) discusses family history, including homesteading near Bagley, Clearwater County, Arthur C. Townley and the Nonpartisan League, the state legislature in the 1920s and 1930s, and Governor Floyd B. Olson.
Interviewer: Russell Fridley

127. DUNN, ROY E. (1886-   ). 1969. 2 hrs. Open for research only.
A state representative (1925-31, 1933-67) from Otter Tail County discusses his political career, role as minority and majority leader in the state house of representatives, and membership on the Republican National Committee (1936-52). He records his impressions of a number of Minnesota governors, including Theodore Christianson, Floyd B. Olson, Elmer A. Benson, and C. Elmer Anderson.
Interviewer: James Bormann

128. GOFF, ROBERT E. (1936-   ). 1965. 105 min. Restricted.
Personal secretary to Democratic-Farmer-Labor Governor Karl F. Rolvaag (1964-67), Goff discusses the gubernatorial election in 1962, Rolvaag's administration, and the DFL leadership meeting at Sugar Hills resort, Itasca County, in 1965. He also comments on the labor movement in Minnesota, the future of the DFL party, and a number of political leaders.
Interviewer: Russell Fridley

129. GRAHAM, CHARLES A. (1905-   ). 1968. 90 min.
An aide to Governors Luther W. Youngdahl, C. Elmer Anderson, Orville L. Freeman, Elmer L. Andersen, Karl F. Rolvaag, and Harold LeVander speaks about his employment and relationships with these men. He also describes life in St. Paul's black community.
Interviewers: Russell Fridley, Robert Goff, Lila Johnson

130. HEANEY, GERALD W. (1918-   ). 1967. 90 min. 29 p. Restricted.
Judge of the U.S. circuit court of appeals in Duluth (1966-   ) recalls his initial interest in politics during the 1928 presidential campaign and discusses his early life, law practice in Duluth in the 1940s, work for the Democratic-Farmer-Labor party, and activities with the Democratic National Committee as finance director and national committeeman. He also comments on political associates, including Hubert H. Humphrey.
Interviewer: Helen White

131. HEFFELFINGER, ELIZABETH BRADLEY (1900-81). 1978, 1979. 11 hrs., 30 min. 246 p. Restricted.
A Republican party activist and civic leader provides information on her family and childhood in Texas; education at Smith College, Mass.; marriage to F. Peavey Heffelfinger, president of Peavey Co., Minneapolis; Minneapolis politics in the 1930s and 1940s; and state and national politics in the 1960s-80s. Heffelfinger served as Republican national committeewoman (1948-60) and secretary

of the Republican National Committee (1958-60), a U.S. delegate to several UNESCO commissions in the 1950s, and head of the women's division of the Office of Civil Defense for Hennepin County during World War II. She comments on the post–World War II U.S. refugee relief operations in Europe, Israel, and India in the 1950s, Harold Stassen, Presidents Dwight D. Eisenhower, Richard M. Nixon, and Gerald Ford, and Hubert H. Humphrey.

Interviewer: James Fogerty

132. HOUGH, SUE M. DICKEY (1890-). 1975. 45 min.

One of the first women to serve as a state representative (1923–25) discusses her family background, her decision to run for the legislature, her campaign, her interests in legislation, and the legislative process.

Interviewer: Ramona Burks

133. HURSH, MORRIS C. (1906–81). 1968. 75 min. 19 p.

The executive secretary of Governors Floyd B. Olson (1931–36), Hjalmar Petersen (1936–37), and Elmer A. Benson (1937–39) compares the personalities and politics of these men. Hursh, appointed commissioner of public welfare in 1955 by Governor Orville L. Freeman, discusses that administration.

Interviewer: Lila Johnson

134. JOHNSON, FRANCIS A. 1973. 60 min. 27 p.

The son of Magnus Johnson (1871–1936) remembers his father's career in the state legislature (1915–17, 1919–23) and the U.S. Congress (1923–25, 1933–35) and as the Farmer-Labor candidate for governor in 1922 and 1926. He also recalls other Farmer-Laborites and Nonpartisan Leaguers of the 1920s and 1930s.

Interviewer: Bruce Larson

135. KING, STAFFORD (1893–1970). 1968. 4 hrs. 30 p. Open for research only.

A state auditor for 38 years discusses his childhood in Bigfork, Itasca County; his military career during the Mexican border dispute and World War I; his career as auditor; and Minnesota politics since the 1930s, including Floyd B. Olson and the Farmer-Labor and Republican parties.

Interviewers: Russell Fridley, Lila Johnson, Lucile Kane

136. LEIRFALLOM, JARLE B. (1913-). 1971. 2 hrs., 30 min. Restricted.

The Minnesota commissioner of conservation (1967–70) discusses his career, the establishment of Voyageurs National Park, management of parks and forests in Minnesota,

and Governor Harold LeVander and his administration.

Interviewers: Lee Anderson, Newell Searle, Robert Wheeler

137. LeVANDER, BERNHARD (1916-). 1974. 3 hrs. 73 p.

An attorney and brother of Governor Harold LeVander recalls his early life and involvement in politics. He discusses Harold E. Stassen's 1938 gubernatorial campaign, directing Stassen's drive for the U.S. presidency (1946–48), Chief Justice Warren E. Burger from Minnesota, Governor Luther W. Youngdahl, and the Republican party in Minnesota during the 1940s and 1950s.

Interviewers: Warren Gardner, James Mulrooney

138. LINDBERGH, FRANK A. (1870–1966). 1964. 30 min. 6 p. Open for research only.

The brother of Charles A. Lindbergh, Sr., was an attorney in Little Falls, Morrison County, and Crosby, Crow Wing County. He discusses Lindbergh and his political career, the sixth congressional district in Minnesota, the Nonpartisan League, and Governor Knute Nelson.

Interviewer: Bruce Larson

139. LUTHER, SARA L. F. (SALLY) (1918-). 1975. 105 min. Restricted.

A state representative (1951–63) and executive assistant to Governor Karl F. Rolvaag (1963–67) discusses her legislative experience; Coya Knutson, first U.S. Congresswoman from Minnesota; and the gubernatorial election of 1966.

Interviewer: Arvonne Fraser

140. MARSHALL, FRED (1906-). 1970. 75 min. 33 p.

Born near Grove City, Meeker County, where he has lived all his life, Marshall recalls his childhood, farming, his father's job with the Minnesota Department of Agriculture, his own work as state director of the Farm Security Administration (1941–48), his campaign as the Democratic-Farmer-Labor candidate for U.S. Congress in 1948, and his service as a U.S. Congressman (1949–63) from the sixth district.

Interviewers: Jean Choate, Lila Johnson, John Massmann

141. PEYTON, JOHN NEWTON (1885–1975). 1967. 45 min. 9 p.

The son of a Duluth banker who arrived in Minnesota in the 1850s discusses his own banking career in Minnesota (1912–52), his career as state commissioner of banks (1931–33) under

Governor Floyd B. Olson, and changes he instituted in the state banking system.
Interviewer: Lila Johnson

142. POPOVICH, PETER S. (1920-   ). 1956. 15 min. Open for research only.
The secretary of the Minnesota delegation to the 1956 Democratic National Convention discusses that convention and efforts to nominate Hubert H. Humphrey as the party's presidential candidate.
Interviewer: James Bormann

143. REGNIER, EMIL L. (1902-80). 1974. 70 min.
A Farmer-Labor state senator (1931-33) recalls his involvement in politics, his impressions of U.S. Congressman Magnus Johnson, whom he assisted in 1933, his work as campaign manager for the Farmer-Labor party in 1932 and 1934, and Governor Floyd B. Olson.
Interviewer: Warren Gardner

144. SLEN, THEODOR S. (1885-   ). 1982. 2 hrs.
An attorney, state legislator (1935-41), and municipal, probate, and county judge (1951-73) from Lac qui Parle County, Slen discusses the Democratic and Farmer-Labor parties of Minnesota, including the 1944 merger, Governors Floyd B. Olson, Hjalmar Petersen, and Elmer A. Benson, Hubert H. Humphrey, and changes in the Democratic and Republican party philosophies from the 1940s through the 1970s. He also comments on the American judicial system, the Minnesota legislature, and the University of Minnesota Law School.
Interviewer: James Fogerty

145. SOMMER, CLIFFORD C. (1908-   ). 1978. 14 hrs., 45 min. 470 p. Restricted.
A banker and politician discusses his childhood in Rush City, Chisago County; education at the University of Minnesota and Rutgers University, New Jersey; his career in banking; Republican politics; and his civic activities. Sommer was president (1955-71) of Security Bank and Trust Co. (later Northwestern National Bank) of Owatonna, Steele County; president of the Minnesota Bankers Assn. (1970-71); member of the Minneapolis Board of Park Commissioners (1953-55); and state senator (1967-71).
Interviewers: James Fogerty, Cheryl Theis

146. WRIGHT, DONALD ORR, SR. (1892-1977). 1974. 60 min. 22 p.
A veteran state legislator from Minneapolis who served both as representative (1927-35) and senator (1935-71) discusses his early

life and entry into Republican politics, his legislative career, and Governor Floyd B. Olson and other Farmer-Laborites.
Interviewers: Warren Gardner, James Mulrooney

[[[[[[[[[[∘]]]]]]]]]]]

MINNESOTA GUBERNATORIAL ELECTIONS OF 1962 AND 1966

The Minnesota gubernatorial election of 1962 was the closest in the state's history. Republican Governor Elmer L. Andersen was first declared the winner by 142 votes, but a recount gave Democratic-Farmer-Labor (DFL) candidate Karl F. Rolvaag a majority of 91 votes.
During Rolvaag's term differences grew between him and his party's leaders. In 1965 at a meeting at Sugar Hills resort in Itasca County the DFL State Central Committee concluded that Rolvaag should not be renominated. At the DFL party's 1966 state convention, Lieutenant-Governor A. M. (Sandy) Keith won the nomination for governor after 20 ballots. Rolvaag, however, won the state primary election but was defeated in the general election by Republican Harold LeVander.
In 1978 Mark Haidet undertook an oral history project for the Minnesota Historical Society to document the gubernatorial elections of 1962 and 1966. Candidates, campaign managers, and leaders of the DFL and Republican parties were among those interviewed. Each discussed his or her involvement in the elections, offering a view of the 1960s political scene. Because of the similarity of subject matter in the interviews listed below, only information about the person interviewed is provided in each entry.

147. ANDERSEN, ELMER L. (1909-   ). 1978. 90 min. Restricted.
The incumbent Republican candidate for governor in 1962 and candidate for endorsement for governor in 1966.

148. FARR, GEORGE A. (1924-   ). 1978. 90 min. Restricted.
State chairman of the DFL party (1961-67).

149. GRAVEN, DAVID L. (1929-   ). 1978. 80 min.
Attorney and one of the organizers of the 1965 Sugar Hills meeting of DFL leaders.

150. HARRIS, FORREST J. (1916-   ). 1978. 90 min.
Professor of social sciences at the University of Minnesota and an active member of the DFL party in the fifth district.

151. HESS, ROBERT E. (1918-   ). 1978. 50 min. Restricted.
Vice-president of the Minnesota AFL-CIO (1956-66) and a negotiator between Keith and Rolvaag prior to the 1966 primary election.

152. KANE, BETTY. 1978. 75 min.
DFL party state chairwoman (1963-68).

153. KEITH, A. M. (SANDY) (1928-   ). 1978. 2 hrs.
Lieutenant-governor (1962-67) and DFL-endorsed candidate for governor in 1966.

154. McLAUGHLIN, MICHAEL (1924-   ). 1978. 2 hrs., 10 min.
Campaign manager for Rolvaag in the 1966 election.

155. SHORT, ROBERT E. (1917-82). 1978. 45 min. Restricted.
Lieutenant-governor candidate on the Rolvaag ticket in 1966.

156. SPANNAUS, WARREN R. (1930-   ). 1978. 45 min. Restricted.
Staff member and later campaign director for U.S. Senator Walter F. Mondale (1965-66); DFL state chairman (1967-69).

157. THISS, GEORGE (1927-83). 1978. 60 min. Restricted.
Republican state chairman (1965-71).

158. WRIGHT, FRANK (1931-   ). 1978. 75 min.
Minneapolis Tribune reporter who broke the news story about the Sugar Hills meeting in 1965.

[[[[[[[[[[[∘]]]]]]]]]]]

HUBERT H. HUMPHREY ORAL HISTORY PROJECT

In 1978 the Hubert H. Humphrey Institute of Public Affairs at the University of Minnesota funded an oral history project to record the memories and thoughts of major figures in the long career of Hubert H. Humphrey (1911-78). The Minnesota Historical Society prepared transcripts of the interviews and is the custodian of the collection. Arthur E. Naftalin, an early Humphrey aide, former mayor of Minneapolis, and professor of public affairs at the Humphrey Institute, interviewed Humphrey's friends, staff members, political associates, and some family members. A few of the interviews were conducted by or with Norman Sherman, staff assistant and later press secretary to Humphrey during his senatorial and vice-presidential years.

The interviews contain information about Humphrey's life, including family history and growing up in South Dakota; education at the University of Minnesota and Louisiana State University; involvement in early Democratic-Farmer-Labor (DFL) party politics; mayorality of Minneapolis (1945-48); U.S. Senate years (1949-64, 1971-78); vice-presidency under Lyndon B. Johnson (1965-69); presidential campaigns of 1968 and 1972; and final illness and death in 1978. Anecdotes related by those interviewed reveal various aspects of Humphrey's personality and provide information about his family and friends, political associates, and staff people. Some of the interviewees analyze Humphrey's political position on several issues, especially Communist influence in the DFL party; federal civil rights legislation; U.S. foreign policy, especially the Vietnam conflict; agriculture; economic affairs, including the Humphrey-Hawkins bill; and labor relations.

In addition to the interviews of individuals listed below, the project included tape recordings of two 1978 discussion groups: (1) the Carnegie Endowment Conference on Humphrey and Foreign Affairs (6 hrs.) and (2) an informal gathering of Humphrey's friends and former employees at the home of Max M. Kampelman (70 min.). The MHS is also the repository of the Hubert H. Humphrey Papers which include, in addition to the records, correspondence, and other files, many tapes and films with or about Humphrey. The Humphrey Papers have some restrictions.

The entries below indentify the people interviewed and indicate how their lives and work intersected with the career of Hubert Humphrey.

159. ALLEN, BYRON G. (BARNEY) (1901-   ). 1978. 4 hrs. 111 p.
DFL gubernatorial candidate (1944) and Democratic national committeeman (1948-55); Minnesota commissioner of agriculture (1955-61); U.S. Department of Agriculture staff member (1961-69).

160. ANDERSON, EUGENIE MOORE (1909-   ). 1978. 2 hrs. 65 p.
Active in DFL and Democratic politics on local, state, and national levels; U.S. ambassador to Denmark (1949-53); U.S. minister to

Bulgaria (1962-65); U.S. delegate to the
United Nations (1965-68).

161. AUERBACH, CARL A. (1915-   ). 1978.
  3 hrs. 82 p.
    Attorney and professor of law; dean,
University of Minnesota Law School (1973-79);
friend and adviser to Humphrey.

162. BACKSTROM, CHARLES H. (1926-   ).
  1978. 60 min. 34 p.
    Congressional fellow (American Political
Science Assn.) assigned to Humphrey's office
(1958); political science professor, University of Minnesota.

163. BARNACLE, TIMOTHY. 1978. 2 hrs. 67 p.
  Restricted.
    Congressional fellow assigned to Hum-
phrey's office (1972); principal economic assistant and speech writer for Humphrey (1973-
78).

164. BERGLAND, BOB S. (1928-   ). 1978.
  60 min. 28 p.
    U.S. Congressman from Minnesota's seventh
district (1971-77); U.S. secretary of agriculture (1977-81).

165. BERMAN, EDGAR F. (1915-   ). 1978.
  2 hrs., 30 min. 79 p.
    Physician; author of Hubert: The Triumph
and Tragedy of the Humphrey I Knew (1979).

166. BESTER, EARL T. (1900-   ). 1978. 30
  min. 16 p.
    Labor union organizer and executive,
United Steelworkers (1930s-   ); active in
Farmer-Labor and DFL parties.

167. BIDEN, JOSEPH R., JR. (1942-   ).
  1978. 30 min. Restricted.
    U.S. Senator from Delaware (1972-   ).
    Interviewer: Norman Sherman

168. BIEMILLER, ANDREW J. (1906-82). 1978.
  90 min. 48 p.
    Wisconsin state legislator (1937-41);
U.S. Congressman (1945-47, 1949-51); director
of department of legislation for the AFL-CIO
(1956-78).

169. BOOKBINDER, HYMAN H. 1978. 60 min.
  30 p.
    Economist and lobbyist for CIO and AFL-
CIO (1952-60); assistant to U.S. secretary of
commerce (1961-63); assistant director of Office of Economic Opportunity and special assistant to Humphrey (1965-67).

170. CONNELL, WILLIAM. 1978. 60 min. 42 p.
    Humphrey's press secretary (1955-56),

administrative assistant (1961-65), and chief
of staff (1966-69).

171. CULVER, URSULA. 1978. 2 hrs. 64 p.
  Restricted.
    Secretary for Humphrey's advance teams
(1966-68) and his personal secretary (1968-
78).

172. DIDIER, CALVIN W. (1925-   ). 1978.
  60 min.
    Minister at House of Hope Presbyterian
Church in St. Paul (1970-   ).

173. DYMALLY, MERVYN M. (1926-   ). 1978.
  45 min. Restricted.
    California state legislator (1962-74) and
lieutenant-governor (1975-79); founder, National Conference of Black Elected Officials;
Humphrey campaign supporter.

174. EAGLETON, THOMAS F. (1929-   ). 1978.
  50 min. Restricted.
    U.S. Senator from Missouri (1969-   );
Democratic vice-presidential nominee (1972).
    Interviewer: Norman Sherman

175. EVANS, ROWLAND. 1978. 45 min. 30 p.
  Restricted.
    Reporter and political columnist for the
Chicago Sun-Times syndicate.
    Interviewer: Norman Sherman

176. FOLEY, EUGENE P. (1928-   ). 1978.
  2 hrs. 84 p. Restricted.
    Humphrey's staff representative on the
U.S. Senate Small Business Committee (1959-
63); Small Business Administration employee
(1963-65); assistant secretary of commerce and
administrator of Economic Development Assn.
(1965-66).
    Interviewers: Arthur Naftalin, Norman
Sherman

177. FRASER, DONALD M. (1924-   ). 1978.
  50 min. 35 p.
    Minnesota state senator (1955-63); U.S.
Congressman from Minnesota's fifth district
(1963-79); mayor of Minneapolis (1980-   ).

178. FREEMAN, ORVILLE L. (1918-   ). 1978.
  30 min. 21 p.
    Governor of Minnesota (1955-61); U.S.
secretary of agriculture (1961-69).

179. FREEMAN, ORVILLE L. AND EVRON M. KIRK-
  PATRICK (1911-   ). 1978. 30 min. 22 p.
    Kirkpatrick, an author and political sci-
entist, was a University of Minnesota professor during Humphrey's student years; executive
director, American Political Science Assn. On
Freeman, see above.

180. GARTNER, DAVID. 1978. 45 min. 29 p.
Humphrey's administrative assistant
(1961-69, 1971-78).

181. GATES, FREDERIC. 1978. 2 hrs. 50 p.
Restricted.
Personal aide to Humphrey (1973-78) and
son of Frederic J. (Freddie) Gates, who was
Humphrey's close friend and personal aide
(1945-71).

182. HART, GARY (1937-   ). 1978. 30 min.
20 p. Restricted.
George S. McGovern's presidential cam-
paign director (1970-72); U.S. Senator from
Colorado (1975-   ).
Interviewer: Norman Sherman

183. HARTT, JULIAN. 1978. 2 hrs. 82 p.
Restricted.
Methodist clergyman; Humphrey's childhood
friend in Doland, S.Dak.
Interviewer: Norman Sherman

184. HEANEY, GERALD W. (1918-   ). 1978.
3 hrs., 30 min. 74 p.
DFL party activist; judge, U.S. circuit
court of appeals, Duluth (1966-   ).

185. HELLER, WALTER (1915-   ). 1978. 2
hrs. 47 p.
University of Minnesota professor of
economics (1946-   ); member, Council of
Economic Advisers to the president (1961-63).

186. HERLING, JOHN (1907-   ). 1978. 60
min. 33 p.
Newspaperman and syndicated columnist re-
porting especially on labor and general affairs; publisher, John Herling's Labor Letter
(1947).

187. HOWARD, FRANCES HUMPHREY (1915-   ).
1978. 55 min. 26 p.
Humphrey's sister.

188. HUMPHREY, HUBERT H., III (SKIP) (1942-
). 1978. 55 min.
Eldest son of Hubert and Muriel Humphrey;
attorney; Minnesota state legislator (1973-
83); attorney general (1983-   ).

189. HYNEMAN, CHARLES. 1978. 60 min. 37 p.
Professor of political science and Hum-
phrey's mentor in graduate school, Louisiana
State University.

190. INK, DWIGHT (1922-   ). 1979. 30
min. Restricted.
Local government administrator, North
Dakota (1948-51); government administrator in
various federal agencies (1951-70s); president, American Society of Public Administrators.

191. JORGENSON, JACK JEROME, SR. (1914-
). 1978. 60 min. 30 p. Restricted.
Labor unionist in Minnesota; president,
Teamsters Joint Council No. 32 (1943-   ).

192. JOSEPH, GERALDINE MACK (GERI) (1923-
). 1978. 80 min. 45 p.
Minneapolis Tribune staff writer (1945-
53), columnist (1971-   ); DFL state chairwoman (1958-60); Democratic national committeewoman (1960-71); U.S. ambassador to the
Netherlands (1978-81).

193. KAMPELMAN, MAX M. (1920-   ). 1978.
30 min. 18 p.
Attorney; Humphrey's legislative assistant on foreign affairs (1949-55).

194. KELLY, HARRY. 1978. 50 min. 24 p.
Restricted.
Reporter for the Associated Press; as-
signed to cover Humphrey's campaigns in 1964
and 1968.
Interviewer: Norman Sherman

195. KUBICEK, WILLIAM G. AND FREDERIC J.
KOTTKE (1917-   ). 1978. 20 min. 26 p.
Kubicek and Kottke, both physicians on
the faculty of the University of Minnesota
Medical School, have been active in the DFL
party since the 1940s. Kubicek was state DFL
party secretary (1950-68).

196. LEARY, D. J. 1978. 110 min. 51 p.
Restricted.
Advance publicity man for Humphrey in
1966, 1968, and 1972.
Interviewer: Norman Sherman

197. LIPPINCOTT, BENJAMIN. 1979. 40 min.
27 p.
Professor and emeritus professor of
political science, University of Minnesota
(1929-   ).

198. LORD, MILES W. (1919-   ). 1978. 60
min. 41 p.
Minnesota attorney general (1955-60);
U.S. attorney, St. Paul (1960-66); U.S. district court judge, St. Paul (1966-   ).

199. MANFRED, FREDERICK F. (1912-   ).
1978. 60 min.
Author; Humphrey campaign worker in 1943.

200. McGOVERN, GEORGE S. (1922-   ). 1978.
60 min. 41 p.
U.S. Congressman from South Dakota (1957-
61); special assistant to the president and

director, Food for Peace (1961-62); U.S. Senator from South Dakota (1963-81); Democratic presidential nominee (1972).

201. McPHERSON, HARRY C., JR. (1929-   ). 1978. 30 min.
Counsel, Democratic policy committee, U.S. Senate (1956-63); special assistant and counsel to the president (1965-69); attorney, Washington, D.C.
Interviewers: Arthur Naftalin, Norman Sherman

202. MINTENER, (JAMES) BRADSHAW (1902-   ). 1978. 60 min. 40 p. Restricted.
Vice-president and general counsel, Pillsbury Mills, Inc. (1933-54); Humphrey campaign worker in 1943, 1945, and 1947; assistant secretary, U.S. Department of Health, Education, and Welfare (1954-56); attorney, Washington, D.C.

203. MITAU, G. THEODORE (1920-79). 1978. 60 min. 25 p.
Political science professor, Macalester College, St. Paul (1940-68); chancellor, Minnesota state university system (1968-76).

204. MOE, RICHARD. 1978. 35 min. 22 p.
State DFL party chairman (1970-72); administrative assistant to Walter F. Mondale (1972-81).

205. MUSKIE, EDMUND S. (1914-   ). 1978. 2 hrs. 57 p. Restricted.
Maine governor (1955-59); U.S. Senator from Maine (1959-80); Democratic vice-presidential candidate (1968); U.S. secretary of state (1980-81).

206. NATHAN, ROBERT. 1978. 60 min. 38 p.
Economist; executive committee chairman (1952-55) and national chairman (1956-58), Americans for a Democratic Society; head of task forces and author of position papers for Humphrey campaign (1968).

207. NEHOTTE, STEPHEN. 1978. 25 min. 16 p.
Labor unionist in Minnesota, Teamsters Union (1940s-   ); DFL activist.

208. NELSON, GAYLORD A. (1916-   ). 1978. 55 min.
Wisconsin Democratic state senator (1949-58), governor (1958-62), and U.S. Senator (1963-   ).

209. NEVINS, RICHARD AND SHIRLEY FILIATROUT. 1978. 90 min. 47 p.
Nevins was a Humphrey campaign supporter in California in the 1960s and 1970s. Filiatrout was secretary, AFL Labor Temple, Duluth (1942-47); organizer, Volunteers for Humphrey (1948, 1954); political campaign worker in California (1958).

210. PETERSON, NEAL. 1978. 30 min. 13 p.
Humphrey campaign worker (1960); counsel to U.S. Senate Small Business Committee (1961-64); vice-president's staff (1964-68).

211. PETERSON, P. KENNETH (1915-   ). 1979. 30 min. 20 p.
Minnesota state legislator (1947-53); chairman, Minnesota Republican party (1949-53); mayor of Minneapolis (1957-61); unsuccessful candidate for U.S. Senate against Humphrey (1960); Minnesota public service commissioner (1967-73).

212. RAMBURG, LEONARD F. (1906-   ) AND W. GLEN WALLACE. 1978. 45 min. 25 p.
Ramburg, a bank officer in Minneapolis, was a Republican alderman, Minneapolis city council (1945-49). Wallace, an architect, was a Democratic alderman, Minneapolis city council (1935-55). Each served on the city council during Humphrey's term as mayor.

213. RAUH, JOSEPH L. (1911-   ). 1978. 75 min. 44 p.
Law secretary to U.S. Supreme Court Justices Benjamin N. Cardozo and Felix Frankfurter (1936-39); counsel to various federal government agencies (1935-42); member and officer, Americans for Democratic Action (1947-   ).

214. RAVNHOLT, EDNA. 1978. 55 min. Restricted.
Office manager for Humphrey (1962-78).

215. REILLY, JOHN. 1978. 60 min. 36 p. Restricted.
Professor of political science, Harvard University; Humphrey's chief foreign policy assistant (1962-69).

216. ROE, DAVID K. 1978. 2 hrs., 15 min. 72 p.
Labor union executive; and president, Minnesota Building and Construction Council (1953-65); president, Minnesota AFL-CIO (1966-   ); active in DFL party.

217. RYAN, WILLIAM E. (ED) (1897-1983). 1978. 60 min. 33 p.
Minneapolis chief of police (1945-47); sheriff, Hennepin County (1947-67).

218. SAUNDERS, ALBERT C. 1978. 30 min. 11 p.
Humphrey's senior legislative assistant

on domestic affairs (1971-74) and director of legislation (1974-78).

219. SCHWARTZ, EDWARD P. (1903-   ). 1978. 60 min. 37 p.
Twin Cities newspaperman (1925-44); president, Minneapolis printing and advertising firm (1944-   ); secretary, Minneapolis Housing and Redevelopment Authority (1959-61).

220. SHORE, WILLIAM B. (1925-   ). 1978. 55 min. 40 p.
DFL organizer (1948-50s); national chairman, Students for Democratic Society (1948-50); research director for Humphrey's campaign staff (1948) and staff member (1949); CIO labor organizer (1949-50); Orville L. Freeman's campaign staff (1952).
Interviewer: Norman Sherman

221. SIMMS, WILLIAM. 1978. 30 min. 17 p. Restricted.
Office manager, Hennepin County Welfare Department (1940s); finance director of Humphrey's campaigns (1943, 1945, 1948); administrative assistant (1946-54).

222. SIMON, PAUL (1929-   ). 1978. 45 min. 31 p. Restricted.
Newspaper publisher; Illinois state legislator (1955-69), lieutenant-governor (1969-73), and U.S. Congressman (1975-   ).
Interviewer: Norman Sherman

223. STEWART, JOHN. 1978. 60 min. 31 p. Restricted.
American Political Science Assn. fellow in Humphrey's Senate office (1961); Humphrey's legislative assistant on domestic affairs (1962-66, 1967-69); executive director, Democratic Policy Council, Democratic National Committee (1969).

224. TOWER, JOHN G. (1925-   ). 1978. 20 min. Restricted.
Republican U.S. Senator from Texas (1961-   ).
Interviewer: Norman Sherman

225. VAN DYKE, FREDERICK T. (TED). 1978. 60 min. 36 p.
European Common Market employee, Washington, D.C. (1960s); volunteer for Humphrey (1963-64) and campaign worker, speech writer, traveling chief of staff (1964-68); campaign worker for George S. McGovern (1972).
Interviewers: Arthur Naftalin, Norman Sherman

226. WATERS, HERBERT J. (1912-   ). 1978. 60 min. 25 p.
California newspaperman; U.S. Department

of Agriculture employee (1949-55); Humphrey's press secretary (1953-55) and administrative assistant (1955-61); assistant administrator, Agency for International Development (1961-68).

227. ZEIDMAN, PHILIP F. (1934-   ). 1978. 105 min. 63 p.
Attorney, special assistant to the administrator and general counsel, U.S. Small Business Administration (1961-68); speech writer and special assistant to Humphrey (1964-68).
Interviewers: Arthur Naftalin, Norman Sherman

[[[[[[[[[[∘]]]]]]]]]]]

THE MINNESOTA SUPREME COURT JUSTICES

The Minnesota judiciary has not been extensively documented over the years. Consequently Mark Haidet of the Minnesota Historical Society staff developed a plan to interview members of the state supreme court. In 1978 Haidet interviewed four justices; a fifth and earlier interview with Justice John J. Todd has been included in this developing oral history collection.

In addition to giving personal backgrounds, Justices Thomas F. Gallagher, Oscar R. Knutson, Walter F. Rogosheske, and Robert J. Sheran discuss the Minnesota state court system, operational problems of the court, changes and proposed changes in the court system, major issues before the supreme court from the 1940s to 1970s, political and public pressures on supreme court justices, and the influence of the U.S. Supreme Court on state supreme courts.

228. GALLAGHER, THOMAS F. (1897-   ). 1978. 75 min.
Born in Faribault, Rice County, Gallagher recalls his early life, his decision to enter the legal profession and early legal career in Minneapolis (1921-42), the effect of the 1930s Depression on the legal profession, and the Minneapolis truckers' strike in 1934. He describes his political activities and affiliation with the Farmer-Labor and Democratic parties, his service as associate justice of the supreme court (1943-66), and his impressions of Justices Charles Loring, Oscar R. Knutson, Henry M. Gallagher, and Roger L. Dell. He also comments on news coverage of court proceedings.

229. KNUTSON, OSCAR R. (1899-1981). 1978.
90 min.
   Born in Wisconsin, Knutson moved with his
parents to a farm near Warren, Marshall County, in 1916. He recalls his early life, the
University of Minnesota Law School in the
1920s, and practicing law during the 1930s
Depression. He discusses the election and
appointment process of Minnesota justices. He
was appointed a judge of the district court in
1941, associate justice of the supreme court
in 1948, and chief justice in 1962, serving
until 1973.

230. ROGOSHESKE, WALTER F. (1914-   ).
1978. 2 hrs.
   Associate Justice Rogosheske was born in
Sauk Rapids, Benton County, and received his
law degree from the University of Minnesota in
1939. He recalls his early life, education,
and law practice in Sauk Rapids and describes
his legislative career (1943-49) and his career as a trial judge. He records his impressions of Chief Justices Oscar R. Knutson and
Robert J. Sheran.

231. SHERAN, ROBERT J. (1916-   ). 1978.
2 hrs.
   Chief Justice Sheran was born in Waseca
County and graduated from the University of
Minnesota Law School in 1939. He recalls his
early life and decision to enter the legal
profession and discusses his impressions of
Chief Justices Henry M. Gallagher, Charles
Loring, and Oscar R. Knutson. He describes
his law practice, service in the state legislature (1947-51), appointment (1962) and res-
ignation (1970) as associate justice of the
supreme court, and his appointment (1973) as
chief justice.

232. TODD, JOHN J. (1927-   ). 1974. 20
min. Open for research only.
   Associate Justice Todd was born in St.
Paul, graduated from the University of Minnesota Law School in 1950, and practiced law until his appointment to the supreme court in
1972. He describes the remodeling of the
court chambers and comments on the judicial
procedures of the court.
   Interviewed by Capitol tour guides, 1974

[[[[[[[[[[[o]]]]]]]]]]]

STATE LEGISLATIVE LEADERS

   The Minnesota Historical Society conducted an oral history project with leaders of
both state houses during each legislative
session from 1969 to 1976. The interviewers
sought to document the decision-making and
legislative processes as viewed from the
inside. The legislators, interviewed before
and after a legislative session, discussed the
issues and problems they anticipated and then
described the operations of the legislature
and analyzed the accomplishments and failures
of that session. They also discussed the jobs
of the leadership: majority leader, minority
leader, speaker of the house of representatives, and president of the senate. While the
areas of concern are similar year after year
-- taxes, education, welfare, environment,
city and state planning, and changes in the
legislative process -- each legislator talks
about his particular way of dealing with the
process of governing.
   The entries below indicate the legislator
interviewed, years of service in the state
senate or house of representatives, and the
leadership positions held.

233. ANDERSON, IRVIN N. (1923-   ). 1973,
1975. 2 hrs., 15 min. Restricted.
   House 1965-83: majority leader 1973-78.
   Interviewers: Lila Johnson (1973),
Joanne Baldwin (1975)

234. ASHBACH, ROBERT O. (1916-   ). 1975.
60 min. Restricted.
   House 1963-65. Senate 1967-83: minority
leader 1975-82.
   Interviewer: Joanne Baldwin

235. COLEMAN, NICHOLAS D. (1925-81). 1969,
1970, 1971, 1973, 1975. 8 hrs., 15 min.
233 p. Restricted.
   Senate 1963-81: assistant minority leader 1967-70, minority leader 1971-72, majority
leader 1973-80.
   Interviewers: Lila Johnson, Joanne
Baldwin (1975)

236. DIRLAM, AUBREY W. (1913-   ). 1969,
1971, 1973. 5 hrs., 45 min. 119 p.
   House 1941-74: minority leader 1957-58,
1973-74; majority leader 1963-70; speaker
1971-72.
   Interviewer: Lila Johnson

237. DUXBURY, LLOYD L., JR. (1922-   ).
1969, 1970. 90 min. 35 p.
   House 1951-69: floor leader 1959-62,
speaker 1963-69.
   Interviewer: Lila Johnson

238. GOETZ, JAMES B. (1936-   ). 1969. 90
min. 34 p.
   Lieutenant-governor 1967-71.
   Interviewer: Lila Johnson

239. GRITTNER, KARL F. (1922-   ). 1969.
    2 hrs. 53 p.
        House 1953-59. Senate 1959-71: minority
    leader 1967-70.
        Interviewer: Lila Johnson

240. GUSTAFSON, EARL B. (1927-   ). 1969.
    2 hrs., 30 min.
        House 1963-67, 1969-71: second assistant
    minority leader 1969-70. Senate 1971-73.
        Interviewer: Lila Johnson

241. HOLMQUIST, STANLEY W. (1909-   ).
    1969, 1971. 2 hrs., 45 min. 41 p.
        House 1947-55. Senate 1955-73: majority
    leader 1967-72.
        Interviewer: Lila Johnson

242. KRIEGER, HAROLD G. (1926-   ). 1973.
    45 min. Restricted.
        Senate 1963-75: minority leader 1973-74.
        Interviewer: Lila Johnson

243. LEE, L. J. (1907-   ). 1969. 30 min.
    15 p.
        House 1961-73: assistant minority leader
    1969-70.
        Interviewer: Lila Johnson

244. LINDSTROM, ERNEST A. (1931-   ).
    1971, 1972. 90 min. 23 p.
        House 1966-75: majority leader 1971-72.
        Interviewer: Lila Johnson

245. SABO, MARTIN O. (1938-   ). 1969,
    1970, 1972, 1973, 1975. 5 hrs., 30 min.
    99 p.
        House 1961-79: minority leader 1969-72,
    speaker 1973-78.
        Interviewers: Lila Johnson (1969-73),
    Joanne Baldwin (1975)

246. SAVELKOUL, HENRY J. (1940-   ). 1975.
    60 min. Restricted.
        House 1969-79: minority leader 1975-78.
        Interviewer: Joanne Baldwin

[[[[[[[[[[[∘]]]]]]]]]]]

VOICES OF THE GOVERNORS

    During the 1960s and 1970s as part of the
oral history program, the Minnesota Historical
Society conducted interviews with twelve Minnesota governors. In some measure the interviews focus on each man's family background
and early life, education, early careers, developing interest in political and civic affairs, campaigns for office, service as gover-

nor, view of the role of governor, assessment
of the relationship between the executive and
the legislature and the judiciary, evaluation
of key issues of the administration, gubernatorial appointments, commentary on party and
opposition party politics, and colleagues on
the state and national levels.
    The interviewers were interested in the
governors' impressions, opinions, and attitudes rather than exact dates and facts. The
entries below list the political party each
represented, the years of service as governor,
and other major political and governmental
offices each man held.

247. ANDERSEN, ELMER L. (1909-   ). 1974,
    1975. 4 hrs., 30 min. 90 p. Open for re-
    search only.
        Republican governor (1961-63), state rep-
    resentative (1949-59).
        Interviewers: Dallas Chrislock (1974),
    Joanne Baldwin (1975)

248. ANDERSON, CLYDE ELMER (1912-   ).
    1964, 1978. 3 hrs., 10 min. 25 p. Re-
    stricted.
        Republican governor (1951-55), lieu-
    tenant-governor (1939-51).
        Interviewers: James Bormann, Russell
    Fridley, Lucile Kane (1964); Mark Haidet
    (1978)

249. BENSON, ELMER A. (1895-   ). 1963,
    1964, 1969. 4 hrs., 15 min. 160 p. The
    1969 interview is restricted.
        Farmer-Labor governor (1937-39), state
    commissioner of banks (1933-35), U.S. Senator
    (1935-37), chairman, Progressive party, 1948.
        Interviewers: James Bormann, Russell
    Fridley, Lucile Kane (1963); Carl Chrislock,
    Lucile Kane (1964); Russell Fridley, Robert
    Goff, Lila Johnson, James Pederson (1969)

250. FREEMAN, ORVILLE L. (1918-   ). 1969,
    1970. 2 hrs. 26 p.
        Democratic-Farmer-Labor governor (1955-
    61), U.S. secretary of agriculture (1961-69).
        Interviewer: Lila Johnson

251. LeVANDER, HAROLD (1910-   ). 1970,
    1977. 2 hrs. 37 p. The 1977 interview is
    restricted.
        Republican governor (1967-71).
        Interviewers: Lila Johnson (1970), Mark
    Haidet (1977)

252. PERPICH, RUDOLPH G. (1928-   ). 1978.
    90 min.
        Democratic-Farmer-Labor governor (1977-
    79, 1983-   ), state senator (1963-71), lieu-
    tenant-governor (1971-77). This interview
    focuses on Croat and Slav communities and fam-

ily life on the Mesabi Iron Range and ethnic politics in Minnesota.
Interviewers: Hyman Berman, Joseph Stipanovich

253. PETERSEN, HJALMAR (1890-1968). 1963. 60 min. 20 p. Open for research only.
Farmer-Labor governor (1936-37), state representative (1931-35), lieutenant-governor (1935-36), railroad and warehouse commissioner (1937-43).
Interviewers: Russell Fridley, Lucile Kane

254. PREUS, JACOB A. O. (1883-1961). 1960. 3 hrs., 30 min. 114 p. Open for research only.
Republican governor (1921-25), state insurance commissioner (1911-14), state auditor (1915-21).
Interviewers: June Holmquist, Lucile Kane

255. ROLVAAG, KARL F. (1913-   ). 1967, 1974, 1978. 7 hrs. The 1967 and 1974 interviews are open for research only; the 1978 interview is restricted.
Democratic-Farmer-Labor governor (1963-67), DFL party state chairman (1950-54), lieutenant-governor (1955-63), U.S. ambassador to Iceland (1967-69), public service commissioner (1973-77).
Interviewers: Russell Fridley (1967), Dallas Chrislock (1974), Mark Haidet (1978)

256. STASSEN, HAROLD E. (1907-   ). 1963. 75 min. 18 p. Open for research only.
Republican governor (1939-43).
Interviewers: Russell Fridley, Arv Johnson

257. THYE, EDWARD J. (1896-1969). 1963. 105 min. 37 p. Open for research only.
Republican governor (1943-47), lieutenant-governor (1943), U.S. Senator (1947-59).
Interviewers: James Bormann, Russell Fridley, Lucile Kane

258. YOUNGDAHL, LUTHER W. (1896-1978). 1964, 1967. 2 hrs., 45 min. 36 p. The 1964 interview is open; the 1967 interview is open for research only.
Republican governor (1947-51), Minnesota supreme court justice (1942-47), federal district judge, Washington, D.C. (1951-78).
Interviewers: James Bormann, Russell Fridley, Lucile Kane (1964); Russell Fridley, Robert Goff, Lila Johnson (1967)

[[[[[[[[[[∘]]]]]]]]]]

BLACKS IN MINNESOTA

In 1974 the Minnesota Historical Society used funds provided by the Northwest Area Foundation to collect and organize materials germane to the history of blacks in Minnesota. During two summers the staff of the Minnesota Black History Project, under the direction of David V. Taylor, collected records of organizations, institutions, clubs, and churches as well as personal papers, genealogies, photographs, and oral interviews. The entries listed below include the oral history interviews conducted for this project as well as some earlier interviews Taylor undertook in doing research for his doctoral dissertation. A more complete description of these interviews and of other material in the society's collections relating to blacks is contained in Blacks in Minnesota: A Preliminary Guide to Historical Sources compiled by David V. Taylor and published by the society in 1976.

259. BANKS, JOHN L. (1907-   ). 1974. 40 min. 16 p.
A retired employee of the Ford Motor Co. discusses family history, the black community in and around Northfield, Rice County, where he moved in 1923, and social and civic activities in the St. Paul black community, where he has lived since 1926.
Interviewer: David Taylor

260. BELL, FRED DOUGLAS (1901-   ) AND LILLIAN VINA BELL (1902-   ). 1975. 90 min. 38 p.
An employee of the United States Steel Corp. for 40 years, Mr. Bell recalls working in the steel-mill town of Gary, St. Louis County. The Bells, who settled in Duluth in 1923, discuss life there and the growth of the black community.
Interviewers: Musa Foster, Malik Simba, David Taylor

261. BLACK, SIDONIA ELIZABETH (1890-   ). 1975. 45 min. 21 p.
Black, who moved to Duluth in 1907, describes her life and community events in that city.
Interviewers: Musa Foster, Malik Simba, David Taylor

262. BROWN, IONE M. (1903-   ). 1974. 40 min. 11 p. Open for research only.
Born in Alexandria, Douglas County, Brown recalls family history, particularly her

grandparents, Mr. and Mrs. Austine O. Hopson, and their life in Alexandria, St. Paul, and Minneapolis.
Interviewer: David Taylor

263. DANIELS, FLORENCE HIBBS (1896-   ). 1974. 45 min. 19 p.
Born in Canada, Daniels moved with her family to Minneapolis in the late 1890s. She discusses family history and recalls black community life in Alexandria, Douglas County; Fergus Falls, Otter Tail County; Minneapolis; and St. Paul in the early 1900s.
Interviewer: David Taylor

264. DOZIER, CARRIE L. (1892-   ). 1975. 40 min. 24 p.
Dozier, who moved to Duluth in 1921, discusses social and economic conditions for blacks; educational opportunities; the lynchings of blacks in Duluth in 1920; the United States Steel Corp. company town of Gary, St. Louis County; NAACP activities since the 1920s; and the religious life of the community.
Interviewers: Musa Foster, Seitu Jones, Malik Simba

265. GIBBS, ADINA ADAMS (1896-   ). 1970. 2 hrs. 50 p.
A resident of Minneapolis and daughter of John Q. Adams (1848-1922), publisher of the Western Appeal, discusses her father and her uncle, Cyrus Field Adams (1857-   ), editor of the Chicago Appeal. She also recalls the St. Paul black community at the turn of the century.
Interviewer: David Taylor

266. HALL, S. EDWARD (1878-1975). 1970, 1972, 1974. 10 hrs. 32 p. Open for research only.
A barber who settled in St. Paul in 1900, Hall was an active Republican and a founder of the St. Paul Urban League and the Hallie Q. Brown community center.
The 1970 interview has information on John Q. Adams and his newspaper, blacks in the state legislature, the NAACP, the Afro-American League, the Niagara movement, interracial marriage in the early 1900s, discrimination in St. Paul hotels, and stories of customers and friends.
The 1972 interview covers family and personal history and many aspects of social life in the St. Paul black community in the early 1900s. Hall also sings a slave song he learned as a child.
The 1974 interview deals with early black migration to Minnesota, the establishment of the St. Paul Urban League, black employment in the early 1900s, blacks in the building

trades, the 1920 lynchings in Duluth, and the 1894 Hinckley fire.
Interviewers: David Taylor (1970), Steve Trimble (1972), Ethel Ray Nance (1974)

267. HELM, WILLIAM (1907-   ). 1975. 30 min. 12 p.
The editor of the Northwest Monitor, a weekly black newspaper published 1930-31, discusses his career.
Interviewer: David Taylor

268. JOHNSON, NELLIE STONE (1905-   ). 1975. 55 min. 20 p.
The founder and organizer of the Hotel and Restaurant Employees International Union, Local 665, a member of the Farmer-Labor party, and the first black and woman vice-president of the Minneapolis Culinary Council discusses her background, including her family's farm near Lakeville, Dakota County, union activity in the Twin Cities, and blacks in the union movement.
Interviewer: David Taylor

269. LYGHT, NORMAN PAUL (1913-   ). 1974. 80 min. 29 p.
The son of homesteaders near Lutsen, Cook County, discusses family history and experiences of other black settlers in northern Minnesota.
Interviewer: David Taylor

270. LYNN, (JAMES) RICHARD (1883-   ). 1974. 2 hrs., 15 min. 39 p.
In 1908 Lynn moved to St. Paul where he worked as a janitor at Maxfield Elementary School. He recalls family history and discusses community life in St. Paul, including the role of fraternal lodges, the NAACP, the Urban League, and black businesses in the early 20th century.
Interviewer: David Taylor

271. MAUPINS, WILLIAM F., JR. (1922-   ). 1975. 50 min. 30 p.
A laboratory supervisor in the chemistry department of the University of Minnesota-Duluth, a past president of the Duluth branch of the NAACP, and a member of the board of the Minnesota American Civil Liberties Union discusses black community life in Duluth, the 1920 lynchings, local NAACP activities, and educational opportunities in the area.
Interviewers: Musa Foster, Seitu Jones, Malik Simba

272. MAXWELL, STEPHEN L. (1921-   ). 1974. 90 min. 18 p.
The Republican candidate for U.S. Congress (1966), assistant Ramsey County attorney (1967), judge of St. Paul municipal court

(1967-68), and judge of the state district court (1968-   ) discusses his family background in St. Paul and personal history.
Interviewer: David Taylor

273. MOORE, LOUIS, SR. (1890-1979) AND CORA MOORE (1897-   ). 1974. 2 hrs., 15 min. 65 p.
Mr. Moore, who moved to St. Paul in 1898, recalls family history and discusses early community life, including various social clubs and the Summit Avenue area of St. Paul. Mrs. Moore moved to St. Paul in 1910. She talks briefly about the St. Paul black community.
Interviewer: David Taylor

274. NANCE, ETHEL RAY (1899-   ). 1974. 90 min. 42 p.
The assistant head resident of Phyllis Wheatley House (1920s), first black policewoman in Minneapolis (1926), first black stenographer in the Minnesota legislature, a member of the Minnesota Negro Council, and associate editor with Cecil Newman of the Timely Digest discusses her family background, the Duluth black community in the early 1900s, the 1920 lynchings in Duluth, the Moose Lake Fire Relief Commission (1918), and her work experiences.
Interviewer: David Taylor

275. NEAL, EVA BELL (1888-1974). 1971. 60 min. 19 p. Open for research only.
A lifelong resident of St. Paul, Neal believes herself to be the first black child born in the Western-Selby neighborhood. She discusses family history and community life in St. Paul, including the visits of prominent blacks.
Interviewer: David Taylor

276. NICHOLS, EDWARD (1900-   ). 1974. 75 min. 31 p.
Born in Tower, St. Louis County, to pioneer parents who arrived in the area in 1884, Nichols recalls family history and discusses early life in Tower, Indian and white relations, the lumber and mining industries, his wife's pioneer family, and his life in Duluth (1936-74).
Interviewer: David Taylor

277. PARKER, FREDERICK L. (1890-   ). Narrative, 1974. 105 min.
Parker, the son of Frederick Douglass Parker and Emma DuBois, was born in St. Paul. He recalls family history and discusses his father's editorship of the weekly Western Appeal and the black community in the Twin Cities.

278. REFF, ALPHONSE (1942-   ). 1975. 35 min. 8 p.
The Reverend Reff who became associated with St. Mark's African Methodist Episcopal Church, Duluth, in 1973 discusses the history of St. Mark's and the black community of Duluth.
Interviewer: David Taylor

279. RHODES, MATTIE VERA JACKSON (1889-   ). 1974. 25 min. 12 p.
Rhodes discusses family history, including her father's migration to Stillwater, Washington County, after the Civil War, blacks in the Stillwater area, the Hinckley fire (1894), and her family's move to St. Paul in 1903.
Interviewer: David Taylor

280. ROBINSON, ALMETRA (1912-   ). 1975. 40 min. 20 p.
Robinson, who moved to Duluth in 1938, discusses her life in that city, particularly her activities in Calvary Baptist Church.
Interviewers: Musa Foster, Malik Simba, David Taylor

281. ROSS, GRACE (1887-   ). 1974. 30 min. Open for research only.
Born in St. Paul, Ross recalls family history and black community life around 1900.
Interviewer: David Taylor

282. SIMMONS, MACEO (1901-   ). 1974. 45 min. 15 p.
A charter member of the St. Paul (now Mount Olivet) Baptist Church discusses the history and growth of this church and its relationship to the black community of St. Paul.
Interviewer: David Taylor

283. SLIGH, TOMMY (1948-   ). 1975. 30 min. 15 p. Open for research only.
The pastor of Camphor Memorial Methodist Church, St. Paul, since 1972 discusses his congregation and touches on the role of the black church in the preservation of Afro-American culture.
Interviewer: Musa Foster

284. STALLING, CHARLES M. (1927-   ) AND GERALDINE H. STALLING (1926-   ). 1975. 65 min. 32 p.
The Stallings discuss growing up in Duluth and offer a contemporary account of community life there in the 1950s and 1960s.
Interviewers: Musa Foster, Seitu Jones, Malik Simba

285. TAYLOR, MAXINE (1928-   ). 1975. 40 min. 23 p. Open for research only.
A lifelong resident of Duluth discusses

recent history and concerns of the black community.

Interviewers: Musa Foster, Malik Simba, David Taylor

286. THOMAS, ZORRA LaVERN SIMS (1924-   ). 1974. 20 min. 7 p.

Thomas discusses the background and life of her great-grandfather, Joseph Edwards (1844-   ), who settled in Lakeville, Dakota County, about 1858.

Interviewer: David Taylor

287. TUCKER, ANITA BRACY (1928-   ). 1974. 70 min. 16 p.

The former director (1953-63) of the teen-age program at Hallie Q. Brown community center, St. Paul, discusses the center and its programs.

Interviewer: David Taylor

288. WEBSTER, POLLETTA VERA LEONARD (1909-   ). 1974. 40 min. 20 p.

Webster recalls family history, including her great-grandparents who lived in the Mendota, Dakota County, area around 1860, and the early black community in Minneapolis.

Interviewer: David Taylor

289. WILKINS, MARJORIE (1923-   ). 1975. 45 min. 15 p. Open for research only.

A registered nurse and past president of the Duluth branch of the NAACP discusses growing up in Duluth and contemporary problems facing the city's black community.

Interviewers: Musa Foster, Malik Simba, David Taylor

290. WRIGHT, BOYD A., SR. (1916-   ). 1974. 75 min. 29 p.

Wright discusses personal history, the family homestead in Crystal, Hennepin County, and connections with the Twin Cities black communities.

Interviewer: David Taylor

[[[[[[[[[[[∘]]]]]]]]]]]

DAKOTA COUNTY

The Dakota County Oral History Project was organized in 1976 by Tom Copeland as part of the Dakota Area Referral and Transportation for Seniors (DARTS), a service program. The project's purpose was to involve older people in both the giving and gathering of reminiscences about Dakota County. All of the people interviewed recalled family and personal his-

tory rich in detail and created a sense of growing up in Dakota County, an area of fertile farm land, and of the changes in farm life during the 20th century.

About a third of the interviews also dealt with a particular change in farm and community life in Dakota County -- the Gopher Ordnance Plant in Rosemount. In 1942 the federal government confiscated 11,600 acres of rich farm land to construct the largest munitions plant in the United States. Farmers were paid an average of $71.00 per acre for their land, although court appeals won some of them slightly increased settlements. The plant was closed after the war, and in 1948 most of the land went to the University of Minnesota for a research facility; some land was sold back to farmers. Members of farm families, lawyers involved in the farmers' appeals, and a few Gopher Ordnance Plant employees discussed the effect of the plant.

The entries below indicate the respondent's place and duration of residence in Dakota County, occupation, and, if applicable, involvement with the Gopher Ordnance Plant. In addition to these interviews the collection includes a tape of a guided bus tour of three townships and a slide-and-tape history of the Gopher Ordnance Plant. Many of the interviews that contain information on the Gopher Ordnance Plant are also available at the North Central Minnesota Historical Center at Bemidji State University.

291. ARNESON, EARL C. (1893-   ). 1976. 60 min.

Born in Farmington; worked at a variety of jobs, including farming, delivery services, plumbing, and his own heating and air-conditioning business.

Interviewer: Wanda Link

292. BARTON-BABCOCK, RUTH FRANCES (1893-   ). 1976. 60 min.

Born in Inver Grove Heights.

Interviewer: Marcella Grover

293. BEADLE, BERNARD VIRGIL (1898-   ). 1976. 3 hrs.

Moved to Dakota County in 1928 to teach agriculture in the South St. Paul schools.

Interviewer: Tom Copeland

294. BERRES, CHARLES. 1976. 2 hrs.

Born in Lakeville and lived there until 1933.

Interviewer: Tom Copeland

295. CARROLL, EMMET C. (1912-   ). 1976. 3 hrs.

Born in Rosemount on his parents' farm,

which in 1942 was taken for the Gopher Ordnance Plant.
Interviewer: Teresa Seliga

296. CASE, ZEPH B. (1899-   ). 1976.
2 hrs.
A farmer; as a child moved with his family to Farmington.
Interviewers: Kim Foster, Teresa Seliga

297. CASSERLY, EUGENE (1905-   ) AND
EVELYN KANE CASSERLY. 1976. 2 hrs.
Mr. Casserly, born in Hastings as was his father, was a clerk of district court in the county. Mrs. Casserly's parents' farm was taken for the Gopher Ordnance Plant.
Interviewers: Helen Davis, Teresa Seliga

298. CASTLE ROCK TOWNSPEOPLE. 1976. 3 hrs.
Open for research only.
Several townspeople talk about the history of their town and community life (1900-45).
Interviewer: Tom Copeland

299. CHELBURG, CLARENCE (1901-   ). 1976.
60 min.
Moved to Dakota County in 1943 to work as a fireman at the Gopher Ordnance Plant.
Interviewers: Kim Foster, Teresa Seliga

300. CIHAK, ANNA GEPHART (1895-   ). 1976.
45 min.
Born in Lakeville; parents ran a grocery store, a farm, a funeral business, and a furniture store.
Interviewer: JoAnn Mako

301. CONZEMIUS, CATHERINE ROWE (1903-   ).
1976. 2 hrs.
A schoolteacher; born in Rosemount Township; father and husband were farmers.
Interviewer: Bonnie DeBoe

302. CORBIN, ROSE CHADIMA (1888-   ) AND
ALBY CHADIMA YOUNT (1890-   ). 1976. 60
min.
The Chadima sisters were born and grew up in Inver Grove Heights.
Interviewer: Marcella Grover

303. DIFFLEY, CORINNE BELAIR (1912-   ).
1976. 80 min.
Diffley's husband worked for the Gopher Ordnance Plant, and the couple rented rooms to other employees. She also discusses her Minneapolis childhood.
Interviewers: Kim Foster, Teresa Seliga

304. EMPEY, IRVING (1886-   ). 1976. 60
min.
Born in rural Northfield, Rice County;

moved to Dakota County in 1919 where he ran Farmington Auto Co.
Interviewer: Mrs. Francis Lagerquist

305. FEATHERSTONE, LOUISE DROMETER (1899-
). 1976. 50 min.
Grew up on a farm in Dakota County; her husband was a farmer and a salesman.
Interviewer: Patricia Schultz

306. FISCHER, ARTHUR (1906-   ) AND LUELLA
T. FISCHER. 1976. 90 min.
Mr. Fischer moved to Dakota County in 1925 to farm near Rosemount; hauled fuel oil to the Gopher Ordnance Plant.
Interviewers: Kim Foster, Nancy Pilgrim, Teresa Seliga

307. FOOTE, MICHAEL H. (1940-   ). 1976.
50 min.
Moved with his family to Sunfish Lake in 1949.
Interviewer: Tom Copeland

308. FRANZMEIER, LOUIS (1900-   ) AND
DOROTHY ELSTON FRANZMEIER. 1976. 60 min.
Mr. Franzmeier, born in Inver Grove Heights, grew up on a farm and became a truck farmer. Mrs. Franzmeier was a schoolteacher.
Interviewer: Patricia Schultz

309. GERAGHTY, H. J. (1898-   ). 1976. 60
min.
Born in Rosemount; followed his father into the general merchandise and grocery business; later worked for Northern Natural Gas Co.
Interviewer: Robert Gottsch

310. HJERMSTAD, ELISABETH KUENZEL (1901-
). 1976. 60 min.
Moved with her Austrian immigrant parents to Hastings as an infant. Her father in 1902 started the Hastings Brewery Co., which he moved to Canada during prohibition.
Interviewer: Bonnie DeBoe

311. HYNES, MARY McANDREWS (1901-   ).
1976. 105 min.
A schoolteacher for 19 years; born in Burnsville to Irish immigrant parents; her husband's land was taken for the Gopher Ordnance Plant.
Interviewers: Helen Davis, Teresa Seliga

312. JOHNSON, MAURICE (1900-   ) AND LIL-
LIAN MOEN JOHNSON (1900-   ). 1976. 90
min.
Mr. Johnson, a farmer, was born in Eureka Center to Norwegian immigrant parents. Mrs. Johnson is also of Norwegian descent.
Interviewer: JoAnn Mako

313. KANE, FRANCIS R. (1903-   ) AND FRAN-
CES KANE. 1976. 2 hrs.
    Mr. Kane, of Irish descent, was born in
Rosemount and worked as a blacksmith and a
mechanic. The Kanes lost their family farm to
the Gopher Ordnance Plant.
    Interviewer: Tom Copeland

314. LeVANDER, HAROLD (1910-   ). 1976.
45 min.
    Governor of Minnesota (1967-71); moved to
Dakota County in 1935 to practice law. In
1943 he represented farmers in their appeal of
the settlement offered by the government for
lands taken for the Gopher Ordnance Plant.
    Interviewers: Helen Davis, Teresa Seliga

315. LOVEJOY, MARY BLANCHE (1905-   ).
1976. 60 min.
    A retired registered nurse; born in
Hastings.
    Interviewer: Sharon Hanson

316. LYON, MABEL ESTHER (1886-   ). 1976.
45 min.
    Moved with her parents to Dakota County
in 1888.
    Interviewer: Sharon Hanson

317. McBRIEN, JOHN J. (1912-   ) AND RUTH
McBRIEN. 1976. 2 hrs.
    An attorney in Farmington, Mr. McBrien
represented a group of farmers displaced by
the Gopher Ordnance Plant in their appeal of
the settlement offered by the government for
their land.
    Interviewer: Tom Copeland

318. McDONOUGH, ANDREW (1909-   ). 1976.
60 min.
    A lifelong resident of Rosemount.
    Interviewer: Robert Gottsch

319. MIKULEWICZ, RUTH VELZORA BENSON (1902-
). 1976. 60 min.
    A retired teacher; born in Inver Grove
Heights.
    Interviewer: Marcella Grover

320. MOELLER, BEN G. (1912-   ). 1976. 25
min.
    Born in Lebanon Township and grew up in
Rosemount; set up a trailer court to house
employees of the Gopher Ordnance Plant and
also worked at the plant as a carpenter and
maintenance man.
    Interviewers: Kim Foster, Teresa Seliga

321. PEINE, HENRY C. AND MRS. PEINE (1898-
). 1976. 75 min.
    Mrs. Peine was born on a farm near Ver-
million, and Mr. Peine was born in New Trier.

Their farm was appropriated for the Gopher
Ordnance Plant.
    Interviewers: Helen Davis, Nancy Pilgrim

322. PIEKARSKI, TED THOMAS (1912-   ).
1976. 60 min.
    A farmer and beef grader; born in Inver
Grove Heights.
    Interviewer: Marcella Grover

323. PIETSCH, HELEN (1915-   ). 1976. 25
min.
    Born on a farm taken for the Gopher Ord-
nance Plant.
    Interviewer unknown

324. ROWE, JOSEPH W. (1882-   ). 1976. 60
min.
    Born in Inver Grove Township; grew up on
a farm and continued farming in the Rosemount
area.
    Interviewers: Tom Copeland, Evelyn
McClung

325. SCHOEN, GILBERT HARRY (1911-   ).
1976. 60 min.
    A trumpet player; born in Hastings and
lived there all his life.
    Interviewer: Bonnie DeBoe

326. SIMON, WILLIAM J. (1911-   ). 1976.
60 min.
    A retired teacher; moved with his parents
to Rosemount as an infant. He also discusses
his grandfather and great-grandfather, who
were circuit-riding preachers in Missouri,
Iowa, and Minnesota.
    Interviewers: Tom Copeland, Agnes Scott

327. SMITH, NORA WALSH (1889-   ) AND
WINIFRED WALSH MALM (1891-   ). 1976.
60 min.
    Smith was born in West St. Paul and her
sister in Inver Grove Township.
    Interviewer: Marcella Grover

328. TOMPKINS, GEORGE (1893-   ). 1976.
2 hrs.
    A farmer; born in Dakota County of Eng-
lish immigrant parents.
    Interviewer: Evelyn McClung

329. TRANSBERG, PETER V. (1907-   ).
1976. 2 hrs.
    A farmer; settled in Dakota County in
1920.
    Interviewer: Robert Gottsch

330. TRUAX, SHIRLEY VANCE (1904-   ) AND
VERNON TRUAX (1897-   ). 1976. 100 min.
    The Truax brothers, born in Hastings, are

descendants of the first settlers in that town.
Interviewer: Patricia Schultz

331. ULBRICH, DELLA JANCOSKI (1899-   ). 1976. 90 min.
Moved to Hastings in 1922 to farm.
Interviewers: Helen Davis, Sue Maher, Nancy Pilgrim, Teresa Seliga

332. WACHTER, ANNA VOLKERT (1889-   ). 1976. 60 min.
Born in Pine Bend; she and her husband lost their farm to the Gopher Ordnance Plant.
Interviewers: Helen Davis, Nancy Pilgrim

333. WALDOW, GEORGE A. (1905-   ) AND RUBY STRATHERN WALDOW (1905-   ). 1976. 2 hrs.
Mr. Waldow, a farmer and truck gardener, was born in Inver Grove Heights of German immigrant parents. Mrs. Waldow moved to Dakota County in 1919.
Interviewer: Evelyn McClung

334. WILHELMY, RUDOLPH (1896-   ). Narrative, 1976. 60 min.
Born in Inver Grove Township; grew up on a farm.

335. ZELLMER, ROY, SR. (1911-   ) AND MILDRED KNEBEL ZELLMER. 1976. 100 min.
A farmer; moved to Dakota County in 1919; hauled materials and equipment for the Gopher Ordnance Plant.
Interviewers: Helen Davis, Teresa Seliga

[[[[[[[[[[[∘]]]]]]]]]]]

JOHN H. DIETRICH AND THE FIRST UNITARIAN SOCIETY OF MINNEAPOLIS

John H. Dietrich (1878-1957) became the minister of the First Unitarian Society of Minneapolis in 1916. Until his retirement in 1938, Dietrich served that congregation with a teaching ministry and built "a community of free minds." As an advocate of pacifism and birth control and as a non-Christian minister exploring what he called a new and humane paganism, Dietrich was considered controversial and thought-provoking.
The interviews listed below were conducted in 1973 by Dorothy Kidder, a Minnesota Historical Society employee and member of the First Unitarian Society. Each person interviewed was an active member of the First Unitarian Society of Minneapolis and reminisced

about Dietrich and the society at the time of his ministry. The entries give a brief listing of the background of the person interviewed.

336. CARLSON, ERIK A. (1891-   ). 1973. 30 min. 13 p. Open for research only.
Emigrant from Sweden in 1911.

337. CASTNER, NINA. 1973. 20 min. Open for research only.
Founder of Inter-racial House, later International House of Minneapolis, and executive director of the Minnesota Memorial Service.

338. CHRISTENSEN, OSCAR A. (1880-   ). 1973. 30 min. 9 p.
Born in Moorhead, Clay County; educated at Concordia College, Moorhead, and the Lutheran Seminary of St. Paul.

339. HARBO, HAROLD F. (1892-   ). 1973. 20 min. Open for research only.
Physician; involved with the Unitarian Society since 1927.

340. JOHNSON, AGNES M. (1896-   ). 1973. 30 min. Open for research only.
Has lived in Minnesota since 1908.

341. REMPEL, WILLIAM (1899-   ). 1973. 25 min. 12 p. Open for research only.
The son of Russian immigrants moved with his family to St. Paul in 1900.

[[[[[[[[[[[∘]]]]]]]]]]]

FINNS IN NORTHERN MINNESOTA

The interviews in this section deal extensively with the experiences of Finnish Americans living in northern Minnesota, their family background, the immigrant experience, homesteading, pioneer life, ethnic pride, and the attempt by many Finns to maintain their cultural heritage while becoming Americanized. These nine people were interviewed in 1975 and 1976 by Lynn Laitala with funds provided by the Comprehensive Employment and Training Act (CETA).

342. AHONEN, ANNA M. (1914-   ). 1975. 90 min. 38 p.
The granddaughter of pioneers in Michigan and South Dakota vividly recalls her childhood, family life in a boardinghouse, community life in Winton, St. Louis County, her edu-

cation at the University of Minnesota, life in the Twin Cities, and her return to the rural Finnish community.

343. DYHR, HELMI SAARI (1885-   ). 1976. 25 min.
   Dyhr recalls her family's immigration to Ely, St. Louis County (1893), homesteading, Ely's first school, and relations with the Ojibway Indians.

344. ERICKSON, IDA PORTHAN (1893-   ). 1976. 60 min. 29 p.
   Born in Ely, St. Louis County, of immigrant parents, Erickson discusses the effort of Finns to perpetuate their culture in Ely, education, domestic life, and medical care at the turn of the century.

345. GAWBOY, HELMI JARVINEN. 1975. 90 min. 48 p.
   Mrs. Robert Gawboy discusses her immigrant parents' backgrounds, their homestead in Ely, St. Louis County, her job as a teacher, her marriage to an Ojibway Indian and life on the Vermilion Lake Indian Reservation (1929-42), and her return to the Ely homestead.

346. KUITUNEN, CECILIA (1895-   ). 1975, 1976. 105 min. 21 p. The 1975 interview is open; the 1976 interview is open for research only.
   Kuitunen describes her parents' life in Russia where she was born, life in rural Finland, emigration in 1900 to Winton, St. Louis County, and the Finnish community in Winton.

347. KUITUNEN, NICK. 1975. 26 min. 13 p.
   Born in Russia, Kuitunen emigrated with his family to Winton, St. Louis County, in 1906. He discusses family history, his education, various jobs including work for the St. Croix Lumber Co., and the diverse ethnic groups in Winton.

348. MAKI, EMILY STARKMAN (1904-   ). 1976. 28 min. 17 p.
   Born at White Iron, St. Louis County, where her immigrant parents homesteaded, Maki recalls family life (her father was a widower with eleven children in 1910), school, and efforts to Americanize while retaining Finnish culture.

349. NORHA, EINO M. (1894-   ). 1976. 60 min. 24 p.
   Norha immigrated to Embarrass, St. Louis County, in 1913. He recalls various jobs as a farmer, lumberman, veterinarian, salesman, and school bus driver and describes the early days of Embarrass, domestic life, his citizenship,

Finnish medical practices, and his writing of Embarrass Township in Historiaa (1960).

350. WACHSMAN, LEMPI MATILDA BECKMAN BIBEAU (1909-   ). 1976. 50 min.
   Wachsman discusses her parents' immigration (1895); homesteading in North Dakota and Nashwauk, Itasca County; her marriage to an Ojibway Indian who was a logger; and Finnish background and values.

[[[[[[[[[[∘]]]]]]]]]]]

FOREST HISTORY AND LUMBERING

   In doing research preparatory to reconstructing a lumber camp at the Forest History Center in Grand Rapids, Itasca County, the Minnesota Historical Society undertook a project to interview local residents and their descendants about work in the lumber industry from the turn of the century to the post-World War II years.
   The people interviewed for this project were foremen, cookees, teamsters, sawyers, swampers, scalers, camp clerks, and other men and women who worked in the woods and in the camps. Also included are homesteaders or their children who farmed the northern Minnesota cutover lands. These interviews provide a wealth of detail about life in the logging camps, camp buildings, food, various tasks, work techniques and tools, log drives, sawmills, wages, accidents in the woods, the special logging vocabulary, and diversions in town.
   In addition to the interviews listed here, the project includes tapes of recollections of the 1918 Moose Lake fire. Six members of the O. E. Carlson family narrated their experiences, and ten other survivors recalled the events at a 50th anniversary commemoration. The entries list the interviewee's residence and indicate how each person participated in the lumber industry and pioneer settlement of northern Minnesota.

351. AHLGREN, CLIFFORD E. (1922-   ). 1976. 2 hrs., 30 min. 61 p.
   The director of the Quetico-Superior Wilderness Center at Basswood Lake, Lake County, describes his Finnish parents' homestead in Brimson, St. Louis County, farming, saunas, schools, home remedies, Finnish craftsmen, land ethic, and forest management.
   Interviewer: Newell Searle

352. ANDERSON, BERGIT I. (1898-   ). 1975. 80 min.

A retired schoolteacher and author of The Last Frontier (1941) and Saga of the Setesdals Laget (1954) talks about her life, including settling east of Bigfork, Itasca County, in 1904 with her father, who was a homesteader, bricklayer, carpenter, logger, and farmer.

Interviewer: John Esse

353. ANDERSON, J. ALBERT (1887-   ). 1975. 60 min. Open for research only.

Born in Sweden, Anderson immigrated to the U.S. as a young man and in 1916 homesteaded near Grand Rapids. He ran a logging camp and had a store in Effie, Itasca County.

Interviewer: John Esse

354. BENSON, DONALD (1908-   ). 1976. 105 min. Open for research only.

Benson came to the Talmoon, Itasca County, area in 1917 when his father acquired a homestead.

Interviewer: John Esse

355. BERG, JHALMER (1897-   ). 1977. 60 min. 26 p. Open for research only.

Berg operated a sawmill near Buyck, St. Louis County.

Interviewer: Robert Wheeler

356. BERGSTROM, ELMER (1899-   ) AND HARLAND TOWLE. 1976. 100 min.

Bergstrom moved to Talmoon, Itasca County, in 1913 and worked in logging camps as a cookee, a teamster, and a blacksmith's helper. Towle arrived in northern Minnesota about 1915 and worked as a teamster in logging camps until 1925.

Interviewer: John Esse

357. BROWN, MARION (1902-   ). 1975. 90 min. 42 p. Open for research only.

Brown lived in Deer River, Itasca County (1903-33). He worked as a clerk in a logging camp and was a brakeman and conductor for the Minneapolis and Rainy River Railway Co. (1920-32).

Interviewer: John Esse

358. BRUNO, CARL (1897-   ). 1975. 75 min.

Born in Cloquet, Carlton County, Bruno was a childhood playmate of Minnesota novelist Walter O'Meara. He worked as a clerk in a lumber camp before World War I.

Interviewer: John Esse

359. BURGESON, CARL. 1978. 45 min.

A lumber cutter in Sweden before immigrating to the U.S., Burgeson worked as a sawyer in a number of lumber camps. He discusses the life of lumberjacks and the saws and other equipment he used.

Interviewer: Robert Wheeler

360. CARNO, ALEXANDER (1890-   ). 1975. 60 min. 71 p.

Carno started working in logging camps in the Grand Rapids area in 1914.

Interviewer: John Esse

361. ERICKSON, SCOTT W. (1899-   ). 1976. 35 min.

Erickson was a sailor on the Great Lakes and worked for the Great Northern Railway Co. and the Minneapolis Steel and Machinery Co. In 1920 he homesteaded near Orr, St. Louis County, entered the forest service for a season, worked for the Virginia and Rainy Lake Lumber Co., and started his own lumber business about 1925.

Interviewer: John Esse

362. EVENSON, OLE (1882-   ). 1975. 30 min.

Norwegian-born Evenson immigrated to Minneapolis in 1905. He moved north to Bigfork, Itasca County, in 1914 where he homesteaded and built lumber camps, including the Washkish and Horseshoe camps.

Interviewer: John Esse

363. FINSTED, MORRIS. 1972. 2 hrs. Open for research only.

A lifelong resident whose parents homesteaded near Buyck, St. Louis County, in 1907 recalls settlement and early life, his work in logging with the Virginia and Rainy Lake Lumber Co., and hunting.

Interviewer: Robert Wheeler

364. HANSON, MAYBELLE (1897-   ). 1976. 90 min. 77 p.

In 1909 Mrs. Allen Hanson moved to Grand Rapids with her parents and in 1931 to Little Fork, Koochiching County, where her husband worked for the International Lumber Co. (1931-72).

Interviewer: John Esse

365. HEINZER, LOUIS (1898-   ). 1976. 2 hrs. 70 p.

Heinzer's family homesteaded in 1904 near Lower Red Lake, Beltrami County. He began working in lumber camps in the area in 1917.

Interviewer: John Esse

366. HERITAGE, ALFRED AND MABEL HERITAGE. 1975. 55 min.

Mr. Heritage and his father started the Red Foley Lumber Co. near Bigfork, Itasca County, about 1905. Mr. and Mrs. Heritage

homesteaded about 1925, and he worked in a sawmill in Koochiching County (1924-60).
Interviewer: John Esse

367. HEZZELWOOD, LILLIAN (1897-   ). 1976. 60 min. 36 p. Open for research only.
Hezzelwood describes the Crane Lake, St. Louis County, area where she lived most of her life.
Interviewer: Robert Wheeler

368. HILDEN, ALFRED M. (1889-   ). 1976. 70 min. 48 p.
Hilden worked for the International Lumber Co. in Koochiching and Itasca counties (1915-58), first as a scaler and later as head lumber purchaser.
Interviewer: John Esse

369. HINES, CHARLES. 1976. 60 min. 16 p. Open for research only.
Charles Hines, the son of Edward Hines who was the principal stockholder in the Virginia and Rainy Lake Lumber Co., discusses life in lumber camps.
Interviewers: Newell Searle, Robert Wheeler

370. HOLMQUIST, ROY (1896-   ). 1973. 60 min. Open for research only.
Holmquist started work for the Cloquet Lumber Co. in 1915 as a swamper.
Interviewer: Robert Wheeler

371. HOLUB, JOSEPH. 1977. 45 min.
Holub, in his nineties at the time of the interview, discusses logging and farming near Gemmell, Koochiching County.
Interviewer: John Esse

372. HUJU, VICTOR (1893-   ). 1975. 60 min.
Huju, who immigrated to Duluth from Finland in 1908, worked as a timber and tie cutter in logging camps before World War I, in the Stephens Mine near Hibbing, St. Louis County, and for the Great Northern Railway Co. and the Minneapolis and Rainy River Railway Co. on a section gang.
Interviewer: John Esse

373. HUNT, BEECHER M. (BERT) (1882-   ). 1975. 85 min.
Hunt began working in the lumber industry in northern Minnesota in 1898 as a cruiser, a teamster, and a river-crew driver.
Interviewer: John Esse

374. JELLISON, CLYDE (1891-   ). 1976. 60 min.
Born in Minneapolis, Jellison moved to

his father's homestead near Bass Lake, Itasca County, about 1903. He worked in a small logging camp near Bass Lake.
Interviewer: John Esse

375. JOHNSON, FRANCIS WILLARD (1903-   ). 1978. 60 min. Open for research only.
A ranger and game warden in the St. Louis County area for the state forest service discusses his work, fish and game laws, illegal hunting, fishing, and trapping.
Interviewers: Slavko Nowytski, Robert Wheeler

376. JOHNSON, HILFRED (1906-   ) AND LESTER POLLARD (1907-   ). 1976. 105 min.
Johnson moved with his family in 1909 to homestead near Nett Lake where his father worked in lumber camps. He worked on log drives in the 1920s and 1930s.
Interviewer: John Esse

377. JOHNSON, JOHANNES (1894-   ). 1977. 60 min. Open for research only.
Born in Sweden, Johnson immigrated to the U.S. in 1913 and the next year went to Big Falls, Koochiching County, to work in the logging camps as a tie cutter.
Interviewer: John Esse

378. JONES, JOHN ALBERT (1876-   ). 1975. 60 min.
Jones, who lived in Pengilly, Itasca County (1910-35), worked in factories, in the iron mines, as a teamster doing roadwork, and on threshing crews.
Interviewer: John Esse

379. KAUKOLA, WILLIAM (1892-   ) AND MRS. KAUKOLA (1904-   ). 1977. 60 min. 57 p.
The Kaukolas emigrated as children from Finland with their families in the early 1900s and have lived in the Crane Lake, St. Louis County, area since 1926. Mr. Kaukola worked in lumber camps, ran a sawmill, and farmed.
Interviewer: Robert Wheeler

380. KINKEL, RAYMOND (1892-   ). 1976. 50 min. 41 p.
Kinkel was born in Minneapolis and moved to the Leech Lake, Cass County, area in 1906 with his family. He worked as a cook's helper and sawyer in logging camps.
Interviewer: John Esse

381. KNIGHT, ESTHER H. 1976. 35 min.
Mrs. James Knight moved to Taconite, Itasca County, in 1910 and taught school in South Dakota (1913) and in Bigfork, Itasca County (1914).
Interviewer: John Esse

382. KNIGHT, JAMES (1893-   ) AND ESTHER H. KNIGHT. 1975. 2 hrs., 45 min.

James Knight, born in Red Lake Falls, Red Lake County, was a hunter and trapper. He homesteaded in the Bigfork, Itasca County, area about 1916 and worked in the logging industry as a river hog.
Interviewer: John Esse

383. KNOX, OLIVER. 1972, 1975. 2 hrs., 30 min. The 1972 interview is open for research only; the 1975 interview is open.

Knox moved to Minnesota in 1904 to work in the lumber industry as a jack and a teamster. He recalls construction of the Kettle Falls Hotel, Rainy Lake, St. Louis County, in 1913 and describes resorts in northern Minnesota in the 1920s.
Interviewers: Robert Wheeler (1972), John Esse (1975)

384. LANE, NELLIE (1874-   ). 1975. 20 min.

The daughter of homesteaders in Deer Creek, Otter Tail County, comments on family life.
Interviewer: John Esse

385. MANNAUSAU, JOSEPH (1904-   ). 1977. 90 min.

Born in the Loman, Koochiching County, area where his parents homesteaded, Mannausau went to work in a logging camp in 1920 and continued logging and farming throughout his life.
Interviewer: John Esse

386. MANNAUSAU, LOUIS (1906-   ). 1977. 40 min.

Louis Mannausau, brother of Joseph, worked at logging (1935-42) but preferred farming.
Interviewer: John Esse

387. MATTICE, ANNE ANDERSON (PEGGY) (1903-   ). 1975. 90 min.

Born in Eveleth, St. Louis County, Mattice ran a tavern in Craigville in the 1940s frequented by lumberjacks and prostitutes.
Interviewer: John Esse

388. NELSON, JOHN (1900-   ). 1976. 90 min. 18 p.

Swedish-born Nelson operated Nelson's Resort in the Crane Lake, St. Louis County, area.
Interviewer: Robert Wheeler

389. O'KONEK, JACK AND HAZEL JOHNSON O'KONEK (1906-   ). 1975. 40 min.

Mrs. O'Konek moved with her parents to the Hill City and Swatara, Aitkin County, area in 1911 and has lived there ever since. Mr. O'Konek arrived in the area in 1921 from Foley, Benton County.
Interviewer: John Esse

390. OLLILA, JOHN (1903-   ). 1976. 60 min. 21 p.

Ollila emigrated from Finland in 1906 with his family, grew up on a farm in St. Louis County, and worked for the Virginia and Rainy Lake Lumber Co. in the 1920s as a swamper, teamster, cookee, and sawyer.
Interviewers: Phil Christianson, Robert Wheeler

391. OLSON, ALICE GUTHRIE (1895-   ) AND BERGIT I. ANDERSON (1898-   ). 1975, 1976. 2 hrs., 20 min.

Olson moved to the Bigfork, Itasca County, area as a child about 1902. Both Olson and Anderson are retired schoolteachers.
Interviewer: John Esse

392. PAULSON, OTTO (1883-   ) AND ELIDA (ELEN) PAULSON (1883-   ). 1975. 30 min.

Mr. Paulson, born in Sweden, immigrated to the U.S. in 1902; Mrs. Paulson immigrated in 1908. They ran a tavern and boardinghouse for lumberjacks in Deer River, Itasca County (1939-41).
Interviewer: John Esse

393. PETE, JACOB L. (1896-   ). 1976. 90 min. 63 p.

Born in Ely, St. Louis County, Pete worked as an errand boy for the St. Croix Lumber Co. office in Ely in 1912. He later built and owned lumber camps in St. Louis and Lake counties on White Iron Lake, Stump Lake, Angleworm Lake (1942), and Bass Lake, as well as a sawmill on Fall Lake. In 1915 he began an outfitting and resort business.
Interviewer: John Esse

394. POLLARD, LESTER (1907-   ). 1975, 1976. 4 hrs., 10 min. 151 p.

Pollard began working in 1924 in the Big Fork River, Koochiching County, area for the American Cedar Co. and in 1927 for the International Lumber Co. in Koochiching and Itasca counties.
Interviewers: Robert Wheeler (1975), John Esse (1976)

395. RAJALA, MABLE (1911-   ). 1975. 90 min.

Mrs. Art Rajala was born of Swedish immigrant parents on a homestead in Itasca County. Her husband and his brothers were loggers and ran a sawmill (1930-60s).
Interviewer: John Esse

396. RAJALA, WILLIAM (1909-   ). 1975. 90 min. Open for research only.
Rajala's parents homesteaded near Effie, Itasca County, in 1910. His father worked for various small logging companies in the area. He and his brother, Art, built their own logging camp in 1947.
Interviewer: John Esse

397. RUD, OLE HILLMAR AND LULA RUD. 1976. 60 min.
The Ruds have lived in northern Minnesota since the early 1900s and farmed in the Birchdale, Koochiching County, area.
Interviewer: John Esse

398. RYAN, JAMES C. (BUZZ) (1900-   ). 1976. 4 hrs. 133 p.
The author of Early Loggers in Minnesota (1973, 1976, 1980) was born in Willmar, Kandiyohi County, and grew up in northern Minnesota. He first went to work in the woods in 1917.
Interviewer: John Esse

399. SALISBURY, MAURICE (1896-   ). 1976. 40 min.
Born in Eden Valley, Stearns County, Salisbury moved to northern Minnesota in 1920. He worked as a bookkeeper and in banks in Aitkin, Aitkin County, and Crosby, Crow Wing County, before starting his own timber business about 1924 and running lumber camps from Grand Rapids to International Falls, Koochiching County.
Interviewer: John Esse

400. SCHOLTA, VEDA (1896-   ). 1977. 60 min.
Mrs. Norman Scholta grew up in Loman, Koochiching County. Her husband was a foreman on river drives.
Interviewer: John Esse

401. SIROTIAK, JOHN (1894-   ). 1975. 50 min.
Sirotiak, born in North Slovakia (now Czechoslovakia), immigrated to the U.S. in 1912. He worked in Minneapolis for the streetcar company, joined harvesting crews in North Dakota, and in 1913 went to Orr, St. Louis County, to work in a logging camp as a sawyer. He later worked for a linseed-oil company and ran a dairy farm near Blackduck, Beltrami County (1927-49).
Interviewer: John Esse

402. SKOV, RAY (1915-   ) AND HELEN SKOV (1918-   ). 1977. 60 min.
The Skovs were born in Minnesota and have lived in the Loman, Koochiching County, area all of their lives.
Interviewer: John Esse

403. SMART, JESSE (1884-   ). 1975. 55 min.
Smart, born in Pelican Rapids, Otter Tail County, grew up on a farm in Morrison County and moved to Hill City, Aitkin County, in 1911. He worked in a pail factory (1911-23) and in logging camps as a sawyer and teamster before World War I.
Interviewer: John Esse

404. SMITH, TENA MACMILLAN (1890-   ). 1975. 50 min.
Smith moved with her parents to Cloquet, Carlton County, in 1898. Her father was a scaler and followed the timber, and the family survived the Cloquet fire of 1918.
Interviewer: John Esse

405. SMITH, WALTER F. (1893-   ). 1975. 105 min.
Smith, who was born in Wadena County and homesteaded with his parents near Pine River, Cass County, about 1905, built lumber camps. His father was a tiemaker and built a stopping ranch (inn) and bunkhouses for lumberjacks.
Interviewer: John Esse

406. STAPLES, HAZEL E. (1892-   ). 1976. 60 min. 25 p.
Mrs. Kenneth Staples lived in Little Fork, Koochiching County, where she raised a family. She also cooked in lumber camps near Nett Lake, where her husband farmed and worked in the woods.
Interviewer: John Esse

407. STILLER, LAURA P. (1882-   ). 1977. 30 min.
Mrs. William Stiller came with her family in 1901 to homestead in Little Fork, Koochiching County. Her husband was a logging camp foreman.
Interviewer: John Esse

408. VIGREN, MARY LITCHKE (1894-   ). 1975. 30 min.
Vigren was born in Grand Rapids and lived there until 1910. Her father was a harness maker and dressed horses for the logging camps.
Interviewer: John Esse

409. VOIGT, EMMA (1884-   ). 1975. 30 min.
Mrs. Gus Voigt moved with her family in 1892 to Elmo, Itasca County, and to Grand Rapids in 1900. In 1909 she went to a logging camp near Cass Lake, Cass County, to join her husband and work as a cook.
Interviewer: John Esse

410. WALKER, HARRIET CHRISTENSEN (1897-
). 1975. 90 min. 67 p.
    A retired schoolteacher, who grew up in
Hill City, Aitkin County, discusses her background and the Moose Lake forest fire of 1918.
    Interviewer: John Esse

411. WERTHNER, FRANK (1887-   ). 1977. 75
    min. 64 p.
    Werthner worked in lumber camps in Wis-
consin until 1908 when he began logging near
Bigfork, Itasca County.
    Interviewers: John Esse, William Rajala

[[[[[[[[[[°]]]]]]]]]]]

THE IZAAK WALTON LEAGUE OF AMERICA IN MINNESOTA

    A group of conservationists who advocated
the restoration and wise use of soil, woods,
water, and wildlife organized the Izaak Walton
League of America (IWLA) in Chicago, Illinois,
in 1922. Eleven members of the Minnesota
chapter discussed the league's influence in
successfully concluding several conservation
projects. The projects included a variety of
local, state, and national undertakings, such
as establishing the Upper Mississippi Wildlife and Fish Refuge in 1924; protection of
the Boundary Waters Canoe Area; completion of
the Tamarac National Wildlife Refuge; creation
of the Minnesota Memorial Hardwood Forest in
1960; support of the Save-the-Wetlands program; campaigns against water, land, and air
pollution; and encouragement of conservation
education of the public.
    Thomas Hayden conducted the interviews in
1972 and donated the tapes to the Minnesota
Historical Society. The entries below list
the interviewee's position in the IWLA and
other conservation-related activities.

412. ANDERSON, ADOLPH. 1972. 20 min. Open
    for research only.
    President of the IWLA's Wilderness
Committee in 1972.

413. AULTFATHER, WILLIAM. 1972. 55 min.
    Open for research only.
    Employee of Minnesota Department of Con-
servation since 1960s; director of the state
Division of Lands and Forestry at the time of
the interview.

414. CLEMENT, PAUL (1892-   ). 1972. 3
    hrs., 30 min. Open for research only.
    Attorney; active in the IWLA since 1930.

415. DORER, RICHARD J. (1889-1973). 1972.
    105 min. Open for research only.
    Past president of the state IWLA; super-
visor of game with the Minnesota Department of
Conservation, 1950s.

416. FRANEY, EDWARD. 1972. 75 min. Open
    for research only.
    Author of articles for the Minneapolis
Tribune supporting the IWLA's conservation
concerns.

417. GREEN, WILLIAM. 1972. 10 min. Open
    for research only.

418. HAIK, RAYMOND. 1972. 40 min. Open
    for research only.
    Past president of the Minnesota chapter
of the IWLA.

419. HEINZELMAN, MIRON (BUD). 1972. 60 min.
    Open for research only.

420. HUBLEY, RAYMOND C., JR. 1972. 10 min.
    Open for research only.
    Employee of the IWLA.

421. LARSON, GOODMAN. 1972. 25 min. Open
    for research only.

422. MINER, NELLIE P. (1899-   ). 1972.
    20 min. Open for research only.
    Attorney; organized the women's Minnehaha
Chapter of the IWLA in 1943.

[[[[[[[[[[[°]]]]]]]]]]]

JEWS IN MINNEAPOLIS

    In 1972 the Minneapolis Federation of
Jewish Services gave the Minnesota Historical
Society four oral history interviews that were
conducted as part of a project to document the
history of the Jewish community in Minneapolis. In 1979 Rhoda Lewin donated seventeen
interviews she conducted in researching her
doctoral dissertation. Many of the people interviewed belong to the second wave of Jewish
immigrants who arrived after 1880 from Eastern
Europe and settled on the North Side of Minneapolis, creating a distinctive Jewish community numbering 8,000 by 1900. Others are first
generation Americans who vividly contrast
their parents' lives with their own. This
collection of memories reveals the growth,
change, and diversity of the community.

423. ARONSON, DAVID. 1967. 3 hrs. Open for
research only.
Born in Russia, Aronson immigrated as a
child to New York City. He became the rabbi
at Beth El Synagogue in Minneapolis in 1924.
He discusses family history, the Jews living
on Minneapolis' North Side, the status of Jews
in the community, and Jewish organizations.
Interviewer: Guida Gordon

424. BARRON, MOSES (1883-1974). 1970. 50
min. Open for research only.
Born in Russia, Barron immigrated to the
U.S. in 1888 to join his father, who had been
a Hebrew scholar in Russia, on a farm in Stevens County. He discusses his family's immigration, their life on the farm, his education
at the University of Minnesota Medical School,
his teaching and practice of medicine, individuals in the Jewish community, literary and
cultural organizations, and his move to Los
Angeles, Calif., in 1964.
Interviewer: Joan Sharp

425. BROCHIN, BEN B. (1909-   ). 1979. 80
min.
The son of Lithuanian immigrants discusses his father's grocery store and delica-
tessen in Minneapolis, immigrants, amateur
boxing, and life in the North Minneapolis
Jewish neighborhood.
Interviewer: Rhoda Lewin

426. COHN, ANGELO (1914-   ). 1976. 60
min. Open for research only.
A reporter for the Minneapolis Star, Cohn
was born in Romania and immigrated to Minneapolis in 1920. He discusses the immigration
of extended family units, early life in Minneapolis, the immigrant community, his education, the 1930s Depression, bootlegging, religious institutions, and anti-Semitism.
Interviewer: Rhoda Lewin

427. COHN, LILIAN BESLER (1895-   ). 1976.
60 min. Open for research only.
Born in Minneapolis of Romanian immigrant
parents, Cohn discusses charitable organizations in the early Jewish community, her
father's work as a miller and at a variety of
other jobs, social life in the Jewish community, and anti-Semitism. She also commments on
a number of prominent citizens in the Jewish
community.
Interviewer: Rhoda Lewin

428. FLIEGEL, ERNIE (1904-82). 1976. 55
min. Open for research only.
Fliegel was born in Romania and immigrated to Minneapolis in 1910. He recalls his
childhood in Romania and Minneapolis, where he
was a paper boy at the age of seven, his amateur and professional boxing career, the 1930s
Depression, bootlegging, the 620 Club, and the
truckers' strike of 1934.
Interviewer: Rhoda Lewin

429. GOLDBERG, BLANCHE HALPERN (1906-   ).
1976. 95 min. Open for research only.
Mrs. Isadore Goldberg, born of Romanian
immigrant parents, grew up in Minneapolis and
Hebron, N.Dak. She discusses the immigration
of her extended family to Minneapolis, life in
a small North Dakota town, anti-Semitism in
Minneapolis, and the 1930s Depression. She
also speaks about child rearing, her husband's
service in World War II, and her son's bar
mitzvah.
Interviewer: Rhoda Lewin

430. GOLDBERG, ISADORE (1900-   ). 1976.
90 min. Open for research only.
Goldberg was born in Minneapolis of Lithuanian immigrant parents. He discusses his
early childhood, his family's poverty, his education and early medical practice, the 1930s
Depression, anti-Semitism, his World War II
service, and religion.
Interviewer: Rhoda Lewin

431. GREENE, FLORENCE GLICK (1900-   ).
1975. 50 min. Open for research only.
The daughter of Lithuanian immigrant parents recalls her early life in a small Iowa
town, the poverty of immigrants, and life in
Minneapolis in the 1920s. She also discusses
the 1930s Depression, anti-Semitism, and
social and cultural activities in the Jewish
community.
Interviewer: Rhoda Lewin

432. HYMES, VIOLA HOFFMAN. 1976. 50 min.
Open for research only.
Hymes, born in Chicago of a Romanian immigrant father and a Swedish mother, moved to
Minneapolis about 1916. She discusses family
history and early family life, her education,
anti-Semitism, and the 1930s Depression. She
also talks about her marriage and family, religion, and her community service activities
as national president of the Council of Jewish
Women and as a founding member of the Citizens
Committee on Public Education (COPE).
Interviewer: Rhoda Lewin

433. LYONS, VERA NISSENSON (1912-   ).
1976. 60 min. Open for research only.
The daughter of an Orthodox rabbi recalls
the flight from Russia with her parents in
1924, life as an immigrant child, and anti-
Semitism and gives a graphic description of a
pogrom. She discusses the 1930s Depression,
working her way through college, the Jewish

communities in Minneapolis, and kosher cook-
ing, which she teaches.
Interviewer: Rhoda Lewin

434. MAYBERG, WILLIAM (1887-1978). 1976.
80 min.
Mayberg, who emigrated from Russia in
1913, operated small grocery stores in Minneapolis and St. Paul. He describes the poverty
of immigrant life and discusses the education
of Jewish children in Russia and the U.S., the
history of the Zionist movement, a Zionist
farm and school in Champlin, Hennepin County,
and religion.
Interviewer: Rhoda Lewin

435. MINDA, ALBERT G. (1895-1977). 1968.
8 hrs. Open for research only.
The rabbi of Temple Israel, Minneapolis,
until 1963 and later rabbi emeritus recalls
personal history, including his education, his
early rabbinical duties in Indiana, his marriage, and his writing. Minda discusses the
history and development of Temple Israel as
well as the Jewish community in Minneapolis,
Talmud Torah, Jewish charity and community
services, anti-Semitism, and the status of
Jews in Minneapolis. He also reflects upon
the duties of a rabbi and his travels, lec-
tures, and participation in Jewish and inter-
faith organizations.
Interviewer: June Stern

436. ROBERTS, SHEPSEL (S. R.) (1914-   ).
1976. 30 min. Open for research only.
Born in Russia, Roberts immigrated with
his family to Minneapolis in 1921. He describes immigration and the poverty of immigrants, the family chicken business and his
being a shochet (ritual butcher), his education at yeshiva in Chicago (1931-33), selling
newspapers as a boy, peddling, and the 1930s
Depression. A mohel (ritual circumciser), he
emphasizes the role religion takes in his
life.
Interviewer: Rhoda Lewin

437. ROSENBLOOM, ESTHER SCHANFIELD. 1976.
20 min. Open for research only.
An active Zionist, who moved to Minneapolis with her family in the early 1900s, recalls family background and cultural affairs
in the Jewish community of the 1940s. She
also describes touring the U.S. and Europe in
the 1920s.
Interviewer: Rhoda Lewin

438. SANDERS, IDA LEVITAN (1900-   ).
1976. 45 min. Open for research only.
A founder of the Young People's Synagogue
and Beth El Synagogue, Sanders was born in
Russia and immigrated to Minneaplis in 1905.

She describes her early childhood, secular and
religious education, the founding and history
of the Minneapolis Talmud Torah, the 1930s
Depression, anti-Semitism, and family and community life.
Interviewer: Rhoda Lewin

439. SCHANFIELD, MAURICE J. (1904-   ).
1977. 90 min. Open for research only.
The Minneapolis-born son of a Romanian
immigrant discusses the Jewish immigrant
neighborhood on Minneapolis' South Side, his
early religious training, and his family and
personal life.
Interviewer: Rhoda Lewin

440. SCHOFF, FLORENCE KARP KUNIAN (1906-
). 1976. 45 min. Open for research
only.
The daughter of Russian immigrant parents, Schoff settled in Minneapolis in 1922.
She discusses family history, her early life
on a South Dakota sheep ranch, working her way
through the University of Minnesota, the 1930s
Depression, and anti-Semitism. She describes
her activities in Temple Israel, Hadassah, the
Minneapolis Federation for Jewish Services,
and the Democratic-Farmer-Labor party.
Interviewer: Rhoda Lewin

441. SCHWARTZ, EDWARD P. (1903-   ). 1976.
60 min. Open for research only.
Schwartz, born in Minneapolis, inherited
and expanded his father's printing business.
He discusses family background, his association with Temple Israel, his early career as a
newspaper reporter, intermarriage, the 1930s
Depression, anti-Semitism, the founding of the
Variety Club Heart Hospital, and the 620 Club
and other Minneapolis restaurants.
Interviewer: Rhoda Lewin

442. SHAPIRO, NATHAN M. (1911-   ). 1976.
80 min. Open for research only.
Born in Minneapolis, Shapiro discusses
family background; his childhood and education; his experiences in the drugstore, night-
club, theater, and insurance businesses, the
break up of a theater-owners' monopoly in Minneapolis in the 1940s; and charitable concerns. He also speaks of Hubert H. Humphrey,
intermarriage, the Unitarian Society, and his
feelings about Jewishness.
Interviewer: Rhoda Lewin

443. WOLFF, MAURICE (1884-   ) AND ANNA
LEE WOLFF (1886-   ). 1969. 60 min.
Open for research only.
Mrs. Wolff, born in Minneapolis, recalls
her early life and discusses her extensive
involvement in the Jewish community and public
affairs, including founding the local National

Council of Jewish Women (1918) and her paci-
fist beliefs. Mr. Wolff, born in Minneapolis,
discusses personal history, a career in advertising, community service, and interest in
social clubs.
Interviewer: Mrs. V. R. Gould

[[[[[[[[[[[∘]]]]]]]]]]]]

LABOR UNION MOVEMENT

Three projects involving labor union
officers and activists are included in this
section. Professor Martin W. Duffy of the
University of Minnesota Industrial Relations
Center conducted a series of interviews with
union leaders for use by his students and
other scholars and for the preparation of a
history of Minnesota labor. In a second
project the Minnesota Historical Society contracted with James Dooley to interview a variety of union members to document their careers
and preserve the story of labor unionism in
Minnesota. As part of a third study Professor
Donald Sofchalk of Mankato State University
donated to the society copies of interviews he
conducted as a part of his research on steelworkers from Minnesota's iron ranges.

In several instances the same person was
interviewed as part of more than one project.
A number of labor leaders were interviewed
individually and are listed in the Reminiscences Section (above). Abbreviations are
used in this section for the American Federation of Labor (AFL), the Congress of Industrial Organizations (CIO), and the Industrial
Workers of the World (IWW).

444. BESTER, EARL T. (1900-   ). 1968,
   1974, 1977. 5 hrs. The 1968 and 1974 interviews are restricted; the 1977 interview
   is open.
   The son of a Michigan copper miner recalls his early life and discusses early labor
organizations on Minnesota's iron ranges and
on the national level. Bester, the first president of the Steelworkers Union, Local 1028,
and district director of the United Steelworkers Union in 1952, talks about Communist party
activity within the union, the 1946 Duluth
harborworkers' strike, and Governor Elmer A.
Benson.
   Interviewers: Helen White (1968), James
Dooley (1974), Martin Duffy (1974, 1977)

445. BJORK, EINAR (1902-   ). 1977. 45
   min.
   Bjork was born in Sweden and immigrated

to the U.S. in 1920. He recalls personal
history and discusses his employment with the
United States Steel Corp. (1922-68); his union
activity including serving as president of
Steelworkers Union, Local 1028, Duluth; and
Socialist and Communist party influences in
the unions in the 1930s and 1940s.
   Interviewer: Martin Duffy

446. CADWELL, L. RUTH. 1976. 90 min. 25 p.
   A charter member of the American Federation of Teachers, Local 561, and a member of
the board of the Minnesota Federation of
Teachers discusses her personal history and
union activities.
   Interviewer: Martin Duffy

447. COUGHTY, FLOYD (1913-   ). 1976. 60
   min. 22 p. Open for research only.
   Coughty discusses personal history and
his labor activities as business representative in the 1950s of the Carpenters Union,
Local 930, St. Cloud, Stearns County, and as
president of the St. Cloud Trades and Labor
Assembly.
   Interviewer: Martin Duffy

448. EBERL, A. P. (SLIM) (1901-   ). 1974.
   60 min. 28 p.
   Born in New Ulm, Brown County, Eberl
began working for the Chicago and Northwestern
Railroad in the carshops in 1918 and was vice-
president of the Tracy, Lyon County, local
union of car men in 1919. He discusses his
involvement in the Teamsters Union, Local 221
(1928-41), and attempts by the Socialist Workers party to gain control of teamster unions
in Minneapolis. He also was a vice-president
of the Minnesota AFL in 1956 and talks about
the merger of the AFL and CIO.
   Interviewer: James Dooley

449. ELLIS, A. FRANK (1888-1976). 1973,
   1974, 1975. 18 hrs., 30 min. 57 p. Open
   for research only.
   Ellis, who began working in a meat-packing plant at the age of eight, discusses conditions in that industry, the IWW, and the
Independent Union of All Workers (IUAW) in
midwestern cities in the 1930s. Ellis helped
organize the United Packinghouse Workers for
the CIO and served that union as president of
Local 9. He talks about organizing strikes,
including the 1933 strike of the Geo. A.
Hormel & Co. plant in Austin, Mower County.
   Interviewer: Martin Duffy

450. GENIS, SANDER D. (1895-   ). 1974,
   1977. 4 hrs. 72 p.
   Genis, an immigrant from Russia in 1912,
started organizing clothing locals in Minneapolis and St. Paul about 1917 and conducted

successful strikes. He discusses trade unionism, particularly his work as vice-president
of the Amalgamated Clothing Workers of America
International (1946-75) and as president of
the Minnesota CIO (1942-45). He talks about
organizing for the International Ladies Garment Workers Union in the Twin Cities, the
Citizens Alliance of Minneapolis, Communist
party influence on the labor movement in the
1930s and 1940s, Governor Floyd B. Olson, labor support for Hubert H. Humphrey as mayoral
candidate in Minneapolis (1945), and the formation of the Democratic-Farmer-Labor party in
1944.
    Interviewers: James Dooley (1974),
Martin Duffy (1977)

451. HARRIS, MYRTLE. 1974. 60 min. Open
    for research only.
    A member of the United Garment Workers
Union since 1920 and a vice-president from the
fifth district of the Minnesota AFL-CIO discusses her organizing activities, the 1934
truckers' strike in Minneapolis, and other
union issues.
    Interviewer: James Dooley

452. KRMPOTICH, NICK (1915-   ). 1974. 70
    min.
    A vice-president for the eighth district
of the Minnesota AFL-CIO, Krmpotich started
work in the mines of Michigan in 1935. In
1950 he joined the union staff, originally the
Steel Workers Organizing Committee and later
the United Steelworkers of America. He discusses the miners' union and its relationship
with United States Steel Corp., management and
labor relations, and union activities and
benefits.
    Interviewer: Donald Sofchalk

453. O'DONNELL, GERALD J. (1898-   ).
    1974. 60 min. 21 p. Restricted.
    O'Donnell, who joined the Steamfitters
Union, Local 455, in 1919, discusses that local and the program of indentured apprenticeship he initiated in 1940 while serving as the
local's business agent.
    Interviewer: James Dooley

454. PETERSON, GLENN E. (1906-   ). 1977.
    90 min.
    The president, vice-president, and chair-
man of the grievance committee of the Steelworkers Union, Local 1028, discusses his union
activites, Communists and steelworkers, labor
organizer Henry Berkheimer, and the inclusion
of iron-ore miners in the Steelworkers Union.
    Interviewer: Martin Duffy

455. PIETRINI, ELIO O. 1971. 90 min. Open
    for research only.

Pietrini discusses changes in working
conditions in Minnesota mines (1930-70), unemployment in the mines during the 1930s Depression, labor and management disputes, and efforts to organize the miners.
    Interviewer: Donald Sofchalk

456. SCHULTZ, FRANK W. (1917-   ). 1977.
    12 hrs. 144 p.
    Schultz, who worked at the Geo. A. Hormel
& Co. plant in Austin, Mower County (1931-73),
and was president of the Packinghouse Workers
Union, Local 9 (1945-70), discusses the Independent Union of All Workers in Austin, the
1933 strike at the Hormel plant, Communists
and unions, the McCarthy era, and the strike
at the Wilson Co. in 1959 in Albert Lea, Freeborn County. He also comments on A. Frank
Ellis, Jay Hormel, and other people involved
in union activities in Austin.
    Interviewer: Martin Duffy

457. SHERBURNE, NEIL C. 1974. 40 min.
    17 p.
    The secretary-treasurer of the Minnesota
AFL-CIO (1956-   ) discusses unions, lobbying
efforts in the state legislature, the labor
movement in Minnesota, and his involvement in
organized labor.
    Interviewer: James Dooley

458. SOLLIE, ALLEN AND VIOLET JOHNSON SOLLIE.
    1974, 1977. 6 hrs., 20 min. 129 p.
    Mr. Sollie emigrated from Norway to the
U.S. in 1905. He recalls his youth, boxing,
and various jobs that led to his being involved in union activities in Minneapolis
since 1924. Mrs. Sollie discusses her education at Hamline University, St. Paul, and the
University of Minnesota; her work as a researcher and clerk for the state house of
representatives in the 1930s; involvement in
Farmer-Labor politics; Governor Floyd B.
Olson; the 1934 truckers' strike in Minneapolis; her work with labor in Minneapolis in the
1940s and 1950s; earning a law degree from
William Mitchell College of Law, St. Paul; and
her law practice (1957-72).
    Interviewers: Warren Gardner (1974),
Martin Duffy (1977)

459. SWANSON, SAM E. (?-1972). 1968, 1969.
    3 hrs., 30 min.
    A labor organizer for the Steelworkers
Union in northern Minnesota during the 1930s
and 1940s and secretary of the Iron Range
Industrial Union Council discusses unemployment and the CIO in the 1930s, newspapers'
opinions of union organization efforts, independent mines, and the benefits of unions.
    Interviewers: Helen White (1968), Donald
Sofchalk (1968, 1969)

460. TEACHERS' UNION, ST. PAUL. 1974. 80
  min. 40 p.
    Four members of the St. Paul teachers'
unions (Federation of Women Teachers, Local
28, and Federation of Men Teachers, Local 43)
describe the St. Paul teachers' strike of
1946, the first organized teachers' strike in
the U.S. Margaret Kelly discusses the benefits she gained as a result of the strike.
Nora Kelly talks about picketing and the attitudes of pupils and parents toward striking
teachers. Albert (Cody) Hanzel, vice-president of Local 43 at the time of the strike,
and John Ryan recall their strike-organizing
activities.
    Interviewer: James Dooley

461. TOBLER, ADOLPH T. (TED). 1974. 60 min.
  25 p. Open for research only.
    Tobler recalls working as a teamster,
factory hand, and machinist; unemployment during the 1930s Depression; his union activities, including service as business agent for
the St. Paul Trades and Labor Assembly in the
1950s and 1960s; and his interest in the Senior Citizens Federation.
    Interviewer: James Dooley

462. TOMASICH, ANDREW. 1971. 75 min. Open
  for research only.
    Tomasich worked in the coal mines in the
eastern U.S. before moving to northern Minnesota. He discusses mining, labor grievances,
his activities as a CIO organizer during the
1930s, the split between the AFL and CIO, and
the Communist party and unionism.
    Interviewer: Donald Sofchalk

463. WIESINGER, JOSEPH F. (1906-   ).
  1974. 45 min. 24 p. Open for research
  only.
    An emigrant from Germany to Duluth in
1926 discusses working as a machinist for a
brewery (1933-71) and his activities in the
Brewery Workers Union, including serving as
vice-president from the eighth district of the
Minnesota AFL-CIO.
    Interviewers: James Dooley, Martin Duffy

464. WILLENBRING, JOHN A. (1882-   ).
  1976. 90 min. 18 p.
    Willenbring started a co-operative cream-
ery and shipping association in Richmond,
Stearns County, in 1912. He describes his
various jobs and discusses the Farm Bureau,
the Stone Cutters Union in St. Cloud, and the
St. Cloud Trades and Labor Assembly.
    Interviewer: Martin Duffy

465. WINN, CARL (1909-   ). 1977. 10
  hrs., 30 min. 123 p.
    A native of Idaho recalls family history

and describes working in logging camps in the
northwest in the 1920s and 1930s as well as
working in mills and on ranches. He discusses
many aspects of labor and unionism, including
the Trade Union Unity League, the United Boom
Workers of America, Communist party efforts to
organize labor in the 1930s, the IWW, the CIO,
the AFL-CIO, and the relationship between
government and labor.
    Interviewer: Martin Duffy

466. WRIGHT, RAYMOND R. (1906-   ). 1977.
  3 hrs.
    Wright describes his early life working
in logging camps, paper mills, sawmills, and
copper mines, on farms, and in various cities
of the Midwest and discusses his work as a
labor organizer and union administrator for
the Hotel and Restaurant Employees Union,
Local 665, Minneapolis (1936-71).
    Interviewer: Martin Duffy

[[[[[[[[[[[[∘]]]]]]]]]]]]

MEXICAN AMERICANS IN MINNESOTA

    In 1975 the Minnesota Historical Society
began a two-year Mexican-American History
Project under the direction of Ramedo J.
Saucedo to collect the historical resources of
this ethnic group: personal papers, records
of organizations, photographs, articles, and
other material, including the oral history
interviews listed below. A description of
these interviews and of other material available at the society is contained in Mexican
Americans in Minnesota: An Introduction to
Historical Sources, compiled by Ramedo J.
Saucedo and published by the society in 1977.
Some of the interviews were conducted in Spanish and are so noted; all of the transcripts
are in English.

467. AGUILAR, DAGOBERTO (1927-   ). 1976.
  In Spanish, 20 min.
    Aguilar, a native of Costa Rica, moved to
Minneapolis in 1973. He discusses the history
and activities of the Primera Igelsia Evangel-
ica Bautista (Baptist Church) in Minneapolis
and his ministry to Spanish-speaking people.
    Interviewer: Ramedo Saucedo

468. ALVARADO, MARÍA ANTONIA (SISTER EN-
  GRACIA) (1947-   ). 1976. In Spanish, 20
  min. Open for research only.
    Sister Engracia was born in Mexico and
assigned to St. Mary's College, Winona, in
1966. She discusses her life in Mexico and

her apostolate in Minnesota as a Lasalian Sister of Guadalupe.
Interviewer: John Sánchez

469. ALVO, STELLA. 1975. 50 min. 16 p.
The assistant director of Mi Cultura, a bilingual and bicultural day-care center for children in St. Paul, discusses the center's origin, program, and growth.
Interviewer: Grant Moosbrugger

470. ANAYA, JOSEPH E. (1927-   ). 1975. 30 min. 10 p.
Anaya, a native of New Mexico who moved to St. Paul in 1939, discusses his role in organizing the St. Paul chapter of the American G.I. Forum and his work with Our Lady of Guadalupe Parish Credit Union, with Brown & Bigelow, and since 1973 with the Metropolitan Economic Development Assn., an organization providing technical services to minority businesss.
Interviewer: Grant Moosbrugger

471. ARELLANO, CARLOTTA F. (1905-   ). 1975. In Spanish, 45 min. 12 p.
Mrs. José Arellano, a native of Mexico, emigrated to the U.S. in 1910 and moved with her husband to Minnesota in 1932. She recalls experiences during the Mexican Revolution and discusses family background, life on the West Side of St. Paul, and traditional Mexican baptismal customs.
Interviewer: Victor Barela

472. AVALOZ, ESTER M. (1911-81). 1975. In Spanish, 80 min. 23 p.
Mrs. Gabriel Avaloz, a native of Kansas, moved to Minnesota in 1935. She describes St. Paul's Mexican community in 1935, her family, her husband and his railroad employment, and his participation in El Comité Patriótico. She also talks about wedding and baptismal customs.
Interviewer: Victor Barela

473. BÓSQUEZ, MARÍA J. (1906-   ). 1975. In Spanish, 80 min. 20 p.
Mrs. Concepción Bósquez was born in Mexico and immigrated with her husband to Minneapolis in 1928. She discusses teaching in Mexico, memories of the Mexican Revolution, participation in the Mexican community of St. Paul, her husband's work with the railroad and as president of a union, and the careers of her eight children.
Interviewer: Victor Barela

474. CAMPA, LUZ (1909-   ) AND VIRGINIA V. CAMPA. 1976. 20 min. 8 p.
Mr. Campa was born in Mexico and immigrated to Texas in 1914. The Campas worked in beet fields near Chaska, Carver County, and settled in the state in 1936. They discuss their family of thirteen children, Mr. Campa's work in various aspects of the food industry, and the establishment of their family restaurant in Brownton, McLeod County, in 1972.
Interviewer: Grant Moosbrugger

475. CAPIZ, HENRY T. (1926-   ). 1975. 30 min. 12 p.
A lifelong resident of St. Paul describes his family background, his work as chief pharmacist at St. Luke's Hospital, and his involvement in civic and social organizations.
Interviewer: Grant Moosbrugger

476. CASILLAS, MATTHEW (1931-   ). 1975. 40 min. 14 p.
The son of pioneer Mexican Americans on St. Paul's West Side discusses community issues and his business, the Riverview Tire Co.
Interviewer: Grant Moosbrugger

477. CASTILLO, LEO VIGILDO (1945-   ). 1976. In Spanish, 20 min. 7 p.
Castillo, a native of Texas, describes settling in Litchfield, Meeker County, in 1969, living conditions for field workers, vocational training in sheet-metal work, and employment with a turkey processing company.
Interviewer: Ramedo Saucedo

478. CHÁVEZ, FRANK (1928-   ). 1975. 30 min. 12 p.
Born in Nebraska, Chávez moved with his family to Beauford, Blue Earth County, in 1932. He discusses patriarchal family structure, work experience, and his business, a printing firm in St. Paul.
Interviewer: Grant Moosbrugger

479. COATES, DIONISIA (NICHA) CARDENAS (1928-   ). 1975. 40 min. 16 p.
Coates, born in Cambria, Blue Earth County, and educated in St. Paul recalls personal history and her work with civic and social organizations and various groups of young people involved in bilingual-bicultural education.
Interviewer: Grant Moosbrugger

480. CONTRERAS, MANUEL J. (1904-   ). 1975. In Spanish, 90 min. 31 p.
Contreras escaped from Mexico during the Mexican Revolution of 1924, moved to Chaska, Carver County, in 1927, and settled permanently in St. Paul in 1933. He vividly recalls the revolution, its leaders, and its effect on his family. He also describes the 1930s Depression years in St. Paul and work in the sugar-beet fields, in meat-packing plants in South St. Paul, Dakota County, and in a muni-

tions plant in New Brighton, Ramsey County.
Interviewer: Victor Barela

481. CORONADO, ARTURO (1905-   ) AND
ELVIRA G. CORONADO (1908-   ). 1975. 110
min. 34 p.
The Coronados, born in Mexico, moved to
Minnesota in 1923. They discuss their family,
the community in St. Paul, Mr. Coronado's work
in the dry-cleaning business and in organizing
a labor union for that trade (1930-46), their
first restaurant in St. Paul in 1938, and
their later restaurant in Minneapolis.
Interviewer: Ramedo Saucedo

482. CRUZ, GUADALUPE J. (1894-   ). 1975.
In Spanish, 80 min. 10 p.
Mrs. Francisco Cruz was born in Mexico
and moved with her husband to Minnesota in
1929. She talks about the Mexican Revolution,
the life of early migrant workers, members of
St. Paul's Mexican-American community, and her
activities as a founder of Our Lady of Guadalupe Society.
Interviewer: Victor Barela

483. DE LEÓN, ALFONSO, SR. (1902-   ).
1975. In Spanish, 80 min. 15 p.
De León, a Mexican immigrant in 1918,
worked winters as a miner in Texas and summers
in the beet fields of Wyoming, Colorado, Iowa,
and Minnesota. He settled in St. Paul in 1929
and worked for 36 years for the Armour and Co.
meat-packing plant. He recalls the Mexican
Revolution, many early leaders in St. Paul's
Mexican community, and his activities in El
Comité Patriótico, Our Lady of Guadalupe Society, and the International Institute.
Interviewers: Ramedo Saucedo, Victor
Barela

484. DELGADO, RALPH (1937-   ). 1976. 20
min. 8 p.
Delgado was born in Hollandale, Freeborn
County. He and his brothers and father bought
farm land in 1953 after many years as farm
laborers. He describes the acquisition and
operation of their 900-acre potato farm in
Freeborn County.
Interviewer: Grant Moosbrugger

485. ELIZONDO, ANGELO (1909-   ) AND
MARCELLA ELIZONDO (1919-   ). 1975. In
Spanish, 60 min. 13 p.
Mr. Elizondo, born in Mexico, immigrated
to the U.S. in 1912; Mrs. Elizondo, born in
Texas, moved to Minnesota in 1929. They
describe their backgrounds and their family of
eight children. Mrs. Elizondo speaks of some
supernatural experiences, the "evil eye," and
Mexican remedies for minor illnesses.

Interviewers: Grant Moosbrugger, Ramedo
Saucedo

486. FERNÁNDEZ, ANGEL M. (1932-   ). 1975.
In Spanish, 2 hrs. 26 p.
An accountant for the Minnesota Department of Public Welfare, Fernández was born in
Mexico, moved to the U.S. in 1956, enlisted in
the U.S. Air Force, and was stationed at Fort
Snelling in 1957. He compares the educational
systems of his native city and St. Paul and
discusses his language adjustments and acculturation.
Interviewer: Victor Barela

487. GALVÁN, ALFONSO (1898-   ). 1975. In
Spanish, 100 min. 14 p.
Galván was born in Mexico, immigrated to
the U.S. in 1919, and settled in St. Paul in
1923. He discusses life in Mexico, the Mexican Revolution, his employment with a railroad
and with several meat-packing firms, the first
Mexicans on the West Side of St. Paul, the
founding of the Anahuac Society, and various
Mexican celebrations.
Interviewer: Victor Barela

488. GALVÍN, GEORGE (1910-   ). 1975. 2
hrs., 30 min. 35 p.
Galvín was born in Texas and moved to St.
Paul in 1920. As a youth he worked summers in
the beet fields. At the age of twelve he
began a boxing career while employed in the
meat-packing industry in St. Paul. He describes his career as a union organizer and
his role in establishing the Minnesota branch
of the League of United Latin American Citizens (LULAC).
Interviewer: Grant Moosbrugger

489. GARCÍA, ANGEL (1921-   ) AND MARÍA
GARCÍA. 1976. 20 min. 6 p.
Mr. García, born in Texas, and Mrs.
García, born in Chicago, moved to Winona Coun-
ty in 1951. They discuss their educations,
Mexican heritage, family trucking business,
their tavern in Stockton, Winona County, and
farm land and other real estate.
Interviewer: John Sánchez

490. GÓMEZ, FRANCISCO (1907-   ) AND
CASIMIRA GÓMEZ. 1976. In Spanish, 45 min.
8 p.
Mr. Gómez, born in Mexico, arrived in the
U.S. in 1922 and in Minnesota in 1927. He
discusses the community on St. Paul's West
Side and his work and family. Mrs. Gómez
talks about holiday celebrations and Mexican
food.
Interviewer: Grant Moosbrugger

491. GONSÁLEZ, BEN P. (1921-   ). 1976. 45 min. 18 p.

Born in Oklahoma, Gonsález moved to Minnesota in 1930 to work in the beet fields and canning industry. He discusses his family, his business enterprises, the Minnesota Citizens for Migrant Affairs, and his work as acting minister and missionary for the Temple de la Fe, a Pentecostal church in Guckeen, Faribault County.

Interviewer: Grant Moosbrugger

492. GONZÁLEZ, GREGORY L. (1920-   ). 1975. 60 min. 10 p.

González was born in Oklahoma and moved to St. Paul in 1924. He discusses personal history and his career in accounting with the Minnesota Department of Revenue and the founding of Our Lady of Guadalupe Parish Credit Union in 1948.

Interviewer: Grant Moosbrugger

493. GUERRERO, MANUEL P. (1935-   ). 1976. 55 min.

The chairman of the Chicano studies department at the University of Minnesota (1974-76) discusses his aspirations for that program as well as personal history.

Interviewer: Grant Moosbrugger

494. GUZMÁN, FRANCISCO (1900-   ) AND DOLORES RODRÍGUEZ GUZMÁN (1907-   ). 1975. In Spanish, 85 min. 18 p.

The Guzmáns were born in Mexico and immigrated to the U.S. in 1922, settling in St. Paul in 1929. They describe the Mexican Revolution; his military service in Mexico; his employment with railroads, sugar companies, and various contractors; and Mexican traditions and food.

Interviewer: Victor Barela

495. GUZMÁN, FRANK C. (1934-   ). 1975. 40 min. 22 p.

The director of Migrants in Action, Inc., discusses that St. Paul organization as well as personal history.

Interviewer: Grant Moosbrugger

496. HERNÁNDEZ, SEBASTIÁN J. (SAM) (1930-   ). 1975. 40 min. 14 p.

The Mexican-American consultant for urban affairs to the St. Paul school system since 1973 discusses family and personal history, teaching in St. Paul schools (1961-71), and his philosophy of cultural pluralism.

Interviewer: Grant Moosbrugger

497. HERRERA, FELICITAS L. (1909-   ). 1975. In Spanish, 2 hrs., 35 min. 33 p.

Herrera was born in Mexico, immigrated to the U.S. in 1920, and settled in St. Paul in

1933. She describes her early life in Mexico, her family, and various jobs as a field worker and in the meat-packing business. She recalls her work as a "Guadalupana," which involves continuing religious customs celebrating the fiesta day of Our Lady of Guadalupe on December 12.

Interviewer: Victor Barela

498. HUERTA, CONCEPCIÓN. 1976. In Spanish, 30 min.

Mrs. Matías Huerta was born in Mexico and moved with her husband to Minnesota in 1916. She recalls life on St. Paul's West Side, her language difficulties, early religious services conducted in Spanish, and the annual Mexican Independence Day celebration.

Interviewer: Nicha Coates

499. JARA, SEBASTIÁN RAMÓN (1906-   ). 1975. In Spanish, 60 min. 14 p.

Jara, born in Mexico, moved to St. Paul about 1925. He discusses family history, various jobs, World War II experiences, the Anahuac Society, and his service as deacon in the Baptist church.

Interviewer: Victor Barela

500. JIMÉNEZ, JESSE (1935-   ) AND JOSEPHINE G. JIMÉNEZ. 1976. 30 min. 11 p.

Mr. Jiménez was born in Hollandale, Freeborn County; Mrs. Jiménez in Iowa. Mr. Jiménez discusses family background, education, employment, participation in social and fraternal organizations, and his restaurant, which he bought in 1969. Mrs. Jiménez speaks of her family, her employment as an office worker, and her children.

Interviewer: Grant Moosbrugger

501. JIMÉNEZ, ROMALDO (1912-   ). 1976. In Spanish, 25 min. 4 p.

Jiménez, born in Mexico, worked in Texas and Kansas before arriving in Walters, Faribault County, in 1933. He discusses working in the beet fields, renting land, and raising his own crops.

Interviewer: Grant Moosbrugger

502. LIMÓN, DAVID B. (1886-   ). 1975. In Spanish, 90 min. 15 p.

Limón was born in Mexico and moved to the U.S. in 1913 and to St. Paul in 1923. He discusses family life, his 38 years of work with the railroad, and some Mexican remedies for physical ailments.

Interviewer: Victor Barela

503. LÓPEZ, LEONARD (1921-   ). 1975. 20 min. 7 p.

López was born in Kansas and moved to St. Paul in 1933. He discusses his early life and

education, work in the beet fields, World War II service, his Spanish and Indian background, and his career as a police officer in St. Paul since 1949.
Interviewer: Grant Moosbrugger

504. MARTÍNEZ, ANGELITA REYES (1927-   ). 1976. In Spanish, 28 min.
Mrs. Román Martínez, born in Iowa, moved to St. Paul in 1930, settling later in Minneapolis with her husband. She discusses family history, the founding of the Twin Cities chapters of the League of United Latin American Citizens, and Mexican customs and holidays.
Interviewer: Rochelle Lopez

505. MARTÍNEZ, LUIS (1931-   ). 1976. 60 min. 21 p.
Martínez was born in Texas and migrated with his family to Minnesota in 1935, settling in East Grand Forks, Polk County, in 1953. He discusses how he became the manager of an automobile dealership, his Spanish-language radio programs on Crookston and East Grand Forks stations, and his role in establishing the first school for migrants in the Red River Valley.
Interviewer: Ramedo Saucedo

506. MARTÍNEZ, TONY (1932-   ). 1975. 20 min. 12 p.
The owner and president of Martinez Ortho Mapping Corp. discusses family background, early farm conditions, work, and personal history as a native of St. Paul's West Side.
Interviewer: Grant Moosbrugger

507. McCLURE, MARILYN E. (1943-   ). 1976. 25 min. 10 p.
Born in New Mexico and educated at Macalester College, St. Paul, and the University of Chicago, McClure describes her work as a school social worker in St. Paul, the genesis of Ramsey County's Mental Health Department's Spanish American Program (since 1976 the Latino Program), and the importance of bilingual personnel to social-service agencies.
Interviewer: Grant Moosbrugger

508. MEDINA, LOUIS G. (1907-   ). 1975. 50 min. 15 p.
Born in Mexico, Medina moved to the U.S. in 1916 and to Owatonna, Steele County, in 1929. He describes family life; his work in the beet fields, with the Twin City Rapid Transit Co., and with the Northern Pacific Railway Co.; and his involvement in fraternal and social organizations, particularly the League of United Latin American Citizens.
Interviewer: Grant Moosbrugger

509. MEJÍA, MATILDE (SISTER MARTA) (1930-   ). 1976. In Spanish, 17 min. Open for research only.
A Lasalian Sister of Guadalupe, born in Mexico, discusses family history, her religious work, and her assignment to St. Mary's College, Winona.
Interviewer: John Sánchez

510. MÉNDEZ, JESÚS A. (1910-   ) AND RAMONA MÉNDEZ (1927-   ). 1976. In Spanish, 20 min. 5 p.
Mr. Méndez was born in Mexico and immigrated to East Grand Forks, Polk County, in 1927 to work for a sugar company. Mrs. Méndez was born in Texas and moved to Minnesota in 1942. They discuss their backgrounds, the education of their ten children, Mexican customs, and his employment with the Migrant Education Program in Crookston, Polk County, during 1976.
Interviewer: Ramedo Saucedo

511. MERCADO, JESÚS (JOHN) (1921-   ). 1975. 20 min. 9 p.
Mercado discusses family history, schooling in Kansas and Minnesota, his service in the U.S. Marine Corps (1942-45), and his career in the St. Paul Police Department after 1948.
Interviewer: Grant Moosbrugger

512. MIES, SANTA (1945-   ). 1976. In Spanish, 15 min. 5 p.
Mies was born in Mexico and crossed illegally into the U.S. in 1953 to work and live in Texas. In 1963 she contracted to work for a food processing company in Litchfield, Meeker County. She discusses her employer's assistance in legalizing her residence in the U.S.
Interviewer: Ramedo Saucedo

513. MONITA, ESIQUIA S. (1902-   ). 1975. In Spanish, 45 min. 14 p.
Born in Mexico, Monita immigrated to the U.S. with her mother in 1906. She recalls family history, early Mexican settlers in St. Paul, and harvesting beets and corn in Kansas, Iowa, and Minnesota.
Interviewer: Victor Barela

514. MORALES, ANTONIO (1934-   ). 1976. 15 min. 8 p.
Morales was born in Texas and moved to Minnesota with his family in 1947. He discusses family background, his early years working in the fields of southern Minnesota, living in Blooming Prairie, Steele County, and his independent trucking business.
Interviewer: Grant Moosbrugger

515. MORÁN, JUANITA R. (1921-   ). 1975. In Spanish, 75 min. 16 p.
   Morán, born in Mexico, immigrated with her parents to Kansas about 1926 and to St. Paul in 1928. An active member of the Mexican-American community, she recalls her childhood, neighborhood celebrations, Our Lady of Guadalupe Church, and the importance of retaining the Mexican language and customs.
   Interviewer: Victor Barela

516. MORÁN, MARÍA RANGEL (1928-   ). 1975. 80 min. 40 p.
   The founder of the Ballet Folklórico Guadalupano, established in the late 1950s, discusses family history, life in St. Paul, and the founding of the troupe, which strives to preserve the regional dances of Mexico.
   Interviewer: Grant Moosbrugger

517. MORENO, PETER (1924-   ). 1976. 45 min. 18 p.
   Moreno, born in Renville, Renville County, moved to St. Paul with his family in 1925. As state director of migrant education, he discusses this federally funded program to educate children.
   Interviewer: Grant Moosbrugger

518. MUÑOZ, TERESA M. (1919-   ). 1975. In Spanish, 90 min. 12 p.
   Mrs. David L. Muñoz was born in Mexico, immigrated to the U.S. in 1944 with her husband, and settled in St. Paul in 1945. She discusses family and community life, her art of making piñatas, and the Mexican-American community celebrations of various religious festivals.
   Interviewer: Victor Barela

519. PALOMO, MARÍA G. (1901-   ). 1976. In Spanish, 40 min.
   Mrs. Francisco Palomo was born in Mexico and moved with her husband to St. Paul in 1930. She describes their early employment as field workers, her husband's job with the railroad, her factory work, the houses they lived in on St. Paul's West Side, and the preparation of Mexican food.
   Interviewer: Ramedo Saucedo

520. PATLÁN, JESÚS ASCENCIÓN (JESSE) (1940-   ). 1975. In Spanish, 95 min. 25 p.
   Patlán was born in Mexico City, immigrated to Minnesota in 1960, and settled in St. Paul in 1962. He discusses the problems of language and culture adjustments and job discrimination encountered by Mexicans in Minnesota and compares living in the Twin Cities to living in Mexico City.
   Interviewer: Ramedo Saucedo

521. RAMÍREZ, DAVID J. (1936-   ). 1975. 41 min. 18 p.
   The director of the Minneapolis Civil Rights Department discusses personal history, his monthly bilingual publication, La Voz, racial discrimination, and the meaning of "Chicano."
   Interviewer: Grant Moosbrugger

522. RANGEL, CRECENCIA O. 1975. In Spanish, 2 hrs. 23 p.
   Mrs. Francisco Rangel was born in Mexico City and settled with her husband in St. Paul in 1928. She discusses her life in Mexico, work in the beet fields, social and religious groups, and the observance of special days among Mexican Americans in St. Paul. She also describes her husband's appointment as Mexican consul (1948) and his involvement in community affairs and in handling language problems and Mexican immigrants in St. Paul.
   Interviewer: Victor Barela

523. RANGEL, FRANCISCO (FRANK, KICO) (1936-   ). 1975. 50 min. 21 p.
   Rangel, born in St. Paul, is employed at the Minnesota Historical Society in the microfilm laboratory. He describes life on the West Side of St. Paul, his family's musical involvement, and his career as a professional musician, orchestra leader, and teacher.
   Interviewer: Grant Moosbrugger

524. RÍOS, JUAN L. (1922-   ). 1975. 20 min. 7 p.
   Ríos was born in Texas and moved to St. Paul in 1960 to serve as minister for a Pentecostal congregation. He outlines the history of his calling to the Assembly of God ministry and the establishment of the Latin American Gospel Mission on St. Paul's West Side.
   Interviewer: Grant Moosbrugger

525. RIVERA, IRENE A. (1910-   ). 1975. 80 min. 23 p.
   Mrs. Marcelino Rivera was born in Texas, moved to Minnesota in 1925, and settled in St. Paul in 1931. She discusses family history, including her husband's life in Mexico, community life on St. Paul's West Side, and Our Lady of Guadalupe Society, established in 1931.
   Interviewer: Richard Juarez

526. RODRÍGUEZ, FRANK J. (1920-   ). 1975. 30 min. 13 p.
   Rodríguez moved to St. Paul in 1922. He describes growing up during the 1930s Depression, his activities with the Democratic-Farmer-Labor party, his work with the Hod Carriers' Building and Common Laborers' Union, Local 132, his involvement in Our Lady of

Guadalupe Church and various civic organizations, and the importance of his Mexican heritage.
Interviewer: Grant Moosbrugger

527. RODRÍGUEZ, JUAN (JOHNNIE) (1930-   ). 1976. In Spanish, 30 min. 7 p.
Born in Texas, Rodríguez worked as a migrant farm laborer harvesting in Minnesota (1941-50). In 1954 he settled in Moorhead, Clay County, as an employee on a wheat farm. He describes migrant work and his activities as a director of Migrant Health Services, Inc., as well as giving personal history.
Interviewer: Ramedo Saucedo

528. SÁNCHEZ, LALO. 1975. 30 min. 9 p.
Sánchez, born in Texas, moved to Minnesota after World War II. He discusses the Azteca Soccer Club he organized in 1969 with Mexican-American youngsters on St. Paul's West Side.
Interviewer: Ramedo Saucedo

529. SAUCEDO, FEDERICO (1891-   ). 1975, 1977. In Spanish, 90 min.
Saucedo was born in Mexico and settled in St. Paul in 1916. He recalls family history and the Mexican Revolution and discusses early Mexican families in St. Paul and organizations such as the Anahuac Society, El Comité Patriótico, and the Comité de Reconstrucción. He also describes his work in the silver and coal mines of Mexico, with a railroad in Illinois, and in a meat-packing firm in St. Paul (1922-52).
Interviewer: Ramedo Saucedo

530. SAUCEDO, FREDERICO (1934-   ). 1976. 70 min. 23 p.
Born on St. Paul's West Side, Saucedo discusses personal history, his church and civic involvements, the role of the Catholic church in his community, patriarchal family structure, differences between first- and second-generation Mexican Americans, and participation in political affairs.
Interviewer: Grant Moosbrugger

531. SAUCEDO, RAMEDO J. (1930-   ) AND CATALINA SAUCEDO (1930-   ). 1977. 60 min. 25 p.
Mr. Saucedo, born in St. Paul, discusses life on St. Paul's West Side, his education and teaching career in Minneapolis, his work as Mexican consul, and the Hispanic Cultural Enrichment Program of the Minneapolis school system. Mrs. Saucedo, born in Texas, moved to St. Paul in 1943. She discusses her husband's work and her career as accountant, tax consultant, and real-estate agent as well as her participation in the Mexican-American community of St. Paul.
Interviewer: John Sánchez

532. SAUCEDO, RUDOLPH, JR. (1951-79). 1976. 25 min. 9 p.
Born on St. Paul's West Side, Saucedo discusses the history, goals, leaders, and future of the Brown Berets, an organization of young Chicano men, as well as police and community attitudes toward the group.
Interviewer: Grant Moosbrugger

533. URVINA, CARLOS (1922-   ) AND MARCELINA R. URVINA (1918-   ). 1975. In Spanish, 75 min. 24 p.
Mr. Urvina was born in Mexico and moved to Minnesota in 1940 under a contract to lay railroad tracks. Mrs. Urvina, born in Texas, moved to Minnesota in 1930 to work with her parents in the beet fields near St. Clair, Blue Earth County. They discuss family history, life in Minneapolis, his employment with the Twin City Rapid Transit Co. and as an iron and metal worker, and her work as a nurse's aide at Harrison Elementary School. Both emphasize the value of education and of being bilingual.
Interviewers: Victor Barela, Grant Moosbrugger

534. VALDEZ, JOSÉ A. (1940-   ). 1976. 100 min. 35 p.
Valdez was born in Texas and moved to Minnesota in 1973 to be director of the Minnesota Migrant Council. He discusses the organization's history, its current structure and funding, and possible future ventures.
Interviewer: Grant Moosbrugger

535. VILLARREAL, ALBERTO (1933-   ). 1976. 9 min. 5 p.
Villarreal was born in Faribault County and grew up in Iowa and Albert Lea, Freeborn County. A member of the Albert Lea Police Department since 1960, he speaks of family history and his involvement with the League of United Latin American Citizens and the Azteca Club.
Interviewer: Grant Moosbrugger

536. VILLARREAL, BILL (1909-   ). 1976. In Spanish, 45 min. 8 p.
Villarreal, born in Mexico, moved to the U.S. in 1923 and settled in Albert Lea, Freeborn County, in 1948. He discusses the League of United Latin American Citizens, his role in founding the Azteca Club, the education and careers of his children, and the need for Mexican Americans to be organized.
Interviewer: Grant Moosbrugger

537. VILLARREAL, DIANA (1928-   ). 1976.
28 min. 11 p.
Villarreal was born in Texas and moved to Minnesota in 1955. As president of the Spanish Speaking Cultural Club, established in 1971, she describes the organization's work, financing, meetings, and plans for the future.
Interviewer: Grant Moosbrugger

538. ZAMORA, ARTURO (1925-   ). 1976. 15 min. 5 p.
Born in Texas, Zamora migrated to Cloquet, Carlton County, in 1931 and settled in Hollandale, Freeborn County, in 1940. He discusses family life, his work in the meatpacking industry, and the restaurant he and three brothers operate in Albert Lea, Freeborn County.
Interviewer: Grant Moosbrugger

539. ZEPEDA, ANTONIO (1902-77) AND PETRA T. ZEPEDA (1906-   ). 1975. In Spanish, 40 min. 15 p.
The Zepedas were born in Mexico and moved to St. Paul in 1923. They describe their early lives, Mexican customs, and their family of twelve children. Mr. Zepeda also explains sugar-beet harvesting techniques.
Interviewer: Victor Barela

540. ZUVEKAS, ANN. 1976. 15 min. 6 p.
The director of Migrant Health Services, Inc. (1974-76), describes the organization of the agency, its work and funding, new programs, and areas that need improvement.
Interviewer: Ramedo Saucedo

[[[[[[[[[[[∘]]]]]]]]]]]

MINNESOTA ART PROJECTS DURING THE DEPRESSION YEARS

"WPA Art" is a term often used to describe the art works created under a number of federal relief projects for artists during the 1930s and early 1940s. Most of the programs operated on a local or regional basis in Minnesota as well as in other states. The projects produced works of art for public use or aided the development of art institutions and community art programs. The Public Works of Art Project (PWAP), the first federal relief program for artists, operated in 1933-34. The Federal Emergency Relief Administration (FERA) provided a follow-up for works begun under PWAP. In 1934 two new programs continued and expanded government patronage of artists, the United States Treasury Section of Fine Arts

Program, 1934-43, and the Works Progress Administration Federal Art Project (WPA/FAP), 1935-43.

In 1977 the University Gallery at the University of Minnesota conducted interviews with nine artists who had taken part in government art projects in Minnesota. Two of these artists, Cameron Booth and Clement B. Haupers, had been interviewed earlier; their reminiscences, which are included, extend both before and beyond the 1930s Depression years.

541. BOOTH, CAMERON (1892-1980). 1971, 1977. 2 hrs. 6 p. The 1971 interview is open for research only; the 1977 interview is open.
Booth arrived in Minnesota in 1921 to teach at the Minneapolis School of Art. He also taught at and directed the St. Paul School of Art (1929-42), was chairman of the PWAP Technical Committee (1933-34), and was affiliated with the University of Minnesota from 1950. He talks about art in Minnesota in the 1920s and 1930s and discusses the selection of artists for PWAP.
Interviewers: Melvin Waldfogel (1971), George Reid (1977)

542. BORATKO, ANDRE (1912-   ). 1977. 30 min. 7 p.
Born in Czechoslovakia, Boratko taught at the St. Paul School of Art and headed the South Dakota FAP (1938-42). He discusses his work with the WPA/FAP as an administrator and as the artist who painted murals at Milaca,
Interviewer: George Reid

543. FOSSUM, SYDNEY G. (SYD) (1909-78). 1977. 30 min. 9 p.
Fossum was born in South Dakota and studied at the Minneapolis School of Art in the early 1930s. He was employed by the local PWAP (1933-34), painted for the University Gallery, and taught art in Minneapolis. He discusses his involvement in the FAP, including the Minnesota Artists Union and the 1938 protests of workers on cultural projects about layoffs.
Interviewer: George Reid

544. HAINES, RICHARD. 1977. 30 min. 7 p.
A FAP artist describes the murals he painted in several Minnesota towns and in the Fort Snelling round tower.
Interviewer: George Reid

545. HAUPERS, CLEMENT B. (1900-82). 1975, 1977, 1979. 5 hrs., 25 min. The 1975 interview is open for research only; the 1977 and 1979 interviews are open.
Haupers studied painting in Paris during

the 1920s before returning to his native St. Paul. He was superintendent of fine arts at the Minnesota State Fair (1931-40), director of FAP in Minnesota and midwest regional director of FAP (1935-41), and taught at the Minnesota Museum and Art School in St. Paul. He discusses Paris in the 1920s, support of the arts in Minneapolis and St. Paul, the WPA/FAP in Minnesota, the artists and their projects, and the two intentions of the FAP — to give employment to artists and to express the validity of art activity to the public.

Interviewers: Lloyd Hackl (1975), Nina Archabal, Mary Harvey, George Reid (1977), Nina Archabal, Jane Hancock, Nick Westbrook (1979)

546. IBLING, MIRIAM (1895-   ). 1977. 30 min. 6 p.

Ibling studied under Cameron Booth at the Minneapolis School of Art and helped to organize the Art League of Minneapolis. She discusses the murals she painted during the 1930s in Stillwater, Washington County; Owatonna, Steele County; and in St. Paul.

Interviewer: George Reid

547. LEWANDOWSKI, EDMUND. 1977. 30 min. 5 p.

Lewandowski discusses the murals he painted in Caledonia, Houston County, and in Wisconsin and Illinois.

Interviewer: George Reid

548. THWAITES, CHARLES. 1977. 30 min. 9 p.

Thwaites discusses the mural he painted in the post office at Windom, Cottonwood County.

Interviewer: George Reid

549. WEDIN, ELOF (1901-   ). 1977. 30 min. 11 p.

Born in Sweden, Wedin was trained at the Chicago Art Institute and the Minneapolis School of Art. He discusses the murals he painted in Minnesota and South Dakota, painting campus scenes for the University Gallery in 1934, and the artists' clubs in Minneapolis in the 1930s.

Interviewers: Nina Archabal, George Reid

[[[[[[[[[[[∘]]]]]]]]]]]

NORTH SHORE FISHERMEN

Fishing has been an industry of the north shore of Lake Superior since the 1830s when the American Fur Co. expanded its activities to include commercial fishing. The industry peaked in the early 1900s. Thereafter, despite a decline brought about by over-fishing, the invading lamprey, and pollution, commercial fishing continued but on a smaller scale.

In 1968 and 1969 Helen M. White of the Minnesota Historical Society staff conducted a series of interviews with Lake Superior north shore fishermen, many of whom started work in the flourishing years of the early 1900s. The fishermen and their wives recall family social life and history, often discussing their parents' or grandparents' immigration to Minnesota. They describe their experiences in the fishing industry, including the boats, clothing, equipment, methods of fishing, marketing, the lamprey problem, and taconite pollution. They also talk about storms and accidents and narrate humorous stories.

The entries listed below identify the people interviewed, their years on the north shore of Lake Superior, and their involvement in the fishing industry.

550. ANDERSON, ANDREW M. (1889-   ). 1968. 90 min. Open for research only.

Emigrated from Norway, 1908; farmed in the Dakotas before becoming a fisherman.

551. CHRISTIANSEN, ALECK. 1968. 70 min. Open for research only.

Owner of H. Christiansen and Sons Co., a Duluth fishery-supply company started by his father.

552. FENSTAD, ALFRED M. (1891-1970). 1969. 2 hrs. Open for research only.

Raised at Little Marais, Lake County, where he was a commercial fisherman (1914-25); later owned Lake Shore Telephone Co., worked for Northwestern Bell Telephone Co., and was active in Little Marais civic affairs.

553. FENSTAD, BEN GRANT (1902-   ). 1969. 2 hrs. Open for research only.

Born at Little Marais, Lake County; brother of Alfred M. Fenstad.

554. GODIN, LARS A. (1884-1970). 1969. 70 min. Open for research only.

Emigrated from Sweden in 1904.

555. GOLDISH, HARRY (1899-   ). 1969. 90 min. Open for research only.

Head of the Lake Superior Fish Co., started by parents (1893); first on north shore to go into trucking (1913).

556. JOHNS, EDGAR (1885-   ) AND GLEN MERRITT. 1968. 90 min. Open for research only.

Johns is the son of a Cornish miner who

came to the Mesabi Iron Range from Michigan in 1861. Merritt is a descendant of the Merritts who searched for and discovered iron ore on the Mesabi in 1890.

557. JOHNSON, FRITZ AND MRS. JOHNSON. 1968. 2 hrs., 30 min. Open for research only.
Born in Sweden, Mr. Johnson immigrated in 1904; worked in the mail-order business started by his father.

558. JOHNSON, JOHN SIGURD (1893-). 1968. 2 hrs., 15 min. Open for research only.
Emigrated from Sweden in 1897; brother of Fritz Johnson; worked in the company his father started, Sam Johnson and Sons.

559. KLEFSTAD, JOHN (1892-). 1969. 2 hrs. Open for research only.
Emigrated from Norway in 1910; worked for Hogstad and Booth Co.; later in insurance business; president, Norwegian-American League.

560. KLUCK, ED (1892-). 1969. 75 min. Open for research only.
Born in Michigan of German parents; moved to the north shore area in 1902.

561. LIND, HOKAN (1906-). 1969. 100 min. Open for research only.
Inspector in the fishing industry (1935-69); includes discussion of co-operative fisheries.

562. LIND, MARCUS (1904-) AND EDGAR LIND (1897-). 1969. 3 hrs. Open for research only.
Sons of a Norwegian immigrant who settled at Castle Danger, Lake County, in 1896; fishermen and farmers.

563. LORNTSON, CONRAD (1896-). 1969. 2 hrs., 50 min. Open for research only.
Fisherman from 1927 to the 1960s.

564. LOVALD, OSCAR (1891-1971). 1968. 2 hrs., 30 min. Open for research only.
Emigrated from Norway in 1910.

565. LOVALD, PETER. 1968. 2 hrs. Open for research only.
Emigrated from Norway in 1911; includes discussion of effects of taconite pollution on the fishing industry.

566. MATHISEN, SVERRE (1891-) AND SEVOLD RISE (1880-). 1969. 90 min. Open for research only.
Emigrated from Norway in 1906; partners in a fishing business.

567. MATTSON, MILTON (1908-). 1968. 2 hrs., 20 min. Open for research only.
Resident of East Beaver Bay, Lake County; includes discussion of north shore area tourism.

568. MICKELSEN, (WILHELM) HERMAN (1885-1972) AND MICKEL MICKELSEN (1889-1969). 1968. 3 hrs., 10 min.
Herman Mickelsen was born in Norway and immigrated to the U.S. in 1900. He was a commercial fisherman for 70 years and director of the North Shore Freight Lines. Mickel Mickelsen immigrated in 1907, joining his brother in commercial fishing.

569. NESS, ED (1912-). 1969. 2 hrs. Open for research only.
Born in South Dakota; son of Norwegian immigrants; moved to Lake Superior area about 1914.

570. RONNING, CHRISTIAN (?-1969). 1968. 2 hrs., 15 min. Open for research only.
Emigrated from Norway in 1909; includes description of his work in construction and boatbuilding. Ronning also plays his violin.

571. SIVERTSON, ARTHUR (1900-). 1969. 2 hrs. Open for research only.
Born in Duluth of Norwegian immigrant parents.

572. SMITH, CLARENCE M. (1900-). 1969. 105 min. Open for research only.
Raised in Schroeder, Cook County, where his Scotch-Irish father ran the Schroeder Lumber Co.

573. THORNGREN, FRANK AND AGNES LIND THORNGREN. 1969. 2 hrs., 20 min. Open for research only.
Worked for a taconite company and fished in Alaska, California, and Lake Superior.

574. TORMONDSEN, CHRISTOPHER (1888-). 1969. 3 hrs. Open for research only.
Emigrated from Norway in 1902; with his wife published _Tofte_ (1968), a booklet on the fishing life.

575. UZZOLO, ARTHUR (1909-). 1969. 60 min. Open for research only.
Vice-president and general manager of the North Shore Freight Lines of Duluth.

576. WAROE, LILLIE JOHANNA (1885-). 1968. 2 hrs. Open for research only.
Discusses her husband, John Waroe, who captained ore boats for United States Steel Corp.; also recalls Ladies Aid Society, church socials, and church bazaars.

577. WICK, ALBIN (1893-   ) AND MRS. WICK.
1968. 110 min. Open for research only.
Norwegian immigrants.

578. WISENER, SAM (1903-   ). 1969. 75
min. Open for research only.
Born at Two Harbors; truck driver for
fish companies in 1925 and later a school-bus
driver.

[[[[[[[[[[[∘]]]]]]]]]]]

NORTHERN PACIFIC RAILWAY COMPANY

In 1968 the Minnesota Historical Society
received a large collection of papers and
materials from the Northern Pacific Railway
(NP). The staff who faced the task of processing these records found it useful to interview NP employees who, having worked with
company files, could explain the organization
and nature of the records. These interviews
offer information about the careers of railroad office employees, a group that, unlike
the famous owners of railroad companies or the
more glamorous train engineers and conductors,
is seldom the subject of notice.
The interviews were conducted by Helen M.
White, then the society's associate curator of
manuscripts. The entries which follow list
the person interviewed and the responsibilities of each with the NP.

579. BROWN, MARTIN AND ROSEMARY MARTIN.
1969. 2 hrs., 30 min. Open for research
only.
Brown worked in the accounting department, in the offices of labor relations and of
the vice-president, and as chief clerk in the
general manager's office (1940-   ). Martin,
whose father was employed by the NP for 47
years, worked in the offices of the general
superintendent of transportation and of the
general manager (1941-   ).

580. GOODYEAR, WALTER H. 1969. 3 hrs. Open
for research only.
Manager of the freight revenue accounting
department in St. Paul; started work for the
NP in 1926 as an agent telegrapher.

581. NICHOLL, DAVID T. 1969. 2 hrs. Open
for research only.
Nicholl started work for the NP in 1942
and became manager of passenger and station
accounting in 1968.

582. ROCHE, CLARENCE. 1968. 2 hrs. Open
for research only.
Roche went to work for the NP at the age
of 17 in the early 1900s and held a variety of
jobs, including that of chief clerk.

583. SCHMID, GEORGE AND GEORGE M. RANGITSCH.
1970. 50 min. Open for research only.
In 1946 Schmid joined the NP's purchasing
department and became a filer about 1965.
Rangitsch started work in 1949 as a file clerk
for statistics in the accounting department
and became statistician in the office of the
chief of engineers about 1965.

584. WIGFIELD, ROBERT M. AND EMIL S. KALLINEN
1970. 60 min. Open for research only.
Wigfield worked for the NP as a steno-
graphic clerk, secretary to the stationer,
personal stenographer in mechanics, and, since
1953, personal stenographer and chief clerk in
the department of the chief of labor relations. Kallinen first worked for the NP in
Montana as a personal stenographer and then in
St. Paul in the offices of the general manager
and vice-president and in the department of
the chief of labor relations.

[[[[[[[[[[[∘]]]]]]]]]]]

THE PRINTING AND GRAPHIC-ARTS INDUSTRY IN THE TWIN CITIES

The Twin Cities printing and graphic-arts
industry had its start in 1849 in St. Paul
when James M. Goodhue unpacked his crate of
movable type, set up a hand press, and issued
the Minnesota Pioneer, the first newspaper in
Minnesota. At the turn of the century, Minnesota's printing industry was fourth in the
nation, and by the 1960s it had grown to be-
come the third largest industry in the state.
Since the 1960s there has been a revolution in
printing equipment. Photocomposition has replaced letterpress, and such things as laser
scanners and computers are the current tools
in printing and graphics operations. Diverse
printing processes and complex technology now
exist.
In 1973 the Minnesota Historical Society
contracted with Nancy Tsuchiya to conduct a
series of interviews with representatives of
the printing and graphic-arts industry. Each
entry identifies the people interviewed and
the subjects discussed.

585. DAVIES, (WILLIAM) JAMES, JR., AND
WILLIAM JAMES DAVIES, SR. 1973. 60 min.
56 p.

James Davies is production manager for
the Minneapolis Star and Tribune Co. His
father joined the Tribune staff in 1911 as an
apprentice on a proof press and later became
composing room foreman. The two men discuss
early printing at the old Tribune building,
printers' unions, tramp printers, future tech-
nological change, and management of that
change.

586. FERLAAK, MELVIN J. (1917-). 1973.
2 hrs. 49 p. Open for research only.

The plant superintendent at Colwell Press
of Minneapolis began his career in 1935 as an
assistant pressman after training at the Dunwoody Institute, Minneapolis. He discusses
the history and development of the printing
and graphic-arts industry, focusing on Colwell
Press.

587. GAWLICK, JOHN A., SR. (1923-).
1973. 30 min. 14 p. Open for research
only.

Gawlick rose from apprentice pressman to
superintendent of printing at Flour City
Press, Minneapolis. As historian of the Twin
City Litho Club, he discusses the history and
function of this craft organization, which was
a place to exchange technical information.

588. LANDON, FRED J. (1890-). 1973. 60
min. 42 p.

As a schoolboy Landon worked in the
Sleepy Eye, Brown County, newspaper office.
He discusses printing at the Minneapolis Tribune (1909-14), tramp printers, his career at
the Dunwoody Institute, Minneapolis, as head
of the printing department (1922-55), the Minnesota Newspaper Assn., unions and management,
printing methods, and vocational training in
public schools and state colleges.

589. MUELLERLEILE, ALFRED G. (1908-).
1973. 2 hrs. 53 p.

Muellerleile joined North Central Publishing Co., St. Paul, in 1927 while still a
student and eventually became chairman of the
board. He discusses the history and development of the printing and graphic-arts industry, focusing on North Central Publishing Co.

590. PAMEL, GEORGE C. 1973. 75 min. 24 p.

The managing director of the Printing
Industry of the Twin Cities, Inc., discusses
this trade association of printing companies
(organized in 1954), labor and management relations, and the printing industry in general.

591. SILHA, OTTO A. (1919-). 1973. 45
min. 23 p.

Silha started as a copyreader for the
Minneapolis Star in 1940 and rose to the presidency of the Minneapolis Star and Tribune Co.
in 1973. He discusses the future of the newspaper industry and its relationship to other
communications media.

592. STEVENS, HEBER JAMES (1914-).
1973. 60 min. 31 p. Open for research
only.

The president of the Graphic Arts International Union, Local 229, entered the printing industry in 1935 as a feeder (assistant to
a lithographic pressman). He discusses efforts in the 1930s to organize labor, strikes,
union benefits, and the Graphic Arts International Union and its predecessors.

[[[[[[[[[[[∘]]]]]]]]]]]

PRIVATE LIBERAL ARTS COLLEGES IN MINNESOTA

Merrill E. Jarchow's Private Liberal Arts
Colleges in Minnesota, published by the Minne-
sota Historical Society in 1973, traces the
history of Minnesota's sixteen private, ac-
credited, four-year liberal arts colleges from
their beginnings to the early 1970s. Jarchow
chronicles the development of Hamline Univer-
sity, Macalester College, the College of St.
Thomas, the College of St. Catherine, Bethel
College, and Concordia College, St. Paul; St.
John's University, Collegeville; Gustavus
Adolphus, St. Peter; Carleton College and St.
Olaf College, Northfield; Augsburg College,
Minneapolis; Concordia College, Moorhead; the
College of St. Teresa and St. Mary's College,
Winona; the College of St. Scholastica, Du-
luth; and the College of St. Benedict, St.
Joseph.

As part of his research, Jarchow conducted oral history interviews with a number
of college administrators and professors.
These interviews touch upon many facets of the
development of private colleges in Minnesota.
Subjects discussed include the concept of private institutions as an alternative to public
education, the varied religious and ethnic
heritages, the enriching diversity of private
colleges, administration and faculty, financing the school, building the campus, innova-
tion and flexibility in curricula, and changes
in the student body.

The following entries list the person

interviewed, educational background, and role in the administration of private colleges.

593. ANDERSON, OSCAR A. (1916-   ). 1969. 45 min. Open for research only.
Educated at Augsburg College, St. Olaf College, and Luther Theological Seminary (St. Paul); president, Augsburg College (1963-80).

594. BARRY, COLMAN J. (1921-   ). 1968. 90 min. Open for research only.
Educated at St. John's University and the Catholic University of America (Washington, D.C.); president, St. John's University (1964-71); president, Assn. of Minnesota Colleges.

595. BOWE, SISTER M. CAMILLE (1903-   ). 1968. 90 min. Open for research only.
Educated at the College of St. Teresa and the Sorbonne (Paris); vice-president (1945-52) and president (1952-69), College of St. Teresa.

596. CARLSON, EDGAR M. (1908-   ). 1968. 60 min. Open for research only.
Educated at Gustavus Adolphus College, Augustana Seminary (Rock Island, Ill.), and University of Chicago; president, Gustavus Adolphus College (1944-68); executive director, Minnesota Private College Council (1968-   ).

597. GALVIN, SISTER EUCHARISTA (1893-   ), SISTER ANTONIUS KENNELLY (1901-   ), AND SISTER ANTONINE O'BRIEN. 1968. 75 min. Open for research only.
Sister Eucharista was educated at the College of St. Catherine and University of Chicago; president, College of St. Catherine (1937-43). Sister Antonius was educated at the College of St. Catherine and University of Munich; president, College of St. Catherine (1943-49). Sister Antonine was educated at the College of St. Catherine and Oxford University; president, College of St. Catherine (1949-55).

598. GIDDENS, PAUL H. (1903-   ). 1968. 90 min. Open for research only.
Educated at Simpson College (Iowa), Harvard University, and Iowa State University; president, Hamline University (1953-68).

599. GRANSKOU, CLEMENS M. (1895-1977). 1968. 60 min. Open for research only.
Educated at St. Olaf College and Luther Theological Seminary (St. Paul); president, Waldorf College, Iowa (1929-32), Augustana College, South Dakota (1932-43), and St. Olaf College (1943-63).

600. HEALY, SISTER MARY EDWARD (1906-   ) AND SISTER MARY WILLIAM BRADY (1906-   ). 1968. 90 min. Open for research only.
Sister Mary Edward was educated at the College of St. Catherine, University of Minnesota, and Catholic University of America (Washington, D.C.); president, College of St. Catherine (1961-64). Sister Mary William was educated at the College of St. Catherine, University of Minnesota, and University of Chicago; president, College of St. Catherine (1955-61).

601. HUBER, SISTER ALBERTA (1917-   ). 1969. 75 min. Open for research only.
Educated at College of St. Catherine, University of Minnesota, and University of Notre Dame; president, College of St. Catherine (1964-79).

602. IDZERDA, STANLEY J. (1920-   ). 1969. 90 min. Open for research only.
Educated at University of Notre Dame, Baldwin-Wallace College (Ohio), and Western Reserve University (Ohio); president, College of St. Benedict (1968-74).

603. KAGIN, EDWIN (1879-   ). 1968. 75 min. Open for research only.
Educated at Centre College of Kentucky, Princeton University, and Boston University; professor of religious education, Macalester College (1926-52).

604. NASON, JOHN W. (1905-   ). 1970. 75 min. Open for research only.
Educated at Carleton College and Yale, Harvard, and Oxford universities; president, Swarthmore College, Pennsylvania (1940-53) and Carleton College (1962-70).

605. RAND, SIDNEY A. (1916-   ). 1968. 75 min. Open for research only.
Educated at Concordia College (Moorhead) and Luther Theological Seminary (St. Paul); president, Waldorf College, Iowa (1951-56); executive director, Board of Christian Education of the Evangelical Lutheran Church (1956-61) and American Lutheran Church (1961-63); president, St. Olaf College (1963-80).

606. REGER, WALTER H. 1968. 60 min. Open for research only.
Educated at St. John's University; teacher, dean, and president of the alumni association of St. John's.

607. RICE, HARVEY M. (1907-   ). 1968. 75 min. Open for research only.
Educated at Concord College (West Virginia), West Virginia University, and Ohio State University; president, New York State College

of Education (1947-51), New York State University College (1951-58), and Macalester College (1958-68).

608. SHANNON, JAMES P. (1921-   ). 1968. 105 min. Open for research only.
Educated at the College of St. Thomas, St. Paul Seminary, University of Minnesota, and Yale University; president, College of St. Thomas (1956-66); auxiliary bishop of St. Paul (1965-69).

[[[[[[[[[[[∘]]]]]]]]]]]

RADICAL POLITICS ON THE IRON RANGES

With funds provided by the Oscar F. and Madge Hawkins Foundation, Irene Paull in 1968 interviewed a number of Finns and others who had participated in radical political and labor movements on Minnesota's iron ranges. The people interviewed were involved in such organizations as the Industrial Workers of the World (IWW), the Congress of Industrial Organizations (CIO), the Communist and Socialist Workers parties, and other radical groups of the early and mid-20th century. They discuss their family backgrounds and Finnish heritage, their growing political awareness, and the efforts of men and women to organize labor and to bring about social, political, and economic changes.

609. ANDERSON, JACOB (JACK) (1902-   ). 1968. 80 min. 43 p.
Born in Aitkin County of Finnish parents, Anderson as a young man worked in lumber camps, joined the IWW, and in the 1920s became involved in the co-operative movement. He discusses his involvement in the Communist party and the labor movement, particularly during the 1930s Depression, and speaks of Gus Hall, Communist party leader.

610. ANTILLA, ANTON (1888-   ). 1968. 105 min. 24 p. Restricted.
Born in Finland, Antilla immigrated to Minnesota in 1906 and worked in the mines until 1913 when he began farming. He recalls family life, the Finnish community in northern Minnesota, and his activities in radical political movements, including joining the Communist party, organizing unions, and supporting co-operative strikes.

611. DAVIS, ELLEN RADIO. 1968. 75 min. Restricted.
Born in Cloquet, Carlton County, of

Finnish parents, Davis recalls family life and growing up in a Finnish-American community. She discusses her activity in the Communist party with her husband, Samuel K. Davis, who was the Communist party candidate for governor in 1934 and a correspondent for the Communist _Daily Worker_. She expresses her views on the struggles of blacks and workers.

612. FOLEY, ALMA. 1968. 90 min. Open for research only.
The secretary of the International Labor Defense League in Minnesota and the Minnesota branch of the American Committee for the Foreign Born during the 1950s discusses these organizations.

613. GREENBERG, MORRIS. 1968. 60 min. Restricted.
Greenberg started his law practice in 1922 in Eveleth, St. Louis County, and with attorney Henry Paull worked on labor cases connected with the development of the CIO and miners' unions in northern Minnesota. He discusses his legal career, his involvement with the labor movement, and Congressman John T. Bernard.

614. HARJU, WALTER (1900-   ). 1968. 60 min. 22 p. Open for research only.
Harju, born on a South Dakota homestead, discusses his organizing activities in the co-operative movement, his involvement in the Communist party and candidacy for the U.S. Congress, the Federal Writers' Project and strike, and his part in Finnish radical activities.

615. HELENIUS, AUNE (1915-   ). 1968. 25 min. Open for research only.
Born in Virginia, St. Louis County, of Finnish parents, Helenius discusses the Finnish cultural movement in northern Minnesota, her attendance at an IWW school in Duluth, her family's involvement in the IWW, and the life of miners and their families.

616. JOHNSON, ANDY (1901-   ) AND HANNAH JOHNSON. 1968. 5 hrs. 97 p. Restricted.
Mr. Johnson, a miner and farmer, is a native of Finland. Mrs. Johnson is the daughter of a Slovene miner from northern Minnesota. They describe the pioneer life of their parents, the efforts of radicals to effect change, and Finnish culture in northern Minnesota.

617. KOIVUNEN, ILMAR (1916-   ) AND EDITH KOIVUNEN. 1968. 4 hrs. 107 p. Restricted.
Mr. Koivunen, born in Mountain Iron, St. Louis County, the son of a miner and farmer,

organizer and president of the Timber Workers Union (later International Woodworkers of America), Local 29, Duluth, and an officer in the Minnesota CIO discusses labor struggles and union organization. Mrs. Koivunen describes Finnish cultural life in northern Minnesota.

618. KOSKI, AILY (1909–   ). 1968. 60 min. 22 p. Open for research only.

The daughter of a miner and farmer describes the community of Iron, St. Louis County, the life of miners, miners' organizations and unions; the farms of black-listed miners, agriculture co-operatives, and the culture of Finns in northern Minnesota.

619. KOSKI, ERO (1905–   ). 1968. 60 min. Open for research only.

Koski's father was a miner and a member of the IWW. Koski, born in Virginia, St. Louis County, discusses the Finnish cultural movement and the miners' struggles to organize labor unions.

620. KUUSISTO, MARTIN. 1968. 75 min. 26 p. Restricted.

The secretary-treasurer of the Timber Workers Union (later International Woodworkers of America), Local 29, Duluth (1947–58), discusses labor organizations, concentrating on the history of that union.

621. MAKI, TOINI. 1968. 30 min. 11 p. Open for research only.

Maki's husband, Martin Maki, was an organizer of the CIO Steel Workers Union and chairman of the Communist party in Minnesota. She recalls personal history and describes Finnish cultural life in northern Minnesota.

622. TUUOMINEN, URHO AND IRMA TUUOMINEN. 1968. 60 min. Open for research only.

Mrs. Tuuominen discusses her activities in left-wing Finnish politics in Minnesota in the 1930s. Mr. Tuuominen describes the Finnish cultural movement in Brimson, St. Louis County, where he grew up.

623. WATSON, CHESTER (1900–   ) AND BETTY FERGUSON WATSON. 1968. 70 min. Open for research only.

Mr. Watson, a social worker, was born in Aitkin, Aitkin County, the son of a miner. He recalls personal history and discusses the 1930s Depression, organization of the unemployed, his presidency of the state Workers Alliance (1936–40) and his involvement in the Farmer-Labor party. The Watsons speak briefly about the Federal Arts Project.

[[[[[[[[[[∘]]]]]]]]]]]

URBAN RENEWAL IN MINNEAPOLIS: CEDAR-RIVERSIDE ASSOCIATES, INC.

During the spring quarter of 1978 as part of an oral history class at the University of Minnesota, three students conducted a series of interviews dealing with urban renewal in the Cedar-Riverside area of Minneapolis near the west-bank campus of the university and donated the tapes to the Minnesota Historical Society. The study focused on the housing project initiated by Cedar-Riverside Associates, Inc. (CRA or UCPI) in the 1960s, the subsequent controversy and criticism surrounding this urban, high-density-living project, and the roles of the developers and of the U.S. Department of Housing and Urban Development (HUD). The entries below identify the respondents, their support of or opposition to the CRA project, and the subjects discussed.

624. BETZLER, WILLIAM. 1978. 70 min.

A resident of the Cedar-Riverside area and an employee of CRA describes his education and interest in urban planning and discusses the principal developers of CRA, the motives for the project, and its problems.
Interviewer: Jon Kerr

625. CANN, JOHN (JACK). 1978. 80 min.

Cann moved to Minneapolis in 1968 to work with the Minnesota Community Union Project that was operating at Franklin and Chicago avenues. He outlines the growth of opposition to the plans of CRA.
Interviewers: Claire Cunningham, Sheila Jordan

626. DREW, ROBERT. 1978. 15 min.

An urban-renewal planner with the Minneapolis Housing and Redevelopment Authority discusses the history of, early plans for, and criticism of the urban-renewal project.
Interviewer: Jon Kerr

627. FEENEY, THOMAS T. 1978. 15 min.

An employee of HUD discusses federal promotion efforts for the high-density-living project.
Interviewer: Jon Kerr

628. HELLER, KEITH. 1978. 65 min. Open for research only.

Heller, who was instrumental in forming CRA in 1969, describes his earlier real-estate interests in the area, the development efforts of CRA, and neighborhood opposition to the project.
Interviewer: Jon Kerr

629. PARLIAMENT, STEVE. 1978. 110 min.

A university graduate school student who arrived in Minneapolis in 1966 discusses community protests against the development plans of CRA, including the Cedar-Riverside Environmental Defense Fund, which initiated a lawsuit against it.

Interviewer: Claire Cunningham

630. RAYMOND, DAVID. 1978. 15 min.

The head of resident relations for CRA discusses internal corporate problems, the idea of CRA as a community-oriented corporation, the rent-increase strike of 1974, and the future of CRA.

Interviewer: Jon Kerr

631. RAPSON, RALPH (1914-   ). 1978. 75 min.

An architectural planner discusses development of the Cedar-Riverside area, his involvement with the planning team of CRA, and the need for change in urban-housing concepts. Rapson responds to criticisms of the CRA project.

Interviewer: Jon Kerr

632. WARNER, CHARLES. 1978. 35 min.

A HUD field representative discusses early skepticism about the CRA housing complex, the intricate financial structure of CRA, and the controversial HUD approval.

Interviewer: Jon Kerr

633. WITCOFF, RALPH. 1978. 90 min.

A member of the New Riverside Cafe Collective discusses this and other community groups that opposed CRA development and describes the 1972 demonstration protesting the HUD secretary's presence at the dedication of Stage I of the CRA project.

Interviewer: Claire Cunningham

634. YU, JOYCE. 1978. 65 min.

A resident of Minneapolis discusses community action groups, the opposition of area residents to development plans of CRA, the 1972 demonstration, and the lawsuit against CRA.

Interviewer: Claire Cunningham

[[[[[[[[[[[○]]]]]]]]]]]

THE WOMEN'S INTERNATIONAL LEAGUE FOR PEACE AND FREEDOM IN MINNESOTA

The Women's International League for Peace and Freedom (WIL) began as a war protest in the early days of World War I. The primary objectives of the WIL were total and universal disarmament, abolition of violence and encouragement of peaceful settlements of conflicts, and the development of a world organization to promote political, social, and economic co-operation of peoples.

In 1972 Gloria Thompson, a Moorhead State College student, conducted for the Minnesota Historical Society this series of eight oral history interviews with members of the WIL. The women interviewed describe their backgrounds and discuss the Minnesota branch of the WIL from its founding in 1922 by Maud C. Stockwell through the 1970s. They comment on the organization's founding principles of peace, support for the United Nations, disarmament, opposition to the Korean and Vietnam conflicts, advocacy of peace candidates, and lobbying for legislation reflecting the human-rights principles of the WIL. The interviewees also mention a Federal Bureau of Investigation scrutiny of the WIL in the 1940s and the WIL resolution criticizing Wisconsin Senator Joseph McCarthy in the 1950s.

635. HAWKINS, MADGE (1882-1980). 1972. 60 min.

Mrs. Oscar F. Hawkins, a retired schoolteacher, has been active in the peace tradition since the Spanish-American War. She was involved in the Nonpartisan League of North Dakota, the Farmer-Labor party, and the WIL, which she joined in the 1930s.

636. HENDRICKSON, VIENA JOHNSON (1898-1980). 1972. 60 min.

Hendrickson immigrated to Minnesota from Finland as an infant with her parents. She was active in the Farmer-Labor party in the 1930s and 1940s, served as a representative of the International Ladies Garment Workers Union (1952-53), and was an active member and president of the WIL (1935-71).

637. MEILI, OLIVE (1895-   ). 1972. 60 min.

Meili joined the WIL in the 1930s and has served as an officer.

638. OTTERNESS, ELEANOR. 1972. 60 min.

President of the WIL at the time of the interview, Otterness moved to Minnesota in 1950 to do post-graduate study in social work.

639. SIBLEY, MARJORIE. 1972. 30 min. Restricted.

A college librarian, Sibley moved to Minnesota in 1948, became active in the WIL, and was state president of the organization during the Joseph McCarthy period.

640. THOMSON, MARGARET. 1972. 60 min. 37 p.

A retired teacher and high school assistant principal, Thomson became active in the WIL in 1955.

641. TILSEN, RACHEL (1928-   ). 1972. 60 min.

A Minneapolis native, Tilsen worked as a secretary. She joined the WIL during the Korean conflict.

642. VISSCHER, GERTRUDE (1889-   ). 1972. 90 min. 29 p.

Visscher moved to Minnesota in 1936 after teaching as a missionary in Japan. She joined the WIL in the 1960s and served as president of the Minnesota branch (1968-70).

PART 2

Regional Research Centers' Collections

INDIVIDUAL INTERVIEWS AND REMINISCENCES

These general reminiscences of farmers, teachers, bankers, business people, clergy, and others cover various aspects of life in Minnesota and the Upper Midwest. Narrators are identified by occupation and geographic area, and subjects discussed are noted under each name. Many of the interviews contain a good deal of rural social history. A large number concern modifications of farm life during the 20th century and concurrent changes in rural institutions.

643. AANESTAD, OTTO HERBERT. 1975. 2 hrs. (S)

An Episcopal priest reflects on his childhood, education, years of teaching, and ministry at St. James Episcopal Church in Marshall, Lyon County, and at churches in the Dakotas and California.

644. ACKMAN, ZINA. 1978. 60 min. (S)

A retired bookkeeper for the Redwood County Rural Telephone Co. (1921-51) from Redwood Falls, Redwood County, comments on the history of the telephone company and the effects of the 1930s Depression.

645. ALBRECHT, CLARA TIMM. 1976. 60 min. (S)

Mrs. Henry Albrecht, a retired teacher and housewife from Taunton, Lyon County, com-

ments on the social life and the role of a minister's wife in Yellow Medicine County (1920-60).

646. ALLEN, GORDON. 1976. 50 min. 12 p. (R)

A counselor at Willmar State Hospital discusses alcoholism in Stevens County.

647. ALLEN, MYRON R. 1975. 90 min. (C)

A retired McGregor, Aitkin County, investor and utilities company executive discusses the operation of several family companies, including the General Minnesota Utilities Co., Eastern Minnesota Power Co., and R. P. Allen Co. He comments on family and local history and the effects of the 1930s Depression on electric utilities.

648. ALSOP, WAYNE. 1975. 60 min. (B)

A retired Beltrami County auditor (1961-74) discusses changes in Bemidji and Beltrami County during his career.

649. AMUNDSON, TOBIAS. 1973. 45 min. 14 p. (R)

The sheriff of Grant County (1938-58) discusses his immigration from Norway (1911) and his career in law enforcement.

650. ANDERSON, ANNA. 1973. 50 min. 28 p. (S)

The sister of S. A. Anderson, who founded O. G. Anderson and Co. (the Big Store) in Minneota, Lyon County, discusses the store's operation and the Icelandic community.

651. ANDERSON, CARL. 1973. 40 min. 13 p. (S)

The son of one of the founders discusses the O. G. Anderson and Co. (the Big Store) in Minneota, Lyon County.

652. ANDERSON, EDITH SEGER. 1975. 60 min. (S)

A resident of Westbrook, Cottonwood County, discusses social life and women's roles in southwest Minnesota (1920-50).

653. ANDERSON, EMIL. 1975. 66 min. 12 p. (R)

A Chippewa County commissioner (1941-65) and farmer comments on his career, work with the Works Progress Administration, and the 1930s Depression.

654. ANDERSON, ERROL AND ALBERTA IHM ANDERSON. 1976. 90 min. 18 p. (R)

Big Stone County farmers discuss farming from World War I to the 1970s; the 1930s Depression; the Nonpartisan League; and the Farm Holiday, Farm Bureau, and Farmers Union.

655. ANDERSON, HELEN ANDERSON. 1977. 110 min. (R)

Mrs. Harvey Anderson, a retired teacher from Evansville, Douglas County, comments on education and religion in rural life and discusses the importance of Melby, Douglas County, as an early business center.

656. ANDERSON, OLIVE BENJAMIN. 1975. 60 min. (S)

Mrs. Alvin Anderson of Lester Prairie, McLeod County, discusses family life and the role of women in rural society.

657. ANDERSON, OSCAR C. 1976. 60 min. (S)

A resident of Dawson, Lac qui Parle County, discusses Swedish settlement in Dawson and Canby, Yellow Medicine County, and changes in farming technology.

658. ANDERSON, THEODORE W. 1973. 50 min. 40 p. (S)

The manager (1943-73) of O. G. Anderson and Co. (the Big Store) in Minneota, Lyon County, recalls the details of its operation.

659. ANDERSON, VALENTINA JASKULSKA. 1976. 90 min. (S)

Mrs. Iver Anderson of Lake Benton, Lincoln County, comments on her education, her career as a lawyer in Poland, the German occupation of Poland during World War II, and her postwar experiences.

660. ANDERSON, WILLARD. 1978. 30 min. (R)

The former manager of the Agralite Cooperative in Benson, Swift County, discusses the formation of the Federated Telephone Cooperative of Chokio.

661. ARNESON, ALVIN. 1973. 60 min. 27 p. (M)

The superintendant of schools in various North Dakota towns during the 1920s, head of the Works Progress Administration in Minot, N.Dak., and an active member of the Democratic party discusses his activities.

662. ARNQUIST, LEN. 1975. 48 min. 18 p. (R)

The operator of a general store in Hoffman, Grant County, discusses farming in the late 19th century and the effects of the 1930s Depression and World War II on small businesses.

663. ASKEGAARD, OSCAR. 1975. 62 min. (M)

A retired farmer from Comstock, Clay County, recalls childhood days in Norway, settlement in the U.S., and the 1930s Depression.

664. ASSENSTAB, ARTHUR F. 1972. 45 min. 36 p. (S)

A banker comments on banking in Wabasso, Redwood County, during the 1930s Depression.

665. AUSEN, IRENE DELLAR. 1976. 45 min. (S)

A housewife from Marshall, Lyon County, comments on life as an immigrant and social activities in Marshall during World War II.

666. AUSTIN, FRANK. 1974, 1975. 2 hrs. 23 p. (R)

A sign painter in Montevideo, Chippewa County, discusses family history, the growth of the town, the 1930s Depression, community reaction to World War II, and the history of the Montevideo community band.

667. BALE, SERINA. 1975. 90 min. (M)

A retired schoolteacher from Moorhead, Clay County, discusses her career, changes in the Lutheran church, and the 1930s Depression.

668. BARTELL, JOHN M. 1974. 30 min. 36 p. (S)

A minister discusses his work and the dissolution of the German Presbyterian Synod of the West.

669. BARTLETT, WINIFRED. 1976. 60 min. (S)

A Pipestone County resident discusses the settlement of the communities of Jasper, Woodstock, and Pipestone.

670. BELL, IONE B. 1976. 45 min. (O)

A feminist and artist from Austin, Mower County, talks about her work.

671. BEAULIEU, CLIFTON. 1979. 100 min. (C)

The former owner of the Fairgrounds Ballroom in Sauk Rapids, Benton County, comments on his life as a traveling musician, the effects of prohibition on his business, and the economics of operating a dance hall.

672. BERG, ELSIE. 1976. 45 min. (C)

A farmwife from Swatara, Aitkin County, comments on life in northern Aitkin County from 1900 to the 1970s.

673. BERG, OLGA LARSEN. 1978. 40 min. (M)

Mrs. Palmer Berg discusses her courtship, marriage, and farm life near Lake Park, Becker County.

674. BOGIE, MARY HAWN. 1975. 52 min. 10 p. (R)

A housewife from Glenwood, Pope County, recalls her emigration from Canada to Minnesota.

675. BORGERDING, THOMAS. ca.1950s. 30 min.
7 p. (B)
A Catholic missionary to the Ojibway at the Red Lake Indian Reservation and a founder of St. Mary's Mission discusses his work among the Ojibway, his acquaintance with Episcopal missionaries, and the effects of the 1863 and 1869 treaties with the Ojibway.

676. BRENDAL, LENA. 1971. 45 min. (R)
A daughter of early settlers in Pope County discusses her father and experiences growing up on the frontier.

677. BRENNING, DOROTHY. 1978. 3 hrs. (B)
A poet and storekeeper from Hines, Beltrami County, comments on her life in one of the state's smallest towns; changes in the religious, social, and economic quality of life in the 20th century; and reads several pieces of her poetry with explanations of their significance to her.

678. BRIGGS, RODNEY A. 1976. 2 hrs. (R)
The president of Eastern Oregon State College and former provost of the University of Minnesota-Morris (1968-69) discusses the development of the University of Minnesota-Morris, phasing out the West Central School of Agriculture, hiring new faculty, and the reaction of the Morris, Stevens County, community to the university.

679. BINGHAM, JAMES L. 1980. 45 min. (M)
Bingham recalls farming near Fosston, Polk County, and life as a cowboy in the North Dakota Badlands.

680. BLACK THUNDER, ELIJAH. 1976. 60 min.
(R)
A Dakota Indian medicine man discusses Indian legends and traditions.

681. BLANKENBERG, AUGUST WILLIAM. 1976. 60
min. (S)
Blankenberg discusses being a farmer and veterinarian in Lakefield, Jackson County.

682. BOLINSKI, HENRY. 1978. 55 min. 19 p.
(C)
Bolinski discusses his service during World War I, the Works Progress Administration, the formation of the Farmer-Labor party, and his work as a Benton County commissioner.

683. BRECHT, ARNOLD. 1972. 90 min. 45 p.
(S)
A Nobles County lawyer, assistant county attorney (1923-26), and county attorney (1931-43) recalls the 1930s Depression and prohibition in Worthington.

684. BROTEN, CHARLES. 1978. 30 min. (R)
The director of the Older American Program at the Morris Senior Citizens Center, Morris, Stevens County, comments on the center's funding activities, programs, and special services.

685. BROWN, MARY BELLE. 1976. 90 min. (S)
Brown discusses medical services in Pipestone County (1870-1900).

686. BROWN, MARY GROSS. 1978. 60 min. (M)
Brown discusses growing up in Logan County, N.Dak., and relatives who emigrated from Germany to the U.S.

687. BRUNS, HENRY. 1974. 90 min. 18 p.
(S)
Bruns comments on the Ebenezer Presbyterian Church, Renville County, on membership in the German Presbyterian Synod of the West, German heritage, and Christian education.

688. BUCK, ELLEN ARNDT. 1975. 60 min. (S)
Mrs. Goodwin Buck discusses farm and family life in Lyon County.

689. BUKOWSKI, EARL. 1978. 75 min. (C)
A bakery and cafe owner describes the bakery business, competition, the effects of inflation on small businesses, the business climate in Sauk Rapids, Benton County, and the development of that community.

690. BURFIEND, HELEN ALLANSON. 1973.
2 hrs., 45 min. 40 p. (R)
The daughter of George G. Allanson recalls her family's political, social, and business activities in Morris, Stevens County.

691. BUSCH, LAWRENCE. 1975. 64 min. 11 p.
(R)
A resident of Pepperton Township, Stevens County, recalls his childhood and his experiences in the Civilian Conservation Corps.

692. BUSCHENA, JOHN F. 1972. 90 min. 48
p. (S)
An electrician discusses the building of the Fulda power plant, the Fulda Light and Power Co., early electrical appliances, and the activities of the Rural Electrification Administration in Murray County.

693. BUSCHMAN, E. H. 1974. 40 min. (S)
A minister discusses churches of the German Presbyterian Synod of the West in Nobles County, their changes from 1915 to the 1930s, and farming in the 1920s.

694. CARBERT, ADELINE OLSON. 1977. 35 min.
(R)

Mrs. Fred Carbert, a retired Cyrus, Pope County, teacher, discusses her career (1928-30) at Stevens County Rural School District No. 8 and service as a school-board member during the 1940s.

695. CARTWRIGHT, MABEL STONE. 1976. 30 min. 9 p. (R)
A former teacher discusses her life and social activities in Morris, Stevens County.

696. CASANOVA, BLANCHE SOULAK. 1977. 60 min. (R)
Mrs. Ralph Casanova of Morris, Stevens County, discusses her childhood near Sisseton, S.Dak.; high-school years in Hibbing, St. Louis County; prostitution in St. Paul during the 1930s Depression; the feelings of Yugoslav Americans in St. Paul during World War II; and the early history of Clara City, Chippewa County.

697. CHAMPAGNE, PETER. 1977. 45 min. 16 p. (O)
A mechanical engineer from Mankato, Blue Earth County, comments on the construction of the Rapidan Dam on the Blue Earth River (1910-11).

698. CHARLES, ERLAND. 1975. 4 hrs. 47 p. (R)
A farmer and pilot from Hancock, Stevens County, discusses politics, farming, and aerial crop spraying.

699. CHUMLEY, G. NATHANIEL. 1978. 100 min. (B) Restricted.
A retired federal and Minnesota state government official discusses the establishment of regional development commissions in the state, in particular that in Region 2 of north-central Minnesota.

700. CITROWSKI, ALBINUS AND LE GRANT VELDE. 1976. 90 min. (S)
Two officers of the Yellow Medicine County National Farmers Organization discuss its growth and activities (1962-75).

701. CLARK, LOREN. 1980. 45 min. 18 p. (R)
An Ortonville farmer discusses the use of German prisoners of war on Big Stone County farms during the war.

702. COLLINS, TERRY P. 1978. 25 min. (R)
A Morris, Stevens County, attorney discusses his involvement in the formation of the Morris Senior Citizens Center.

703. COMSTOCK, ALVIN. 1974. 90 min. 52 p. (S)
The postmaster of Lakefield, Jackson County (1925-64), discusses small-town life and the activity of the local Red Cross.

704. CORNEILUSSEN, ALICE. 1973. 60 min. 29 p. (M)
A retired Moorhead schoolteacher comments on the role of women in higher education in the 1920s and on the growth of the city of Moorhead, Clay County.

705. COY, ROBERT B. 1976. 28 min. 10 p. (R)
The former manager of a general store in Danvers, Swift County, discusses life in the early 1900s and his role as a businessman during the 1930s Depression and World Wars I and II.

706. CRANE, GUY. 1975. 80 min. (O)
The former stage manager of the Old Wonderland and Unique vaudeville theaters in Mankato, Blue Earth County, reminisces about his life in vaudeville.

707. CUNNINGHAM, AGNES O'LEARY. 1973. 60 min. 14 p. (R)
An elementary schoolteacher from Wheaton, Traverse County, discusses her teaching experiences and rural life in Traverse and Big Stone counties.

708. DAELLENBACH, OSWALD. 1976. 60 min. (M)
A retired Moorhead, Clay County, agricultural extension service agent discusses his work and comments on his teaching career in Ulen, Clay County.

709. DAHLSTROM, RUBEN AND DONNAL WILKES. 1978. 105 min. (C)
Dahlstrom and Wilkes discuss the history of Milaca, Mille Lacs County, and the impact of the automobile on rural communities.

710. DALLMAN, OTTO. 1977. 50 min. (M)
A retired farmer from Fergus Falls, Otter Tail County, discusses emigration from Germany during the 1930s and his experiences in farming.

711. DALY, MICHAEL JAMES. 1975. 5 hrs. 45 p. (M)
A Perham attorney discusses the history of the Perham and Fergus Falls areas of Otter Tail County.

712. DeLANGHE, RAFHAELLE VAN HOVERBEKE. 1975. 60 min. (S)
Mrs. Jules DeLanghe of Marshall, Lyon County, discusses emigration from Belgium in 1905 and farm life in the 1920s.

713. DOLAN, JOHN. 1973. 50 min. 27 p. (S)
A farmer discusses the development of the Milroy, Redwood County, area.

714. DOSDALL, HENRY A. 1976. 50 min. (R)
A Stevens County farmer discusses farm life, his early schooling, the 1930s Depression, the Farmers Union Oil Station in Starbuck, Pope County, and his ideas on co-operatives.

715. DOSLAND, GOODWIN L. 1975. 40 min. (M)
A probate court judge in Moorhead, Clay County, recalls the development of that area and discusses national and regional trends in the legal profession.

716. DRAHMANN, CATHERINE. 1977. 30 min. (M)
A retired grocer from Perham, Otter Tail County, comments on her family's history, their movement from Ohio to the Perham area, and the early development of Perham.

717. DREWES, OTTO. 1975. 60 min. 10 p. (R)
A farmer and former president of the Stevens County Farmers Union (1963-67) discusses that organization and his work with it.

718. DZIUK, BERTHA. 1978. 35 min. 14 p. (C)
A pharmacist from Foley, Benton County, discusses the operation of her business, the Foley Drug Store, and her service on the Foley city council.

719. EAMES, CAMILLA HENDRICKS. 1975. 71 min. 19 p. (R)
A Stevens County housewife discusses her activities with the American Legion Auxiliary, the First Lutheran Church Board, and the League of Women Voters.

720. EAMES, EARL. 1976. 75 min. (R)
The owner of a grain elevator and seed distributing company in Morris, Stevens County, discusses the Farmers Coop Grain Elevator, the Morris electric power dispute (1932-34), public sentiment prior to World War I, his experiences in World War I, farming, prohibition, and the 1930s Depression.

721. EBELING, LOUIS. 1974. 60 min. 35 p. (S)
A farmer from Rushmore, Nobles County, discusses the German Presbyterian Synod of the West and farming in the early 1900s in southwestern Minnesota and northern Iowa.

722. EBELING, WIARD. 1977. 60 min. (S)
A farmer from Rushmore, Nobles County, discusses education, religion, and the effects of the 1930s Depression and World War II on farming.

723. EBERLIN, ELLEN McLACHLAN. 60 min. (R)
The widow of Dr. Edward A. Eberlin of Glenwood, Pope County, discusses the work of a rural physician, the operation of a private hospital, and social life in Glenwood.

724. ECKLUND, HORACE KENNETH. 1975. 56 min. (M)
A retired telephone company employee from Moorhead, Clay County, comments on his Swedish heritage, his education at Moorhead Normal School (1910-21) and Moorhead State Teachers College (1922-26), and athletics at the college.

725. EDDY, JOSEPHINE. 1975. 55 min. 11 p. (R)
A former teacher and social worker in Morris, Stevens County, discusses her work, organizations in which she has been active, and the changes in the status of women.

726. EEKHOFF, WIERT. 1973. 90 min. 34 p. (S)
A Presbyterian minister from Rushmore, Nobles County, comments on his work with the Navaho Indian missions in Arizona.

727. EGGERS, RUSSELL. 1974. 45 min. (B)
The general manager of the Nu-Ply Corp. plant in Bemidji, Beltrami County, discusses the development of a wood-treatment process.

728. ELLIS, A. FRANK. 1974. 40 min. (O)
A labor organizer and the first president of United Packinghouse Workers of America, Local 9, discusses the union's 1933 strike against the Geo. A. Hormel & Co. in Austin, Mower County.

729. ELSING, HERMAN. 1974. 60 min. (S)
A farmer from Rushmore, Nobles County, discusses farming with horses, the effects of the 1930s Depression on farming, the history of the East Freesland Presbyterian Church, and the German Presbyterian Synod of the West.

730. ELSING, JOHN. 1974. 45 min. (S)
A retired Rushmore, Nobles County, farmer discusses farming and the German Presbyterian Synod of the West.

731. ENGBRETSON, JOHN. 1973. 50 min. 28 p. (S)
A Luverne banker comments on banking in Rock County during the 1930s Depression.

732. ENGEL, JOSEPH JOHN. 1974. 45 min. 29 p. (S)

A former resident of Vesta, Redwood County, discusses rural and small-town life, transportation, electricity, Farm Holiday Assn. activity in Marshall, Lyon County, the Swift Dairy and Poultry Co. of Marshall, and the Watergate political scandal. Engel farmed near Vesta and owned a shoe-repair shop and hardware store in that town.

733. ENGEL, MINNIE SCHROEDER. 1975. 60 min. (S)

Engel discusses early settlement of Yellow Medicine County.

734. ERNST, WILLIAM H. 1977. 60 min. (R)

A retired Alberta, Stevens County, farmer discusses school consolidation and its effect on the town, social activities involved with the school, the Manse (teacher's home) and its relation to the school system, a model of the school exhibited at the 1915 World's Fair, and the growth of Alberta. He comments on his activities as an athlete, bus driver, and school-board member.

735. FISHER, HAROLD. 1978. 100 min. (C)

The former postmaster and mayor of Royalton, Morrison County, discusses that town, his work, and the county's ethnic background.

736. FLEMING, HAROLD D. 1978. 45 min. (B)

A professor emeritus discusses his role as director of the Division of Education and of the Laboratory School at Bemidji State Teachers College.

737. FORDE, ASTRID FLACK. 1976. 20 min. (R)

A music teacher and widow of a minister from Starbuck, Pope County, discusses her work and her husband's ministry.

738. FORTUNE, WILLIAM, SR. 1977. 75 min. (M)

A retired building contractor from Fargo, N.Dak., and Moorhead, Clay County, comments on his family and the general-construction business in the Fargo-Moorhead area and reminisces about early area businessmen.

739. FOSLIEN, FRED. 1978. 110 min. (R)

The retired manager of the Production Credit Assn. in Alexandria, Douglas County, discusses the association's operations, Minnesota highway legislation in the 1930s, the Democratic-Farmer-Labor party, the Nonpartisan League, and the development of the Victoria Heights area of Alexandria.

740. FRICKE, ACHSAH. 1974. 30 min. 17 p. (S)

The wife of a railroad worker discusses small-town life in Bingham Lake, Cottonwood County, and railroads in southwestern Minnesota.

741. FROMELT, HERBERT. 1978. 42 min. 19 p. (C)

An implement dealer discusses his business, the mechanization of farming, his first experience with electricity, uses of advertising, and the history of Rice, Benton County.

742. FROST, SIGRID. 1973. 50 min. 40 p. (S)

The former cashier and bookkeeper for O. G. Anderson and Co. (the Big Store) in Minneota, Lyon County, discusses its operation.

743. FULTS, LEWIS. 1975. 58 min. 12 p. (R)

A farmer and former president of the Stevens County Farm Bureau (1953-57) discusses the bureau and other farm organizations.

744. GADE, FLORENCE. 1975. 60 min. (S)

A housewife from Heron Lake, Jackson County, comments on the settlement of the county and on women's history and social life in southwest Minnesota (1920-60).

745. GAIDA, LARRY. 1975. 60 min. (D) Restricted.

A service-station operator from Duluth, St. Louis County, comments on his career (1939-75).

746. GARRITY, JAMES E. 1977. 45 min. (M)

A county court judge in Clay County discusses the growth and development of Moorhead, Clay County, and the career of his father, James A. Garrity, as county attorney and probate court judge.

747. GAVIN, EMMET J. 1974. 45 min. (O)

A former employee reminisces about work at the Geo. A. Hormel & Co. meat-packing plant in Austin, Mower County, including information on labor organizations and strikes during the 1930s.

748. GAWBOY, ROBERT. 1975. 75 min. 10 p. (R)

An Ojibway medicine man from Ely, St. Louis County, discusses his work, remedies and spells, and Indian legends and traditions.

749. GAYLORD, MARGARET GRANNIS. 1975. 60 min. (D) Restricted.

A resident of Duluth, St. Louis County, comments on family history, including information on Paul Gaylord, her father-in-law and the first photographer in Duluth.

750. GILBERTSON, SELMA FALLA. 1976. 45 min. (S)
   Mrs. Gerhard J. Gilbertson from Montevideo, Chippewa County, discusses women's history and social life in southwest Minnesota (1920-60).

751. GLASRUD, CLARENCE. 1976. 72 min. (M)
   A retired English professor from Moorhead, Clay County, discusses his years at Moorhead State University as a student and faculty member, including comments on changes in student attitudes and the contributions of past university presidents.

752. GODFREY, CHARLES H. 1973, 1975, 1976. 3 hrs. 61 p. (B)
   An Itasca County land commissioner (1942-62) comments on the operation of the steamboat "Frank S. Lane" on Lake Winnibigoshish in the early 1900s and his experiences as a logger in the Cass Lake area.

753. GORMAN, LABERTA ENGEBRETSON. 1975. 60 min. (M)
   A retired restaurant operator from Moorhead, Clay County, recalls her experiences during the 1930s Depression.

754. GRAMM, MARGARET. 1975. 41 min. 11 p. (R)
   A Stevens County resident discusses the customs, philosophies, activities, and roles of women in the Apostolic Christian church.

755. GRANGER, STEPHEN. 1976. 90 min. (R)
   The assistant provost of the University of Minnesota-Morris discusses the history of the university and the closing of the West Central School of Agriculture.

756. GREEN, MAUDE LITTLE. 1976. 60 min. (S)
   A retired Redwood County teacher discusses the education system and social history of Redwood Falls.

757. GROVER, DONOVAN. 1978. 31 min. (R)
   A retired rural mail carrier comments on his work with the Ashby, Grant County, school board, his English great-grandparents, and the activities of the Nonpartisan League.

758. GUNDERSON, EMMA BAKKEN. 1975. 45 min. (S)
   Mrs. George Gunderson of Minneota, Lyon County, comments on education and homesteading in Lyon County.

759. GUTTARNSSON, STEPHEN. 1978. 60 min. (S)
   A Lutheran minister discusses the Icelandic church in Minnesota, the development of Icelandic communities in western Minnesota, and the impact of World War II.

760. HAALA, RAYMOND S. 1976. 60 min. (S)
   A retired printer from Comfrey, Brown County, talks about the Comfrey newspaper, the printing trade, and newspaper work (1920-76).

761. HAGG, HAROLD T. 1978. 60 min. (B)
   A professor emeritus at Bemidji State University discusses his career, the growth of the university, and student-teacher relations.

762. HAMILTON, ARTHUR. 1978. 35 min. (M)
   A businessman from Thief River Falls, Pennington County, discusses his childhood in Langdon, N.Dak., the impact of World War I on the Red River Valley, speakeasys during the 1920s, and business during the 1930s Depression and World War II.

763. HAMILTON, MILDRED ENGEN. 1978. 30 min. (M)
   Mrs. Arthur Hamilton comments on life in Thief River Falls, Pennington County, college life during the 1920s, the 1930s Depression, and her 30 years as organist for Trinity Lutheran Church.

764. HAMMETT, ANNE G. 1974. 82 min. 16 p. (M)
   A retired schoolteacher from Glyndon, Clay County, discusses her education, the influence of her Norwegian heritage, and life during the 1930s Depression.

765. HANSEN, ERNIE H. 1978. 55 min. (R)
   A retired rural mail carrier discusses his work, the effects of the 1930s Depression on the Ashby, Grant County, area, and his father's blacksmith shop.

766. HANSEN, PIERRE T. 1978. 60 min. (C)
   A farmer from Rockville, Stearns County, comments on his family, the history of Rockville, including the development of local churches, the effects of prohibition and the 1930s Depression, the growth of the granite industry, and changes in farming.

767. HANSON, BERT. 1976. 75 min. 30 p. (O)
   A Blue Earth County farmer discusses family history and developments in agriculture during the past 60 years.

768. HANSON, ETHEL ELLINGSON. 1973. 25 min. 7 p. (R)

A farmer discusses rural life near Hoffman, Grant County.

769. HANSON, HERBERT M. AND NEIL HARCUM. 1978. 2 hrs. (R)
A farmer discusses rural life near Hoffman is a retired store owner; Harcum worked for a stone and monument company. They discuss the Minnesota Republican party; the Nonpartisan League; social and civic clubs in Browns Valley, Traverse County; the 1912 corn and alfalfa exposition in Morris, Stevens County; and operation of a dry-goods store.

770. HANSON, LAURA WOLFE. 1977. 45 min. (R) (S)
A retired Chippewa County farmer discusses the Co-op Canning Co. and store in Montevideo, activities of the Farmers Union, and her views of farm life.

771. HANSON, NORMAN AND REGINA HAGENE HANSON. 1978. 60 min. (M)
Farmers from Morken Township, Clay County, discuss their Norwegian heritage and farming.

772. HAROLDSON, CLINT. 1974. 90 min. 30 p. (S)
A Farm Holiday Assn. organizer in central and northern Minnesota discusses the association's activities and life during the 1930s Depression.

773. HARRIS, HANNAH HAUGSLAND. 1976. 60 min. (M)
A retired insurance agent from Fargo, N. Dak., comments on her parents' emigration from Norway and her childhood experiences in Goodhue County and Fargo.

774. HARRIS, WALLACE. 1976. 60 min. (S)
A lifelong resident of Cambria, Blue Earth County, talks about the Welsh settlement, the influence of various Welsh churches, and the mergers that formed the Cambria Federated Church.

775. HARVEY, DORA ASKDAL AND CORA MONSETH. 1977. 45 min. (S)
Two retired teachers from Minneota, Lyon County, discuss social life, religion, and education in Minneota; the Icelandic language; the development of the Minneota Public Library; O. G. Anderson's general store (the Big Store); and the Riverside Farm.

776. HEDBLOM, CLARENCE. 1978. 60 min. (C)
An auctioneer and insurance agent from Freedham, Morrison County, discusses his family; early career in farming; the history of the Swanson Brothers' store, the creamery,

and churches in Freedham; and changes in the ethnic background of the county's population.

777. HEGGEN, REUBEN. 1973. 20 min. 4 p. (R)
A retired farmer from Wheaton, Traverse County, discusses incidents surrounding the removal of the county seat from Browns Valley to Wheaton in 1886.

778. HEIM, LEONARD. 1978. 50 min. (C)
The owner of Heim Milling Co., St. Cloud, Stearns County, comments on the flour-milling industry, the Heim family, and the operation of the Heim mill.

779. HERBERGER, G. ROBERT. 1973. 60 min. (C)
The founder of the Herberger Department Stores of St. Cloud, Stearns County, discusses the operation of the chain of stores and family history.

780. HERFINDAHL, GRANT. 1979. 60 min. (R)
A farmer discusses Norwegian settlement patterns in Swift County and the importance of the church in Norwegian communities.

781. HICKMAN, O. J. 1974. 60 min. 31 p. (S)
A farmer from Ellsworth, Nobles County, recalls the German Presbyterian Synod of the West, anti-German feelings during World War I, and the change to an English-language church service.

782. HILDE, KATIE. 1974. 56 min. 14 p. (M)
A Ulen, Clay County, housewife discusses education, health care, home remedies, and the experiences of her family as they emigrated from the Netherlands to Russia and finally to the U.S.

783. HILFERS, HENRY. 1975. 48 min. 7 p. (R)
A Murray County farmer discusses railroads in Murray and Pipestone counties.

784. HISKEN, GERTRUDE. 1974. 25 min. (S)
A minister's wife discusses the German Presbyterian Synod of the West.

785. HOFF, CHRISTIAN. 1975. 60 min. (M)
A retired railroad worker discusses Minnesota Governor Floyd B. Olson (1931-36), politics during the 1930s Depression, and his work.

786. HOGENSON, HAZEL. 1978. 45 min. (B)
A retired professor discusses the growth

and programs of the Laboratory School at Bemidji State Teachers College.

787. HOLZER, HARRY. 1975. 60 min. 11 p. (R) Restricted.
A journalist and community activist from Montevideo, Chippewa County, discusses World War II, prohibition, and the development of Montevideo businesses.

788. HOVERSTEN, MARTHA JOHNSON. 1976. 60 min. (S)
A farmer from Marshall, Lyon County, recalls her emigration from Norway at age fifteen, her experiences during the voyage, and her life in Norway and the U.S.

789. HOWELL, IRENE IRONHEART. 1977. 60 min. (S)
A Yellow Medicine County housewife comments on Dakota Indian history in southwest Minnesota, including information on the Lower Sioux Indian Reservation.

790. HUBLEY, JAMES. 1974. 45 min. (S)
A Vietnam War veteran discusses his experiences and the antiwar movement.

791. HULL, HENRY, JR. 1975. 43 min. 11 p. (R)
The chief of police in Morris, Stevens County, talks about the crime rate, new developments in law enforcement, and the nature of police work.

792. HUSTAD, TEGNER. 1975, 1978. 100 min. (R)
A retired Minnesota state park ranger from Starbuck, Pope County, discusses the preservation and management of prairie lands, the settlement of Starbuck, the founding of the Pope County Bank, and Norwegian immigration to Minnesota.

793. IMHOLTE, JOHN Q. 1976. 75 min. (R)
The provost of the University of Minnesota—Morris, Stevens County, discusses his decision to teach at the university, his first classes and students, and the university's growth and development.

794. JACOBS, HENRY. 1974. 50 min. (S)
A retired farmer from Ellsworth, Nobles County, discusses the German Presbyterian Synod of the West.

795. JENSEN, IDA AND ANNA WELTER. 1973. 50 min. 27 p. (S)
Two officers of the Milroy, Redwood County, Women's Christian Temperance Union discuss its activities.

796. JOHNSON, CLARENCE. 1976. 60 min. 13 p. (B)
A resident of Bemidji, Beltrami County, discusses the operation of the Civilian Conservation Corps camp at Big Lake during the 1930s.

797. JOHNSON, E. V. 1973. 50 min. 49 p. (S)
A businessman discusses the history of the town of Arco, Lincoln County.

798. JOHNSON, HARVEY. 1978. 32 min. (S)
A farmer discusses the American Agriculture movement in Minnesota and its objectives in planning a national farm policy.

799. JOHNSON, LENORA ISAACSON. 1973. 60 min. 22 p. (M)
A schoolteacher discusses Norman County schools, teaching during the 1930s Depression, Minnesota politics, and the rural economy.

800. JORDAN, KATHLEEN SMITH. 1976. 60 min. (S)
A physician from Granite Falls, Yellow Medicine County, discusses the operation of the Riverside Tuberculosis Sanatorium (1930-63) and the development of tuberculosis treatment and testing programs.

801. JORGENSON, ALMA. 1980. 75 min. (M)
A resident of Ulen, Clay County, recalls her childhood.

802. KAMPMEYER, GEORGE F. 1975. 43 min. 7 p. (R)
A retired Chicago and Northwestern Railway Co. agent in Currie, Murray County, comments on the railroad and his work.

803. KEANY, PATRICK. 1976. 90 min. (S)
A Roman Catholic priest discusses the problems faced by rural churches and education and changes within the church.

804. KENFIELD, JOHN W. 1975. 60 min. (B)
A Bemidji, Beltrami County, businessman discusses the founding and operation of the Bemidji Box Factory (1900-20) by his family. Kenfield owns and operates the Kenfield Lumber Co.

805. KIVI, KAREN. 1973. 60 min. 25 p. (M)
The librarian at Moorhead State University discusses the activities of the Finnish community in Crosby, Pine County, during the 1930s Depression.

806. KLOKSETH, EDYTHE BOEHMER. 1978. 58 min. (M)
A retired farmer from Morken Township,

Clay County, discusses her childhood and memories of the 1930s Depression and World War II.

807. KOCH, MABEL. 1979. 25 min. (R)
A retired housekeeper discusses her work, Norwegian heritage, and the use of the Norwegian and English languages in the Nora Lutheran Church in Pope County.

808. KOHN, KATHRYN. 1975. 25 min. 7 p. (R)
A German immigrant compares her life in Grant County with that in Germany.

809. KOOPEMEINERS, LINUS. 1978. 40 min. (C)
The general manager of Gran-A-Stone, Inc., Waite Park, Stearns County, comments on the granite industry and his grandparents' emigration from Germany.

810. KOSER, RODNEY. 1975. 36 min. 12 p. (R)
A Grant County farmer discusses the state's prairie land and wetlands management programs.

811. KRAGNES, CORA KLOKSETH. 1978. 60 min. (M)
Mrs. Alvin Kragnes discusses her Norwegian heritage, emigration from Norway, and her family's settlement in Morken Township, Clay County.

812. KRAMER, ARNOLD. 1972. 60 min. 70 p. (S)
A Wabasso, Redwood County, farmer and painter -- called the "Grandpa Moses of Southwest Minnesota" -- discusses farm life.

813. KREBS, NETTIE BELL. 1973. 30 min. 19 p. (S)
Mrs. Arthur Krebs, the wife of a banker from Appleton, Swift County, reflects on social life and customs (1920s-50s).

814. KRIEG, OSCAR. 1978. 36 p. (C)
An insurance agent from Sauk Rapids, Benton County, discusses the development of Sauk Rapids, the effects of the 1930s Depression, changes in the insurance industry, and local school board administration.

815. KRYZSKO, SYLVESTER J. 1977. 4 hrs., 30 min. 72 p. (W)
A retired bank president from Winona, Winona County, discusses his family, education, banking career, and work for the Republican party. He comments on St. Mary's and St. Teresa's colleges, of which he is a trustee, and his service on the Minnesota State University Board (1951-65).

816. LaFAVE, EDWARD J., JR. 1975, 1978. 84 min. (R)
The managing officer of the Citizens Bank of Morris, Stevens County, comments on rural medical care and the work of the Area Health Care Committee of which he is a member. He discusses the West Central Education Development Assn. and its role in establishing the University of Minnesota-Morris.

817. LAMPMAN, CLAUDE L. 1975. 60 min. 12 p. (B)
A retired Bemidji, Beltrami County, resident discusses the logging industry and his 35 years as a cook in logging camps.

818. LARSON, BLANCHE SHEFLOE. 1978. 39 min. (R)
A retired teacher from Morris, Stevens County, comments on the operations of the Morris Senior Citizens Center.

819. LARSON, CHRIS. 1978. 39 min. (R)
A retired teacher comments on the operations of the Morris Senior Citizens Center in Stevens County.

820. LARSON, GEORGE O. 1973. 90 min. 68 p. (S)
A retired Minneota, Lyon County, farmer discusses the effects of the 1930s Depression and Nonpartisan League activity in the county.

821. LARSON, HARLAN. 1979. 45 min. (M)
The founder of the Larson Transfer Co. discusses its growth from 1906 through its sale in 1957 and the development of the towns of Breckenridge, Wilkin County, and Wahpeton, N.Dak.

822. LARSON, IDA HARKNESS. 1974. 103 min. 31 p. (M)
Mrs. Walter Larson of Moorhead, Clay County, recalls her experiences as a teacher and as a participant in the girls' basketball programs at Winona State College, Winona County, and the University of Minnesota.

823. LATTIN, JOANNE SCHAUMBERG. 1978. 60 min. (M)
Mrs. Charles D. Lattin recalls summering at Lake Minnetonka, Hennepin County, during the 1930s and 1940s, the 1930s Depression, and World War II.

824. LE BLANC, STELLA HOULE. 1973. 90 min. 41 p. (M)
A retired teacher recalls the local history and French-Canadian customs of Belle Prairie, Morrison County.

825. LEE, ALMA KOPLIN. 1978. 45 min. (R)
A retired restaurant owner discusses the effects of prohibition, the 1930s Depression, and World War II on her business in Morris, Stevens County.

826. LEE, MARCUS. 1976. 45 min. (R)
A carpenter from Erdahl, Grant County, discusses his experiences in World War II as a member of the "Devil's Brigade," a forerunner of the Green Berets.

827. LEINUM, EVERT. 1977. 60 min. (M)
A West Fargo, N.Dak., resident discusses family history, his childhood in the state of Washington, work in a Washington Civilian Conservation Corps camp, and service in World War II.

828. LEWIS, ALVIN AND FAMILY. 1975. 90 min. (O)
Lewis family members reminisce about life in Medo Township, Blue Earth County, their Norwegian ancestry, the Lutheran church, farming, social life, and college days at St. Olaf College in Northfield, Rice County.

829. LINDELAND, BEN. 1973. 60 min. 12 p. (O)
A farmer reminisces about life near Pemberton, Blue Earth County, during the 1930s Depression.

830. LINDGREN, CARL V. 1976. 90 min. (B)
A retired farmer discusses dairy farming in Lammers Township, Beltrami County, and his father's life as a logger and farmer.

831. LOUK, IONE MITCHELL. 1976. 45 min. (O)
Mrs. Harry E. Louk of Mankato, Blue Earth County, discusses her experiences as the first student to graduate with a minor in women's studies from Mankato State University.

832. LYSFJORD, CHARLES. 1977. 60 min. (M)
A farm manager from Kennedy, Kittson County, discusses his career with Keine Farms, Inc., one of Minnesota's largest farms. He comments on Frank Keine, the founder of that corporation, and on current trends in large-scale farming.

833. MacDONALD, HARRIET. 1977. 65 min. (O)
A retired elementary teacher from Mankato, Blue Earth County, discusses the Jessie Irving family with whom she lived after moving to Mankato in 1926 and the Irving house, built in 1873. She includes autobiographical information.

834. MACK, JOHN. 1978. 90 min. (S)
A lawyer from New London, Kandiyohi County, discusses his involvement as attorney for the Willmar Bank Employees Assn. during its strike against the Citizens National Bank of Willmar. He includes information on the discrimination lawsuit, the formation of the union, relations with the bank, and political attitudes toward the strike.

835. MANTHEY, DOLORES. 1978. 90 min. (C)
The president of Sentinel Printing Co., Sauk Rapids, Stearns County, provides information on the printing business, company history, and labor relations.

836. MARC, JOHN AND PEDER MARC. 1976. 2 hrs. (B)
Two pioneer loggers discuss the settlement of Roosevelt Township, Beltrami County, logging for the Crookston Lumber Co., and homesteading cutover land in northern Minnesota.

837. MARKS, TINA LEONARD. 1977. 60 min. (S)
A farmer from Milroy, Redwood County, discusses rural family life and the influence of the Roman Catholic church.

838. MARTIN, FLORENCE EBELING. 1976. 60 min. (S)
Mrs. C. Paul Martin of Worthington, Nobles County, comments on the role of women in the county.

839. MARTIN, RICHARD AND HELMER BENSON. 1978. 36 min. (R)
Two school board members discuss the consolidation of the Kerkhoven and Murdock, Swift County, schools.

840. MATSON, GEORGE A. 1976. 60 min. (S)
A retired farmer and former Minnesota state and national officer of the National Farmers Organization discusses the development and growth of that group.

841. MATTSON, AXEL. 1974. 40 min. 18 p. (S)
A retired Lyon County farmer discusses farming during the 1930s Depression, the Farmers Union, and political issues related to farming.

842. MAUGHAN, WILLIAM E. 1977. 55 min. (R)
A former resident of Morris, Stevens County, discusses his education in the schools of that town.

843. MEADE, F. J. 1972. 50 min. 25 p. (S)
A Lyon County agricultural agent (1934-

54) discusses the Rural Electrification Administration and New Deal farm programs.

844. MEYER, ULRICH. 1974. 45 min. 29 p. (S)
A retired farmer from Marshall, Lyon County, discusses rural and small-town life; transportation, electricity, and Farm Holiday Assn. activity in Marshall; the Swift Dairy and Poultry Co.; and the Watergate political scandal.

845. MEYERS, MILDRED YOUNG. 1978. 90 min. (R)
A retired nurse from Wheaton, Traverse County, comments on nursing, school board politics, and the activities of the Traverse County Republican party.

846. MICKLISH, WILLARD. 1978. 40 min. (R)
The branch manager of the Golden Cream Dairy, Morris, Stevens County, and an active member of the West Central Education Development Assn. discusses the founding of the University of Minnesota-Morris, which replaced the West Central School of Agriculture, and community reaction to its operation.

847. MOEN, JERRY. 1974. 60 min. 15 p. (B)
The chief of the Bemidji, Beltrami County, fire department (1964-   ) comments on the department's growth and the Rural Fire Protection Agency.

848. MOHR, ELSIE SCHLUETER. 1974. 42 min. 12 p. (R)
A housewife from Morris, Stevens County, discusses rural life, her move to a small city, and the post-World War I economy in west central Minnesota. She comments on her experiences during World Wars I and II as a person of German ancestry.

849. MOORE, RUSSELL. 1975, 1976. 2 hrs. 25 p. (B)
A retired lumberman from Akeley, Hubbard County, discusses brickmaking, the growth of the towns of Akeley and Walker in Cass County, and the Red River Lumber Co. of Akeley.

850. MORK, GORDON. 1971. 85 min. (B)
A professor emeritus at the University of Minnesota discusses the development of the Laboratory School at Bemidji State Teachers College.

851. MURPHY, LAWRENCE W. 1974. 45 min. (O)
A retired manager comments on work at the Geo. A. Hormel & Co. meat-packing plant in Austin, Mower County (1923-64) and on the 1933 strike there.

852. MURPHY, TESSIE BUCKLEY. 1974. 75 min. 26 p. (M)
A retired elementary teacher from Felton, Clay County, discusses her career, her 20 years of service as a township clerk, the 1930s Depression, and farming.

853. NELSON, AGNES. 1976. 90 min. 24 p. (R)
A retired teacher and superintendent of the Big Stone County rural school system (1934-58) discusses her career, education in a rural school, and the use of Swedish as a second language at home and in school.

854. NELSON, ALFRED E. 1976. 60 min. 11 p. (B)
A resident of Bemidji, Beltrami County, recalls life at Camp Rabideau of the Civilian Conservation Corps. The camp was located on Rabideau Lake near Blackduck, Beltrami County.

855. NELSON, DONALD. 1977. 60 min. (M)
A farmer and cafe owner from Abercrombie, N.Dak., comments on his pioneering ancestors and the early history of the Christine and Hickson areas of North Dakota.

856. NELSON, EDWARD. 1975. 45 min. 13 p. (R)
A Stevens County resident discusses his 50 years of work for the Great Northern Railway Co.

857. NEMZEK, JOHN P. 1975. 60 min. (M)
A Moorhead, Clay County, policeman and carpenter discusses his work.

858. NICHOLSON, RICHARD W. 1977. 60 min. (S)
A retired businessman from Lynd, Lyon County, discusses Lynd businesses, telephone company, school system, and churches.

859. NORMAN, ROWLAND AND GERTRUDE BRANUM NORMAN. 1975. 30 min. 7 p. (R)
Two retired Chippewa County farmers describe the Swensson House, which is operated as a historic site by the Chippewa County Historical Society.

860. NELSON, HERMAN. 1978. 90 min. (C)
A retired farmer and machinist from Milaca, Mille Lacs County, discusses his heritage, education, careers, and the early history of the town.

861. NOLTE, FRED A. 1974. 45 min. (S)
Nolte discusses education in Nobles County, the German Presbyterian Synod of the West, and World War I.

862. NORGANT, ANSEL. 1974. 60 min. 30 p.
(S)
    A businessman discusses the Swedish
Lutheran Church in Lakefield, Jackson County.

863. NORMAN, JOHN P. 1978. 55 min. (M)
    A Swedish immigrant discusses his voyage
to America in 1910 and the 1930s Depression
and contrasts his memories of Sweden with
Swedish society of the 1970s.

864. NYBERG, LEONORA McCRACKEN. 1980. 50
min. (M)
    Mrs. Carlton Nyberg recalls her childhood
in Scotland, immigration to America in 1954,
and life in Benson, Swift County. She discusses comparative lifestyles of Scotland and
the U.S. and her first impressions of America.

865. NYSTROM, WILLIAM. 1972. 75 min. (S)
    A farmer and state legislator (1935-37)
from Worthington, Nobles County, discusses the
Farmers Union and its interests in the Farm
Holiday Assn., New Deal legislation, and the
Rural Electrification Administration.

866. OLSEN, HAROLD J. 1975. 48 min. 18 p.
(R)
    A city councilman and butcher in Hoffman,
Grant County, discusses the community's chang-
ing needs.

867. OLSEN, WESLEY. 1976. 36 min. (R)
    A farmer from Clinton, Big Stone County,
discusses farming and government grain-storage
programs.

868. OLSON, FLORENCE PETERSON. 1975. 48
min. 14 p. (R)
    Mrs. Joseph Olson of Granite Falls,
Yellow Medicine County, discusses the Olaf
Swensson family of Wegdahl, Chippewa County.

869. OLSON, MYRTLE. 1978. 60 min. (R)
    A retired principal and teacher from
Glenwood, Pope County, comments on rural
school systems, school consolidation, and the
Norwegian heritage.

870. OLSON, PETER. 1975. 2 hrs. (D) Restricted.
    An architect from Duluth, St. Louis Coun-
ty, discusses his career.

871. OLSON, WILLIAM M. 1976. 31 min. (B)
    A retired farmer discusses farming cut-
over land in Beltrami County, his father's
life as a logger and sawmill operator, and the
history of Eckles Township.

872. OTTERSTAD, CARL J. 1957, 1975. 2 hrs.
10 p. (B)

    A retired railroadman from Turtle River,
Beltrami County, discusses his career with the
Minnesota and International Railroad Co., the
history of Turtle River, and his father's work
as a timber cruiser.

873. PALM, JAMES. 1978. 30 min. (R)
    A school superintendent discusses his
role in the consolidation of the Kerkhoven and
Murdock, Swift County, schools.

874. PANKONIN, MINNIE SCHWANKE. 1975. 60
min. (S)
    Mrs. Charles J. Pankonin reflects on her
experiences as a German immigrant and as a
Cottonwood County farmer and mother.

875. PARSONS, EDITH BURMEISTER AND WINIFRID
BURMEISTER AUSTBO. 1973. 50 min. 23 p.
(S)
    The daughters of August C. Burmeister,
owner of the Redwood Falls Milling Co., Redwood Falls Electric Light Plant, and president
of the First National Bank of Redwood Falls,
discuss family history and the development of
electric power in their Redwood County community.

876. PARSONS, LILLIAN. 1974. 80 min. 26 p.
(R)
    One of the first women physicians in
Grant County discusses her medical training
and practice.

877. PARTA, RUSSELL. 1972. 65 min. 16 p.
(M)
    A newspaper publisher from New York
Mills, Otter Tail County, discusses Finnish
newspapers in the Midwest and the contributions of the Finnish community to Minnesota.

878. PAUL, EUGENE. 1976. 60 min. (S)
    Paul discusses the development and organ-
ization of the Faribault County National Farmers Organization (NFO) and the role played by
the Roman Catholic church in the formation of
the NFO.

879. PEDDYCOART, JESSE. 1973. 60 min.
33 p. (M)
    A retired laborer discusses homesteading
in Canada, logging in British Columbia, and
the development of Moorhead, Clay County.

880. PEDERSON, MABEL KNUTSON. 1976. 22 min.
(R)
    Mrs. Elmer R. Pederson of Starbuck, Pope
County, discusses Norwegian folk dancing and
customs.

881. PERALA, LEMPI ANDERSON. 1975. 30 min.
(M)

A housewife in New York Mills, Otter Tail County, discusses growing up during the 1930s Depression and her service on the New York Mills school board.

882. PETERSON, EDA LIEN. 1976. 75 min. (O)
A farmer from Delavan, Faribault County, discusses farm life, education, and marriage.

883. PETERSON, ROY A. 1973. 90 min. 26 p. (S)
A physician discusses work as a general practitioner in Vesta, Redwood County.

884. PETRICK, JOSEPH AND MAZELLE GRICE PETRICK. 1976. 107 min. (R)
A retired rural mail carrier (1927-69) and his wife discuss his career and mail route near Ortonville, Big Stone County, and his service in the National Guard.

885. PIEPER, OTTO. 1975. 50 min. 11 p. (R)
A German immigrant and retired farmer from Clara City, Chippewa County, comments on farm life, the Farmers' Co-op Elevator and Farmers' Co-op Telephone Co. of Clara City, the Farm Holiday Assn., and the Nonpartisan League.

886. PIERI, FRED. 1976. 40 min. (C)
A farmer from Swatara, Aitkin County, discusses farming in Anoka County and comments on the use of draft horses.

887. PIERSON, BEN J. AND LENORA ROMSDAHL PIERSON. 1974. 60 min. 47 p. (S)
The Piersons discuss Ellburgh Lutheran Church; the Norwegian language and Norwegian Bible school; the Current Lake Creamery Co., Murray County; Austin Normal College; farming; and the installation of electricity.

888. PIHL, HARRY. 1974. 45 min. (B)
The mayor (1953-54) of Bemidji, Beltrami County, discusses the founding and development of the Nu-Ply Corp. there.

889. PONSTEIN, JOHN. 1974. 30 min. 20 p. (S)
A Dutch immigrant discusses farming near Lynd, Lyon County, during World War I and the 1930s Depression.

890. POULSEN, WILLIAM. 1976. 60 min. (S)
The president of the Redwood County Farm Bureau and Bureau Service Co. (1934-62) discusses farming, the county extension office, 4-H clubs, and the University of Minnesota Agricultural Experiment Station at Lamberton.

891. QUAAL, GORDON. 1978. 30 min. (S)
A farmer discusses the American Agriculture movement in Minnesota and its aims for a national farm policy.

892. QUANDALL, HELEN EVERETT. 1976. 60 min. (S)
Mrs. Theodore Quandall of Redwood Falls, Redwood County, comments on education, the influenza epidemic of 1918, woman suffrage, and prohibition.

893. QUIGGLE, ARTHUR W. 1974. 80 min. (O)
The president of the H. H. King Flour Mills Co. discusses the history of the Sheffield-King Milling Co. and the King flour mills in Faribault, Rice County, and the development of the macaroni processing industry during the first half of the 20th century.

894. RANKIN, GEORGE. 1973. 50 min. 38 p. (S)
The Lyon County sheriff discusses law enforcement during the 1930s Depression.

895. RASMUSSEN, ALMA HALDORSON. 1979. 55 min. (R)
Rasmussen discusses Norwegian customs, education, and family life in Stevens County.

896. RAVELING, WILLIAM. 1973. 50 min. 42 p. (S)
A farmer in Redwood County comments on farming during the 1930s Depression and the federal crop insurance program.

897. RAY, GLADYS. 1976. 95 min. (M)
An American Indian educator and nurse from Fargo, N.Dak., discusses racial discrimination, her careers in the U.S. Army and as a nurse, her efforts to help Indian people, her grandparents' arrival in 1912 at the White Earth Indian Reservation, her father's tribal political activities and adherence to traditional religion, life on the reservation, and her education at Mahnomen High School, Mahnomen County, and the Flandreau Indian Boarding School, Flandreau, S.Dak.

898. REESE, JOHN. 1974. 60 min. 32 p. (S)
A farmer from Swede Prairie Township, Yellow Medicine County, reminisces about World War I, anti-German sentiment and the use of German prisoners of war on area farms, the 1930s Depression, and the Farm Holiday Assn.

899. REID, JAMES. 1973. 60 min. 26 p. (B)
A lumberman from Deer River, Itasca County, discusses his work as a superintendent of Civilian Conservation Corps camps (1929-37) and logging in the Deer River area.

900. REITAN, HALVAR. 1976. 45 min. (D)
Restricted.
A retired Wisconsin fisherman discusses
the sinking in 1924 of his tugboat on Lake
Superior off Port Wing, Wis.

901. REMLEY, FRANCIS. 1975. 50 min. (M)
A retired fireman from Moorhead, Clay
County, discusses famous fires and the growth
of the fire department.

902. RICHTER, ERVIN F. 1976. 60 min. (S)
A Brown County farmer discusses the effects of the 1930s Depression and prohibition
on Comfrey, Brown County.

903. RIENSTRA, LENA EBELING. 1976. 60 min.
(S)
Mrs. Andrew Rienstra of Worthington,
Nobles County, discusses education and women's
history in southwest Minnesota (1920-60).

904. ROBARDS, HUGH B. (PAT). 1976. 43 min.
12 p. (R)
The owner of an Alexandria, Douglas
County, hardware store discusses the growth of
his business, his World War I experiences in
France, and the economic impact of tourism on
Alexandria.

905. RODE, OTTO. 1978. 31 min. (M)
A Russian immigrant recalls his childhood
in the Ukraine and Siberia, World War I, the
Russian Revolution of 1917, and his family's
reunion in Nebraska in 1919.

906. ROGSTAD, LOLA PETERSON. 1975. 80 min.
(M)
Mrs. Ferdinand Rogstad of Detroit Lakes,
Becker County, comments on family history and
the effects of the 1930s Depression.

907. ROSE, ROBERT D. 1976. 79 min. 19 p.
(R)
A pharmacist and administrator of the
Stevens County Memorial Hospital in Morris
discusses the development of rural medical
care programs in that county.

908. ROUST, HENRY A. 1975. 45 min. 9 p.
(R)
A physician and former mayor of Montevideo, Chippewa County (1953-56), discusses
the Chippewa County Hospital and growth of the
city.

909. RYAN, MARQUENTE BRIDGEMAN. 1976. 45
min. (S)
A resident of Minneapolis, Hennepin County, discusses the role of women in the World
War II job market and the social history of
southwest Minnesota (1920-60).

910. SAIKI, SUE OKAMATO. 1975. 45 min.
14 p. (O)
Mrs. Ty Saiki discusses family history,
the treatment of the Japanese in the U.S. during World War II, and the family's move from
California to Blue Earth County.

911. SALTNES, NELS J. 1975. 60 min. 9 p.
(B)
A lumberman from Solway, Beltrami County,
discusses changes in Bemidji and Beltrami
County since 1911, his involvement in the
Beltrami County Historical Society, and his
collaboration with Dr. Charles Vandersluis on
the book, Mainly Logging (1974).

912. SANDERSON, ARNOLD. 1973. 50 min.
17 p. (S)
The principal (1943-   ) of the Worthington High School, Nobles County, comments
on the development of the school and its programs.

913. SATERSMOEN, ALMA. 1975. 31 min. (M)
A retired nurse from Otter Tail County
comments on family history, her childhood in
Pelican Rapids, dealings with Indians, the development of medicine during the 1918 influenza epidemic and World Wars I and II, and life
during the 1930s Depression.

914. SAUER, PHILIP R. 1978. 40 min. (B)
A professor emeritus at Bemidji State
University discusses that institution's growth
and development and its relationship with the
community of Bemidji, Beltrami County. Sauer
taught at Bemidji from 1937 to 1975.

915. SCHAEFFER, ELAINE C. 1975. 50 min.
12 p. (R)
A retired educator discusses the history
of Pomme de Terre, Grant County, family history, her childhood, and her work in education.

916. SCHARF, JOHN A. 1975. 35 min. 10 p.
(R)
The manager of the Minnesota Department
of Natural Resources fish and wildlife station
at Morris, Stevens County, discusses the
acquisition of Helsene Prairie and its management.

917. SCHMIDGALL, FLOYD AND DORA ZELTWANGER
SCHMIDGALL. 1975. 80 min. (R)
The owners of a drugstore in Morris,
Stevens County, discuss the Apostolic Christ-
ian church.

918. SCHMIDT, IRENE POWERS. 1977. 30 min.
(R)
A retired farmer from Morris, Stevens
County, discusses her service on the board of

the Stevens County Rural School District No. 8 (1942-54).

919. SCHMIDT, JERRY. 1978. 29 min. (R)
A member of the Morris Fire Department discusses fires in Stevens County and the department's training programs.

920. SCHUILING, JOHN. 1971. 32 min. (B)
A retired assistant superintendent of schools in Bemidji, Beltrami County, discusses the Laboratory School at Bemidji State Teachers College.

921. SCHUMAKER, MARY. 1973. 50 min. 13 p. (R)
A former teacher and principal in Ortonville, Big Stone County, discusses the development of that town and anti-German sentiment during World War I.

922. SCOTT, KATHRYN FRUEGELL. 1978. 60 min. (R)
A retired nurse discusses her work, the operation of a private hospital, and changes in medical care in Appleton, Swift County.

923. SHEW, FERN M. GIBBS. 1976. 40 min. (S)
Mrs. Adelbert Shew of Brainerd, Crow Wing County, discusses education and women's history in southwest Minnesota (1920-60).

924. SINNER, RICHARD. 1977. 60 min. (M)
A Roman Catholic priest from Kent, Wilkin County, discusses his great-grandparents' settlement in Casselton, N.Dak., his career as a priest, and his interest in politics.

925. SKRIEN, CHARLOTTE SKALLET. 1976. 60 min. (M)
A church member discusses the construction and activities of the Keene Norwegian Evangelical Lutheran Church, Clay County.

926. SMEDLEY, WALTER L. 1975. 98 min. 22 p. (R)
A retired veterinarian in Herman, Grant County, comments on his work and the management of prairie lands he owned.

927. SMITH, GLANVILLE. 1976. 2 hrs., 45 min. 22 p. (C)
An architect discusses family history and the history and businesses of Cold Spring, Stearns County.

928. SMITH, RALPH. 1973. 80 min. 41 p. (M)
A secondary school instructor (1920-30) in New York Mills, Otter Tail County, discusses his teaching career.

929. SMITH, WILLIAM G. M. 1976. 60 min. (S)
A resident of Redwood Falls, Redwood County, discusses education and social life in that community.

930. SORBY, OSCAR. 1973. 55 min. 8 p. (R)
A railroadman in west central Minnesota who worked for the Chicago, Milwaukee, St. Paul and Pacific Railroad Co. for 71 years in a variety of jobs discusses his experiences.

931. SPANOS, GUST. 1978. 75 min. (C)
A retired store owner from St. Cloud, Stearns County, discusses his immigration to the U.S. from Greece and his careers as a popcorn-wagon driver, railroad worker, and operator of a gas station and store.

932. SPICER, MARY GRAVLEY. 1976. 45 min. (S)
The secretary of the Redwood County Farm Bureau (1966-   ) discusses its growth and activities.

933. SPRING, W. DONALD. 1976. 75 min. (R)
The chairman of the humanities division at the University of Minnesota-Morris, Stevens County, discusses the growth of the university, his role in shaping the curriculum, and his perceptions of students and faculty.

934. STAPLETON, C. L. (PAT). 1975. 60 min. 16 p. (B)
The Beltrami County school superintendent (1933-75) discusses school consolidation, requirements for teaching, teachers' salaries, retirement, and curricula.

935. STEBNER, HERMAN W. 1978. 60 min. (C)
A retired automobile salesman and factory worker from Waite Park, Stearns County, discusses his family and education, careers, service in World War II and readjustment to civilian life, and the history of Waite Park and the Waite Park Methodist Church.

936. STEVENS, MARGARET BROOKMEYER. 1976. 60 min. (S)
Stevens discusses women's education and suffrage and the effects of the 1930s Depression on family life.

937. STITT, MILDRED LAUFFER. 1977. 60 min. (M)
Mrs. Dale Stitt of Fergus Falls, Otter Tail County, discusses the history of the Stitt family in Pennsylvania, her husband's dentistry work on South Dakota Indian reservations, and life in the Fergus Falls area.

938. STOCK, JOHN F. 1975. 55 min. 13 p.
(R)
   A physician in Morris, Stevens County, discusses rural medical care and his work with the Doctor Procurement Committee.

939. STORDAHL, RICHARD (ROY). 1977. 60 min.
(M)
   The president of Silver Line, Inc., a boatbuilding firm in Clay County, and mayor of Moorhead (1964-72) discusses his family background and changes in the recreation boat industry and the city of Moorhead.

940. STRANDNESS, ELISABETH. 1975. 37 min.
8 p. (R) Restricted.
   A retired U.S. Forest Service employee and farm owner discusses the management of the Strandness prairie land.

941. STROMWALL, CLEM F. 1978. 90 min. (C)
   A retired farmer, miner, and postmaster discusses his work, the 1930s Depression, bootlegging, and the history of Foreston, Stearns County.

942. STRONG, MARK AND GAIL WATKINS. 1978.
60 min. (S)
   Two union stewards in the American Federation of State, County and Municipal Employees Union, Local 701, at Willmar State Hospital, Kandiyohi County, discuss union support for the Willmar Bank Employees Assn. strike (1977-78), feminists in union ranks, changes in union membership activities, and collective bargaining in public employee unions.

943. SUNDE, ELIZABETH LANGSETH. 1975. 45
min. (M)
   Mrs. Knut Sunde recalls life during the 1930s Depression and the history of various buildings in Moorhead, Clay County.

944. SUNQUIST, KATHRYN SCHMIDT AND ROSALIE
SCHMIDT ANDERSON. 1977. 30 min. (R)
   Two sisters, both residents of Morris, Stevens County, discuss their education during the 1920s in Stevens County Rural School District No. 8.

945. SWANKE, ANNA KAUFMAN. 1973. 3 hrs.
(R)
   A teacher from Browns Valley, Traverse County, comments on World War I, the 1930s Depression, and rural life.

946. SWANSON, HENRY. 1973. 3 hrs. 32 p.
(R)
   A farmer near White Rock, S.Dak., and Monson, Traverse County, recalls farming experiences and local history.

947. SYLVESTER, MAUDE. 1974. 35 min. 23 p.
(S)
   An elementary schoolteacher discusses early 1900s farm life, teaching in a rural school (1920-40), teacher education, and recent changes in the teaching profession.

948. TEIG, CLARA BARKHEIM LARSON. 1976. 50
min. (S)
   Mrs. Alfred Teig recalls farm life and church activities in Belmont Township, Jackson County.

949. THOMPSON, GORDON. 1972. 50 min.
22 p. (S)
   A city clerk (1938-69) discusses the 1930s Depression and the development of the city of Worthington, Nobles County.

950. THORTVEDT, EVA. 1974. 46 min. 20 p.
(M)
   A retired clerk and telegraph operator from Glyndon, Clay County, recalls her experiences as a telegrapher for Western Union, her visits to Yellowstone National Park, and the teaching of Norwegian in early Clay County schools.

951. TIEDEMAN, MINNIE KLOKSETH. 1978. 55
min. (M)
   Mrs. Henry Tiedeman recalls her emigration from Norway, settlement in Morken Township, Clay County, and Norwegian customs in America.

952. TIFFANY, DOUGAL. 1973. 50 min. 24 p.
(S)
   A farmer near Redwood Falls, Redwood County, discusses rural life, the Rural Electrification Administration, and the National Farmers Organization.

953. TOLMAN, THOMAS. 1973. 2 hrs. (B)
   The Beltrami County sheriff (1966-   ) discusses his career and his work with the Indian police on Ojibway reservations.

954. TWETEN, STANLEY. 1978. 30 min. (B)
   Tweten recalls life at the Beltrami County Poor Farm near Solway and the farm's operations and residents.

955. UHDEN, MARTHA. 1974. 30 min. 16 p.
(S)
   The wife of a minister in the German Presbyterian Synod of the West discusses her husband's work, the use of the German language at home and at church, the activities of the church's women's organizations, and the 1930s Depression.

956. VAN DAM, SILVA. 1976. 60 min. (S)
    A resident of Okabena, Jackson County, discusses pioneer life and the activities of the Nonpartisan League.

957. VAN UDEN, BEATRICE BOT AND DEBORAH BOT VAN NEVEL. 1974. 45 min. 25 p. (S)
    Mrs. Hubert Van Uden and Mrs. Edward Van Nevel recall farm life in southwestern Minnesota during the 1930s Depression, farm foreclosures, and Rev. Charles E. Coughlin's radio program.

958. VIRNALA, RUDOLPH. 1975. 60 min. (M)
    A farmer from New York Mills, Otter Tail County, describes his experiences during the 1930s Depression and World War II.

959. WALLIN, IRENE PETERSON AND GLENNIS TER WISSCHA. 1978. 50 min. (S)
    Two employees of the Citizens National Bank of Willmar comment on their membership in the Willmar Bank Employees Assn. and the organization's strike (1977–78). The strike was the first against a bank in Minnesota.

960. WARFIELD, HERBERT C. 1975. 60 min. 24 p. (B)
    A resident of Bemidji, Beltrami County, discusses local history, the Ojibway Indian leader Bemidji, and the 1924 fire at the Bemidji mill of the Crookston Lumber Co.

961. WETHERILL, FRED E. 1977. 2 hrs. (O)
    The Nicollet County agriculture extension director discusses his career, technological developments in agriculture, and the impact of economic and political changes on the American farmer.

962. WHITTEMORE, D. D. 1975. 60 min. (B)
    A retired physician from Bemidji, Beltrami County, comments on the founding and operation of the Bemidji Clinic.

963. WIECKING, EMMA. 1977. 45 min. (O)
    A retired librarian from Mankato, Blue Earth County, discusses Mankato in the early 1900s, her youth and school days at Mankato Normal School, faculty and student activities, the development of the library at Mankato State University, and changes in education.

964. WILLENBRING, JOHN ALOIS. 1976. 80 min. (C)
    A retired farmer, co-operative organizer, boiler inspector, machinist, and labor leader from Richmond, Stearns County, discusses family history, life in Stearns County from the late 1880s to the 1970s, and his work in the farm co-operative movement and as a labor organizer in St. Cloud during the 1930s.

965. WILLIAMS, RALPH. 1978. 60 min. (R)
    A retired professor of music at the University of Minnesota-Morris discusses his compositions and the development and growth of the university.

966. WILSON, GEORGE. 1957. 30 min. 4 p. (B)
    A retired logger from Park Rapids, Hubbard County, discusses logging in Beltrami County, the Brainerd Lumber Co., the Gull River Lumber Co., and various logging procedures.

967. WILSON, H. WATSON, JR. 1977. 90 min. 33 p. (D)
    An accountant and former secretary of the Duluth Board of Trade discusses the Northeast Minnesota Historical Center's collection of records from the board, explains the various documents found in the collection and their use and significance, and describes the interrelationship of the board's various bureaus.

968. WILSON, SANFORD. 1976. 28 min. 7 p. (R)
    A physician and chairman of the Board of Citizens who organized to build a new hospital in Starbuck, Pope County, discusses the problems involved in that project.

969. WINDEY, HENRY. 1973. 35 min. 19 p. (S)
    A Belgian immigrant discusses farming near Edgerton, Rock County (1895–1917).

970. WOLLMAN, SAMUEL AND SAMUEL HOFER. 1974. 110 min. (R)
    Two members of the Hutterite community near Graceville, Big Stone County, discuss its operation, farming methods, manufactures, and social structure.

971. WOOLRIDGE, LEROY. 1975. 30 min. 12 p. (R)
    A pilot discusses the first airplane in Stevens County, barnstorming, and his views on early aviation.

972. WRIGHT, HANNY LUND. 1975. 53 min. (M)
    A retired nurse from Moorhead, Clay County, discusses her emigration from Norway, her nursing career including teaching experiences during World War II, and the organization of the Clay County Camp Fire Girls in 1946.

973. YOCK, GORDON A. 1977. 2 hrs., 30 min. (R)
    The founder of VSC, Inc. (originally Variety Supply Co.), and chairman of the Minnesota Republican party (1953–55) from Clara City, Chippewa County, discusses the founding and operation of the company, Clara City his-

tory, the Clara City Telephone Co., and his political activities.

974. ZECK, OTTO. 1973. 60 min. (M)
The curator of the Becker County Historical Museum discusses the history of the county and of Detroit Lakes and conditions on the White Earth Indian Reservation (Ojibway).

975. ZUEHLSDORF, OTTO. 1973. 30 min. (M)
A retired railroadman from Clay County discusses farm life and Democratic-Farmer-Labor party politics in the 1950s and 1960s.

976. ZYLLA, PAUL. 1978. 2 hrs. (C)
A Roman Catholic priest from Rockville, Stearns County, discusses his family; early work as a shoe shiner in his father's barbershop; life in the seminary during World War II; reminiscences of postwar study in Washington, D.C., and Rome; his duties as vice-chancellor and chancellor of the diocese of St. Cloud (1960-70); his parish in Rockville; and contemporary changes in the Catholic church.

[[[[[[[[[[[∘]]]]]]]]]]]

THE PUBLIC AFFAIRS CENTER COLLECTION

Political involvement on the local, state, and national levels is a hallmark of life in Minnesota. The oral histories in this series reflect that concern. The collection consists of interviews with persons active in numerous capacities in local politics, including many who have served or are serving in the Minnesota legislature. Virtually all of the legislators discuss their political careers and give their views on legislation passed during their terms of office. Each entry contains information on the narrator's residence, occupation, and terms of office, if any.

977. ALDERINK, GEORGE. 1973. 30 min. 7 p. (C)
Minnesota state legislator (1955-57) from Pease, Mille Lacs County. Includes family history.

978. ALLEN, BYRON G. 1973. 5 hrs. (M)
Minnesota commissioner of agriculture (1955-61), Iowa state legislator, Democratic national committeeman for Minnesota (1948-55), and first Democratic-Farmer-Labor party candidate for governor of Minnesota (1944).

979. ANDERSON, C. ELMER. 1978. 90 min. (C)
The mayor of Brainerd, Crow Wing County,

and former governor of Minnesota (1951-55) comments on his personal and educational background, early jobs, political influences and service as governor, changes in campaigning, years as mayor of Nisswa and later as mayor of Brainerd, and changes observed in the office of governor since his term.

980. ANDERSON, ERNEST J. 1977. 50 min. (O)
A Minnesota state legislator (1955-73) and farmer from Frost, Faribault County, discusses family history, farm and community affairs, including his directorship of the Minnesota Farmers Elevator Co., the dairy and creamery in Frost, and his membership on the Frost school board.

981. ANDERSON, JERALD. 1977. 70 min. (C)
A Minnesota state legislator (1971-   ) and dentist from North Branch, Chisago County, discusses family history, political views, his decision to run for the Minnesota senate, campaigns, impressions of the legislature, and his views on school consolidation.

982. ANGSTMAN, GEORGE L. 1973. 60 min. (C)
Minnesota state legislator (1957-59) and lawyer from Mora, Kanabec County.

983. BARR, SAMUEL R. 1973. 50 min. 11 p. (R)
Minnesota state legislator (1961-73) and electrical contractor from Ortonville, Big Stone County.

984. BARSNESS, EDWARD E. 1973, 1976. 98 min. 22 p. (R)
A Minnesota state legislator (1927, 1961), editor of the Pope County Tribune, and Pope County judge of probate court from Glenwood discusses his family history, the Tribune as a political and moral force, the Farm Holiday Assn., and his activities in the Nonpartisan League.

985. BASFORD, HARRY. 1973. 75 min. 37 p. (M)
Minnesota state legislator (1949-61) from Wolf Lake, Becker County. Founder of the Grass Roots Fund for Farmers and the Becker County Farmers Union.

986. BEAUCHAMP, DAVID. 1974. 2 hrs. 18 p. (M) Restricted.
Minnesota state legislator (1975-79) from Moorhead, Clay County.

987. BENSON, ELMER A. 1973. 80 min. 17 p. (R) 1974. 60 min. 27 p. (M)
The Minnesota governor (1937-39) and U.S. Senator (1935-36) from Appleton, Swift County, discusses the Farmer-Labor party, the Works

Progress Administration in Minnesota, and legislation during the 1930s Depression.

988. BERGESON, BURNETT J. 1977. 115 min. (M)

A Minnesota state legislator (1955-61) from Hallock, Kittson County, discusses his childhood near Twin Valley, Norman County, work in agriculture, his role in the Farm Security Administration in the 1930s, the building of the Farmers Union and Democratic-Farmer-Labor party in Norman and Mahnomen counties, and the establishment of the University of Minnesota Technical College at Crookston, Polk County (1965).

989. BERGLAND, SAM AND MABLE EVANS BERGLAND. 1976. 60 min. (M)

Retired Roseau County farmers discuss their involvement in the Farmer-Labor and Democratic-Farmer-Labor parties in Minnesota, the 1930s Depression, their activities in the farm co-operative movement, and the career of their son, Bob Bergland, U.S. Congressman (1971-77) and secretary of agriculture (1977-80).

990. BORDEN, WINSTON. 1973. 90 min. (C)

Minnesota state legislator (1971-78) and lawyer from Brainerd, Crow Wing County.

991. BRINKMAN, BERNARD J. 1973. 85 min. (C)

Minnesota state legislator (1965-   ) and businessman from Richmond, Stearns County.

992. CARLSON, DOUGLAS W. 1973. 75 min. (C)

Minnesota state legislator (1971-   ), veterinarian, and farmer from Sandstone, Pine County.

993. CHMIELEWSKI, FLORIAN W. 1973. 60 min. (C)

Minnesota state legislator (1971-   ) and orchestra leader from Sturgeon Lake, Pine County.

994. DE CHAINE, JAMES. 1980. 60 min. (C)

An administrative assistant to U.S. Congressman Richard Nolan discusses his work, impressions of Washington, D.C., and the congressional political process, and Nolan's campaigns.

995. CLAWSON, JOHN T. 1977. 80 min. (C)

A Minnesota state legislator (1975-   ) and Lutheran clergyman from Center City, Chisago County, discusses his campaigns and legislative activities.

996. DuBOIS, BENJAMIN F. (PAT), JR. 1973. 80 min. (C)

Minnesota state legislator (1963-67) and banker from Sauk Centre, Stearns County. Includes family history.

997. DUNN, ROBERT G. 1973. 90 min. (C)

Minnesota state legislator (1965-81) and businessman from Princeton, Mille Lacs County.

998. ERICKSON, CHRIS LOUIS. 1977. 45 min. (O)

A Minnesota state legislator (1951-61), Martin County attorney (1934-46), and lawyer from Fairmont discusses his family history, law practice, public service, and Republican party politics during his legislative career.

999. GAARENSTROOM, CONRAD F. 1977. 85 min. (O)

An attorney and probate court judge from Fairmont, Martin County, discusses his family history, law career, ethnic heritage, lobbying activities, and the political and professional career of his father, Christian Frederick Gaarenstroom, also a Fairmont lawyer. He comments at length on his father's Farmer-Labor party involvement, friendship with Governor Floyd B. Olson, views on the formation of the Democratic-Farmer-Labor party in 1944, and campaigns for county attorney, attorney-general, and U.S. Congress in the 1920s and 1930s.

1000. GESELL, RAYMOND L. 1973. 80 min. 41 p. (M)

Minnesota state legislator (1945-49) from Moorhead, Clay County. Includes comments on Red River Valley farm life during the 1930s Depression.

1001. GRUENES, DAVID. 1980. 58 min. (C)

A Minnesota state legislator (1981-   ) from St. Cloud, Stearns County, discusses his political campaigns and his family.

1002. GRUSSING, GEORGE P. 1973. 45 min. 9 p. (R)

Minnesota state legislator (1955-67) and farmer. Includes information on the Clara City, Chippewa County, area.

1003. GUTAW, WARREN. 1975. 45 min. (M)

A businessman from Moorhead, Clay County, discusses his work with area chambers of commerce, the impact of the New Deal on the Red River Valley, that region's Communist party in 1931, and McCarthyism.

1004. HOBERG, DWAINE. 1975. 47 min. 22 p. (M)

The mayor of Moorhead, Clay County (1972-77), discusses the growth of that city and general political issues affecting the operation of city government.

1005. HUGHES, KEITH F. 1973. 2 hrs. (C)
Minnesota state legislator (1965-71) and lawyer from St. Cloud, Stearns County.

1006. IVERSON, CARL M. 1973. 102 min. 22 p. (R)
Minnesota state legislator (1919-33, 1939-65), founder of the Ashby Cooperative, and farmer near Ashby, Grant County.

1007. JOHN, EDA SWENSON. 1977. 80 min. (O)
A retired St. Paul, Ramsey County, state employee discusses her family and especially her father, Oscar A. Swenson, who operated a dairy business in New Sweden Township, Nicollet County. She includes information on Swenson's community activities, his service in the Minnesota state legislature (1913-31, 1937-49), and the Republican party.

1008. JOHNSON, WALTER. 1973. 20 min. 12 p. (M)
Otter Tail County farmer and Progressive party candidate for governor of Minnesota (1948).

1009. JOSEFSON, J. A. (JOE). 1973. 45 min. (S) Restricted.
Minnesota state legislator (1955-77) and farmer from Minneota, Lyon County. Includes information on his service in a number of township and county agricultural organizations.

1010. KELLY, J. J. 1973. 60 min. 46 p. (S)
Minnesota state legislator (1957-61) and veterinarian from Marshall, Lyon County.

1011. KOSLOSKE, JOHN T. 1974. 45 min. (C)
A Minnesota state legislator (1949-53) and former mayor of Sauk Rapids, Benton County, discusses his family background and political career.

1012. LONG, VERNE E. 1977. 2 hrs. (S)
A Minnesota state legislator (1963-75) from Pipestone County comments on the founding of the Pipestone County Township Officers Organization, the county Republican party organization, the role of a rural legislator, and the founding of Southwest State University, Marshall, Lyon County.

1013. McGRATH, THOMAS. 1973. 50 min. 22 p. (M)
A former member of the Communist party in the U.S. comments on its development and on the 1930s Depression as it affected the Red River Valley near Moorhead, Clay County.

1014. MAHOWALD, ROBERT A. 1973. 90 min. (C)
Minnesota state legislator (1961-65) and insurance broker from St. Cloud, Stearns County.

1015. MARTINSON, HENRY R. 1973. 45 min. 28 p. (M)
Martinson discusses the Socialist party in North Dakota, the Nonpartisan League, and labor unions.

1016. MARVIN, MARGARET. 1976. 55 min. (M)
A Warroad, Roseau County, housewife comments on her 20-year involvement in the Republican party.

1017. MUELLER, AUGUST BENJAMIN. 1977. 35 min. (O)
A Minnesota state legislator (1941-75) and farmer from Sibley County discusses his family history and farm operation.

1018. NATWICK, HERMAN. 1976. 60 min. (M)
A farmer from Twin Valley, Norman County, comments on his involvement in the county Republican party (1960-74).

1019. NELSEN, MARLIN B. 1980. 60 min. (C)
A Minnesota state legislator (1977-81) from Aitkin, Aitkin County, discusses the Minnesota powerline construction controversy, fluoridation, the legislative seniority system, and the role of lobbyists.

1020. NIEHAUS, JOSEPH T. 1973. 45 min. (C)
Minnesota state legislator (1969-83) and farmer from Sauk Centre, Stearns County.

1021. NOBLITT, HARDING. 1976. 2 hrs. (M)
A political science professor at Concordia College, Moorhead, Clay County, discusses his 20-year involvement in the Democratic-Farmer-Labor party.

1022. NOLAN, RICHARD M. 1973. 80 min. (C)
U.S. Congressman (1974-80), Minnesota state legislator (1969-73), and educator from St. Cloud, Stearns County.

1023. NYCKLEMOE, HENRY. 1973. 65 min. 41 p. (M)
A Minnesota state legislator (1955-57) and district judge from Fergus Falls, Otter Tail County, discusses his opposition to World War II.

1024. NYGAARD, KARL E. 1973. 60 min. 21 p. (M)
The first Communist mayor in the U.S. (Crosby, Crow Wing County, late 1930s) discusses the Communist party in the U.S., his

mayoral campaign, the New Deal, and World War
II as it affected American Communists.

1025. NYSTROM, WILLIAM. 1972. 60 min.
22 p. (S)
    A Minnesota state legislator (1935-37)
and orchard owner from Worthington, Nobles
County, comments on New Deal legislation, the
Rural Electrification Administration, and the
Farmers Union.

1026. ONNEN, TONY. 1979. 80 min. (C)
    A Minnesota state legislator (1977-   )
from Cokato, Wright County, discusses the role
of government in rural affairs and his work as
an accountant.

1027. PATTON, AL. 1973. 90 min. (C)
    Minnesota state legislator (1973-81) and
businessman from Sartell, Stearns County.

1028. PAULSON, HARVEY N. 1977. 60 min. (O)
    A Minnesota state legislator (1957-61),
sergeant-at-arms of the Minnesota house of
representatives (1963-73), and farmer from
Sleepy Eye, Brown County, discusses his Nor-
wegian-Danish ancestry and farming and business activities; membership on the board of
Brookville Township, Redwood County; the council of Evan Lutheran Church, Evan, Brown County; directorships of Evan Coop Creamery and
Livestock Shippers Assn.; and work as supervisor of the Redwood County Soil Conservation
District.

1029. PEDERSON, DONALD E. 1975. 60 min.
(S)
    A Minnesota state legislator (1963) dis-
cusses his farm implement business in Dawson,
Lac qui Parle County.

1030. PEHLER, JAMES C. 1973. 100 min. (C)
    Minnesota state legislator (1973-   )
and co-ordinator of television services at St.
Cloud State University.

1031. PETERSEN, MEDORA GRANDPREY. 1973. 90
min. (C)
    The widow of Hjalmar Petersen, Minnesota
governor (1936-37), discusses his political
career.

1032. PETERSON, ROY. 1973. 2 hrs. 22 p.
(R) (S)
    A milk deliveryman from Benson, Swift
County, comments on his involvement in the
Nonpartisan League, Farm Holiday Assn., and
other 1930s political organizations.

1033. REGAN, ROBERT M. 1977. 90 min. (O)
    A Mankato, Blue Earth County, lawyer dis-
cusses the life of his father, John E. Regan,

a Minnesota state legislator (1931) and Democratic party candidate for governor in 1932
and 1934 and comments on politics in Minnesota
in the 1920s and 1930s.

1034. REGNIER, EMIL L. 1974. 60 min. (S)
Restricted.
    A Minnesota state legislator (1931-33)
and railroad and warehouse commissioner (1936-
66) from Marshall, Lyon County, discusses the
1931-33 session of the legislature, the 1934
state elections, the Farmer-Labor party, Senator Magnus Johnson, and Governor Floyd B.
Olson.

1035. RICHARDSON, HERVEY M. 1975, 1977.
4 hrs., 45 min. 24 p. (R)
    A retired Morris, Stevens County, farmer
and Minnesota state legislator (1961) discusses Democratic-Farmer-Labor party politics,
the Minnesota state elections of 1948, agricultural co-operatives, and the Federated Telephone Cooperative of Chokio, Stevens County,
of which he was president (1953-66).

1036. RICHARDSON, JOHN L. 1973. 45 min.
(C)
    Minnesota state legislator (1955-61) and
retired insurance broker from St. Cloud,
Stearns County.

1037. ROSENMEIER, GORDON. 1973. 65 min.
(C)
    Minnesota state legislator (1941-71) and
lawyer from Little Falls, Morrison County.

1038. RUED, DAVID E. 1980. 75 min. (C)
    A Minnesota state legislator (1978-83)
from Aitkin, Aitkin County, discusses the role
of government in agriculture.

1039. SAND, ARTHUR. 1974. 65 min. 19 p.
(R)
    A farmer from Wendell, Grant County, dis-
cusses the effects of the 1930s Depression on
the Democratic party, the Nonpartisan League,
and the Farmer-Labor party.

1040. SCHONBERGER, GEORGE. 1973. 75 min.
52 p. (M)
    The North Dakota state chairman of the
Nonpartisan League (1932-55) and farmer from
Ogema, Becker County, provides information on
league political activities.

1041. SCHROM, ED. 1973. 80 min. (C)
    A Minnesota state legislator (1971-81)
from Albany, Stearns County, discusses his
family background and political career.

1042. SCHUMANN, MARVIN C. 1973. 90 min.
(C)

Minnesota state legislator (1955-67) and farmer from Rice, Benton County.

1043. SILLERS, DOUGLAS H. 1974. 2 hrs. 50 p. (M) Restricted.
Minnesota state legislator (1963-81) and farmer from Moorhead, Clay County.

1044. SLEN, THEODOR S. 1973. 100 min. 73 p. (S)
A Minnesota state legislator (1935-39) and district court judge from Madison, Lac qui Parle County, recalls events surrounding the merger of the Democratic and Farmer-Labor parties.

1045. SULLIVAN, RUTH HISLEFF. 1973. 90 min. (C)
The widow of Henry H. Sullivan (1889-1959), Minnesota state legislator (1935-53) from St. Cloud, Stearns County, discusses her husband's career.

1046. SUNDET, ARMIN O. 1977. 90 min. (O)
A Minnesota state legislator (1953-69), farmer, and businessman from Faribault, Rice County, discusses his Norwegian ancestry, his farming and business activities, and his legislative career.

1047. THORSON, LOWELL. 1976. 55 min. (M)
A banker from Ada, Norman County, discusses his 20-year involvement in the Republican party and comments on local and presidential elections (1955-76).

1048. TIEMANN, EDMUND C. 1973. 105 min. (C)
Minnesota state legislator (1951-61) and businessman from Melrose, Stearns County.

1049. WEFALD, MAGNUS. 1973. 60 min. 32 p. (M)
A Minnesota state legislator (1947-57), lawyer, and mayor of Hawley, Clay County, during the 1930s Depression comments on the political career of his father, U.S. Congressman Knud Wefald.

1050. WELCH, RICHARD. 1977. 75 min. (C)
A Minnesota state legislator (1977-   ) from Cambridge, Isanti County, discusses family history, campaign strategy, and political opponents.

1051. WELLS, THORNLEY. 1980. 38 min. (M)
A businessman discusses his work as mayor of Moorhead, Clay County (1954-57), and county commissioner (1957-73) and provides information on the growth and development of Moorhead.

1052. YOUNGDALE, JAMES M. 1973. 2 hrs. 22 p. (R) (S)
A Swift County farmer, author, and politician discusses the Democratic-Farmer-Labor party, the 1930s Depression in western Minnesota, his political campaigns, and the National Farmers Organization. He is the author of Third Party Footprints (1966) and several times was a candidate for the U.S. Congress.

[[[[[[[[[[∘]]]]]]]]]]]

BUSINESS AND LABOR IN DULUTH

The interviews in this project document the history of Duluth area businesses and labor unions. Narrators comment, where appropriate, on the founding and growth of various businesses or labor organizations, the formation of corporate policies, labor-management relations, urban renewal, union philosophy and strategy, government regulation, binding arbitration, and the relationship of business and labor to political and civic affairs. Barbara J. Sommer, Northeast Minnesota Historical Center, University of Minnesota-Duluth, conducted the interviews.

1053. ANDRESEN, JOHN C. 1980. 2 hrs. (D) Restricted.
The president of the Andresen-Ryan Coffee Co. discusses its history, the coffee business, and the business climate in Duluth.

1054. BEUKEMA, CHRISTIAN F. 1980. 92 min. (D) Restricted.
A retired vice-president of the United States Steel Corp. discusses his work as president of the Oliver Iron Mining division of United States Steel, the relationship of that company's policies to public policy in Minnesota, the Minnesota Taconite Amendment, and Great Lakes shipping.

1055. BRIDGES, RUSSELL AND HELEN WINGROVE BRIDGES. 1981. 60 min. (D)
Two union activists discuss the organization of the Retail Clerks Union, Local 1116, Duluth; the 1937 and 1946-47 union strikes against the Glass Block Department Store; and the International Head of the Lakes Council.

1056. HUNNER, JOHN C. 1981. 78 min. (D) Restricted.
The director of research and planning for the city of Duluth (1946-68) discusses the growth of Duluth and freeway development.

1057. JOHNSON, EDMUND W. 1981. 75 min. (D)
A carpenter and official of the Carpenters, Millwrights, Pile Drivers, and Floor Coverers Union, Local 361, Duluth, discusses struggles against nonunion workers and changes in union philosophy and strategy.

1058. JOSEPHS, ARTHUR C. 1980. 2 hrs. (D)
The retired chairman of the Zalk-Josephs Co. discusses the steel-fabrication business and the impact of anti-Semitism on business in Duluth.

1059. KYYHKYNEN, ALEXANDER. 1981. 60 min. (D)
The owner of the Dove Clothing Store discusses the growth of his men's clothing business, his emigration from Finland, business philosophy, clientele, and work as Finnish vice-consul and later consul in Minnesota.

1060. LASKIN, SYLVESTER. 1980. 90 min. (D)
The retired chairman of Minnesota Power and Light Co. discusses changes in the electric utility industry, the effects of government regulation on business, and the relationship of utility companies to the communities they serve.

1061. LIVINGSTON, ROBERT E. 1980. 60 min. (D)
A clothier comments on his business, the Big Duluth Men's & Boys' Clothing Store, which was founded in 1881.

1062. McMILLEN, PATRICK. 1980. 92 min. (D)
A retired ship's cook describes his work for the Industrial Workers of the World (IWW), the organization's objectives, his attempts to recruit members, the role of women in the IWW, changes in IWW ideology, and his work as a cook for various shipping lines.

1063. MILETICH, ELI J. 1981. 60 min. (D)
The president of the International Union of Police Associations, Duluth local, discusses the Duluth Central Labor Body; relations with the American Federation of State, County, and Municipal Employees; Minnesota Public Employees Labor Relations Act; binding arbitration; and the role of police officers in the labor movement.

1064. MILLER, CURTIS. 1981. 75 min. (D)
The former editor of Labor World (1951-65) and president of the Lake Superior Newspaper Guild discusses the Duluth Industrial Union Council, the National Right to Work Committee, and the relationship of Labor World to the major Duluth daily newspapers.

1065. RAMSLAND, ODIN S. 1980. 75 min. (D)
A communications consultant discusses the establishment and operation of the KDAL radio and television stations.

1066. RAMSLI, M. KENNETH. 1980. 60 min. (D)
The president of Duluth Tent and Awning Co. describes the firm's development.

1067. SLAUGHTER, EDWARD L. 1980. 2 hrs. (D)
A union employee describes his work with the International Longshoremen's Assn., the impact of World War I on union activities, organizing the waterfront in Duluth during the 1930s, and union attitudes toward the Industrial Workers of the World and the Communist party.

1068. STEPHENSON, CONRAD. 1980. 60 min. (D)
The retired chairman of the Insurance Service Agency discusses the company's business, its relationship with the John A. Stephenson and Co. real-estate firm, changes in the insurance industry, and the sale of the family firms to outside interests.

1069. STEPHENSON, WILLIAM R. 1980. 60 min. (D)
The retired president of John A. Stephenson and Co., a Duluth real-estate firm, discusses the firm's involvement in the growth of Duluth.

1070. SWANSTROM, JOHN E. 1980. 58 min. (D)
The president of the Diamond Tool and Horseshoe Co. discusses the patented horseshoe calk developed by Otto Swanstrom, company diversification, and the impact of the St. Lawrence Seaway on Duluth business.

1071. TAYLOR, A. W., JR. 1980. 90 min. (D)
The retired president of the Stewart-Taylor Co. discusses the firm's development, changes in the printing industry, and the impact of Duluth's location on business.

1072. WAGNER, LEWIS J. 1981. 90 min. (D)
The former president of the Order of Railway Conductors and Brakemen (1962-67) discusses the railroad industry, wage negotiations, changes in work rules, the relationship with the Brotherhood of Railroad Trainmen, and the formation of the United Transportation Union.

1073. WISOCKI, STEPHEN. 1980. 88 min. (D)
A restaurateur discusses the effects of the 1930s Depression, prohibition, and commun-

ity growth on his business, the Pickwick Restaurant.

[[[[[[[[[[[∘]]]]]]]]]]]

THE FARM HOLIDAY ASSOCIATION

The Farm Holiday Association was a farmers' movement sparked by the poor economic conditions of the early 1930s. The association's actions were designed to increase farm prices and secure relief from mortgage foreclosures. Participating farmers dramatized their plight in 1933 by picketing, forcibly halting the delivery of foreclosure notices, and marching on the state capitol in St. Paul. This project documents the activities of the association as seen by both supporters and opponents. The interviews were conducted by Professors H. Warren Gardner, David L. Nass, and Maynard Brass of Southwest State University, Marshall.

1074. BOSCH, JOHN. 1972. 50 min. 36 p. (S)
A retired Kandiyohi County insurance executive and former president of the Minnesota Farm Holiday Assn. discusses the economic and social conditions that gave rise to the Farm Holiday movement and his work with it.

1075. BRECHT, ARNOLD. 1972. 90 min. 45 p. (S)
A lawyer from Worthington, Nobles County, discusses prohibition and the effects of the 1930s Depression and World War II on the farm economy of southwestern Minnesota.

1076. DAHLQUIST, OSCAR. 1973. 50 min. 23 p. (S)
A farmer from the Slayton, Murray County, area discusses the Rural Electrification Administration.

1077. EBELING, LOUIS. 1973. 50 min. 33 p. (S)
A Rushmore, Nobles County, farmer comments on the Rural Electrification Administration.

1078. GOEDE, WILLIAM C. 1974. 60 min. 17 p. (S)
A former secretary of the Jackson County Farm Holiday Assn. discusses the Nonpartisan League.

1079. GOLD, DONALD W. 1973. 60 min. 23 p. (S)
A Redwood County insurance broker recalls the early years of Sears, Roebuck and Co. in Redwood Falls and farm loans during the 1930s Depression.

1080. HANSON, N. P. 1976. 45 min. (R)
A county agent from Pope County discusses the Farm Holiday Assn. movement and his work during the 1930s.

1081. HAROLDSON, CLINTON. 1974. 60 min. (S)
A Renville County farmer discusses his involvement in organizing the Farm Holiday Assn. movement (1932–33).

1082. HASSENSTAB, ARTHUR F. 1972. 45 min. 36 p. (S)
A banker from Wabasso, Redwood County, discusses the effects of the 1930s Depression on the banking industry.

1083. JAEHNING, GROVER C. 1973. 45 min. 14 p. (S)
A Morton pharmacist discusses changes in pharmacy, New Deal legislation, prohibition, and the effects of the 1930s Depression in Renville and Redwood counties.

1084. JOHNSON, ERNEST. 1972. 50 min. 24 p. (S)
A farmer in Jackson and Watonwan counties recalls the Farm Holiday Assn. march on the Minnesota State Capitol in 1933.

1085. JOHNSON, WILLIAM N. 1972. 50 min. 34 p. (S)
The owner and editor of the Ivanhoe Times, Lincoln County.

1086. LANGE, WALTER R. 1975. 61 min. (S)
The retired president of the Pipestone National Bank discusses banking during the 1930s Depression and the Farm Holiday Assn. in Pipestone County, farm prices, farm mortgage foreclosures, and the New Deal.

1087. LUND, CLARENCE. 1973. 50 min. 26 p. (S)
A farmer near Lake Lillian, Kandiyohi County, recalls the Farm Holiday Assn. march on the Minnesota State Capitol in 1933.

1088. LUND, GUY H. 1975. 60 min. (S)
A seed-corn salesman recalls his work for the Farmers Union in southwest Minnesota and activities of the Farm Holiday Assn. in Lincoln County.

1089. MEEHL, PERCY. 1973. 90 min. 45 p. (S)
A Lyon County judge and former county at-

torney discusses his work, the 1930s Depression in southwest Minnesota, and the 1934 Farm Holiday Assn. march on the Swift Packing Co. meat-packing plant in Marshall.

1090. MOSS, ROY. 1973. 50 min. 41 p. (S)
A farmer and former school board member from Rushmore, Nobles County, discusses education during the 1930s Depression.

1091. NYSTROM, WILLIAM. 1972. 50 min. 22 p. (S)
An orchard owner from Worthington, Nobles County, comments on New Deal legislation and the Rural Electrification Administration.

1092. OLSON, DAVID E. 1973. 50 min. 29 p. (S)
A farmer in Jackson County comments on New Deal legislation.

1093. PETERSON, ROY. 1973. 60 min. 23 p. (S)
A dairy-products distributor from Benson, Swift County, discusses the Farmer-Labor party, the 1935 convention of the Minnesota Farm Holiday Assn., Governor Elmer A. Benson (1937-39), and the activities of the Nonpartisan League and the National Farmers Organization.

1094. PFINGSTON, ERHEART. 1976. 2 hrs., 30 min. (S)
The former national vice-president and Iowa state officer of the National Farmers Organization (NFO) discusses his work, the growth of the NFO, and the founding of NFO chapters in Minnesota.

1095. RUNHOLT, VERNON. 1973. 50 min. 42 p. (S)
A Lyon County farmer discusses rural life, country schools, Ku Klux Klan activities during the 1930s, and the Protective Land Use Assn.

1096. SANDERS, PARKER. 1973. 50 min. 18 p. (S)
A farmer near Redwood Falls, Redwood County, comments on New Deal farm programs and the Rural Electrification Administration.

1097. TATGE, ORVILLE. 1973. 2 hrs., 30 min. 30 p. (R) (S)
The former president of the Swift County National Farmers Organization (NFO) discusses NFO activities, agricultural conditions during the 1930s Depression, and political activity in west central Minnesota.

1098. TKACH, ANDREW. 1972. 90 min. 46 p. (S)

A farmer in Jackson County comments on the Nonpartisan League.

1099. TOPEL, CHARLES. 1972. 45 min. 23 p. (S)
A Balaton, Lyon County, farmer discusses the 1930s Depression and the establishment of the Rural Electrification Administration.

1100. TORSTENSON, OSCAR. 1973. 50 min. 36 p. (S)
A Dawson, Lac qui Parle County, farmer and director of the Minnesota Valley Electric Light and Power Cooperative discusses the Rural Electrification Administration.

1101. WECK, A. D. 1973. 50 min. 17 p. (S)
A real-estate broker discusses farm foreclosures in Murray County during the 1930s Depression and the history of the State Bank of Slayton.

[[[[[[[[[[[∘]]]]]]]]]]]

THE IRISH-AMERICAN COMMUNITY OF CLONTARF

This collection of interviews documents the history of Clontarf, Swift County, its settlement by Irish immigrants, brought to Minnesota through the efforts of Roman Catholic Archbishop John Ireland, and their relations with the French Canadians already living there. The interviews were conducted by Peg Michels-Peterson, University of Minnesota-Morris.

1102. BENOIT, ALEX J. AND LEONA BOUTAIN BENOIT. 1977. 44 min. (R)
Retired farmers discuss the Farm Holiday Assn., the 1930s Depression, and French-Catholic influence in Clontarf.

1103. COONEY, JOHN. 1977. 90 min. (R)
The priest of St. Malachy's Catholic Church discusses the history of Clontarf, recent visits to Ireland, seminary training, the Irish Republican Army, and Archbishop John Ireland.

1104. DOHERTY, MARY. 1977. 76 min. 23 p. (R)
A retired teacher discusses childhood in Clontarf, work as a rural schoolteacher, and small-town social life in the early 1900s.

1105. FENNEL, ROBERT. 1977. 44 min. (R)
A businessman discusses social life, the history of his grocery business, and relations

between French-Canadian and Irish settlers in Clontarf.

1106. GILBERTSON, ADDIE DANIELS. 1977. 53 min. (R)
A retired businesswoman and farmer discusses church, school, and social life in Clontarf and French-Canadian influence in that community.

1107. GOULET, MARIA BOUTAIN. 1977. 46 min. 18 p. (R)
Housewife.

1108. LANGAN, JACK. 1977. 52 min. (R)
A farmer and Swift County commissioner discusses political and social life in Clontarf and relations between the French-Canadian and Irish communities.

1109. PERRIZO, ROSE HUGHES AND ANNE HUGHES. 1977. 59 min. (R)
Mrs. Roy Perrizo and her sister discuss the Perrizos' general store in Clontarf, the formation of the Variety Supply Co. of Clara City, Chippewa County, and social life in Clontarf.

1110. REARDON, GEORGE. 1977. 90 min. (R)
A retired farmer, school bus driver, and janitor discusses politics and the role of the Roman Catholic church in political and social life in Clontarf.

1111. SHINNICK, ANNE. 1977. 60 min. 20 p. (R)
A retired schoolteacher compares and contrasts public and parochial school education in Clontarf.

[[[[[[[[[[∘]]]]]]]]]]]

LAKE SUPERIOR: THE NORTH SHORE COMMERCIAL FISHING INDUSTRY

These interviews concern the history of commercial fishing on the Minnesota north shore of Lake Superior. The narrators comment on fishing industry finance, women in the industry, fishing equipment, boatbuilding, the effects of weather on Great Lakes fishing, clothing, and the history of individual fishing businesses. The interviews were conducted by Barbara J. Sommer, Northeast Minnesota Historical Center, University of Minnesota-Duluth.

1112. CHRISTIANSEN, ALECK. 1977. 60 min. 22 p. (D)
A businessman and former fish dealer from Two Harbors, Lake County, provides information on credit terms used in the commercial fishing business and changes in local and national markets.

1113. HOLTE, INGABORG JOHNSON. 1977. 90 min. 39 p. (D)
The daughter, sister, and wife of commercial fishermen discusses summer life on Isle Royale, Mich., food preservation, the responsibilities of women in the fishing industry, and the effects of the industry's decline on the north shore economy. Holte is the sister of Edwin C. Johnson.

1114. JOHNSON, EDWIN C. 1977. 95 min. 29 p. (D)
A retired fisherman and steelworker from Duluth, St. Louis County, discusses fishing methods and equipment. Johnson is the brother of Ingaborg Holte.

1115. JOHNSON, MILFORD, JR. 1977. 60 min. 21 p. (D)
A mining company employee from Two Harbors, Lake County, discusses smelt fishing, prices, and the relationship of smelt fishermen to the rest of the commercial fishing industry.

1116. LORNTSON, CONRAD. 1979. 92 min. 36 p. (D)
A retired fisherman and carpenter comments on fishing in Beaver Bay, Lake County, nets used, fish prices, and commercial fishing in Alaska during the 1950s.

1117. MATTSON, HJALMER. 1977. 55 min. 18 p. (D)
A fisherman and boatbuilder from Duluth, St. Louis County, comments on his father's career in commercial fishing around 1900.

1118. OBERG, ROY. 1977. 60 min. 20 p. (D)
A boat captain from Grand Portage, Cook County, discusses the types of boats used in the commercial fishing industry, the effects of weather on fishing, special clothing needed, and the work of hauling fish for dealers.

1119. STROM, EINAR AND ARTHUR SIVERTSON. 1977. 90 min. (D)
Two fishermen from Duluth, St. Louis County, discuss the development and growth of Sivertson Fisheries.

1120. SVE, RAGNVALD AND RAGNHILD JACOBSON SVE. 1977. 90 min. 35 p. (D)

Two retired fishermen and resort operators from Two Harbors, Lake County, discuss lumbering, farming, and the tourist industry.

1121. TORMONDSEN, CHRISTOPHER. 1977. 75 min. 17 p. (D)
A retired fisherman from Tofte, Cook County, comments on emigration from Norway in 1929.

1122. TORGESON, GEORGE. 1977. 90 min. 27 p. (D)
An ore-dock foreman from Knife River, Lake County, discusses commercial fishing in New Jersey and Alaska during the 1950s.

[[[[[[[[[[[o]]]]]]]]]]]

THE MINNESOTA POWERLINE CONSTRUCTION ORAL HISTORY PROJECT

The interviews in this project document construction of a controversial high-voltage transmission line across Minnesota farmland. The powerline and the protest it generated became a national cause célèbre and the subject of a television motion picture and several books. The oral history project was recorded over a two-year period during the height of the controversy and includes interviews with persons representing the major opposing positions. Among them are farmers whose land was affected by the line, state legislators, power company officials, a county sheriff, powerline supporters, and organizers of the major groups. The interviews are at the Minnesota Historical Society and at the University of Minnesota-Morris. Edward P. Nelson of the society conducted the interviews.

1123. ANDERSON, CHARLES L. 1979. 90 min. 48 p. MHS and (R) Restricted.
A farmer from Litchfield, Meeker County, and president of the board of directors of Cooperative Power Assn.

1124. ANDERSON, WILLARD. 1978. 50 min. 24 p. MHS and (R) Restricted.
Manager, Agralite Cooperative, Benson, Swift County.

1125. BANKS, ROBERT S. 1978. 70 min. 38 p. MHS and (R) Restricted.
A Minnesota Department of Health official and author of a health-study report on powerline construction and operation.

1126. BARSNESS, NANCY C. 1979. 3 hrs., 55 min. 154 p. MHS and (R) Restricted.
A farmer from Cyrus, Pope County, and a free-lance reporter for local newspapers and a radio station.

1127. BERG, CHARLES. 1977. 45 min. 20 p. MHS and (R) Restricted.
A farmer and former Minnesota legislator from Chokio, Stevens County.

1128. BRADLEY, WENDELL. 1978. 85 min. 38 p. MHS and (R) Restricted.
A professor of physics and environmental studies at Gustavus Adolphus College, St. Peter, Nicollet County, and an organizer of the Coalition of Rural Environmental Groups.

1129. BROOKS, RONNIE. 1979. 55 min. 95 p. MHS and (R) Restricted.
An aide to Governor Rudy Perpich (1976-79, 1983-   ) and the governor's representative to the Minnesota Environmental Quality Board.

1130. CROCKER, GEORGE. 1979. 2 hrs., 15 min. 64 p. MHS and (R) Restricted.
A powerline protest leader from Lowry, Pope County.

1131. EMMONS, IRA DALE. 1977. 20 min. 11 p. (R) Restricted.
Resident of Glenwood, Pope County, and county sheriff.

1132. FJOSLIEN, DAVID. 1978. 40 min. 20 p. MHS and (R) Restricted.
A farmer and Minnesota legislator from Brandon, Douglas County.

1133. FUCHS, VIRGIL AND JANE H. FUCHS. 1977. 2 hrs., 25 min. 88 p. MHS and (R) Restricted.
Farmers and protest leaders from Belgrade, Stearns County.

1134. GELBMAN, JAMES. 1978. 30 min. 18 p. MHS and (R) Restricted.
The co-ordinator of the Minnesota Public Interest Research Group at the University of Minnesota-Morris, Stevens County.

1135. HAGEN, HAROLD. 1977. 3 hrs., 20 min. 61 p. MHS and (R) Restricted.
A farmer from Pope County and president of Counties United for a Rural Environment.

1136. HANSON, RICHARD A. 1979. 3 hrs. 110 p. MHS and (R) Restricted.
A Pope County farmer and university student who managed the Minnesota gubernatorial campaign of Alice Tripp (1978).

1137. HARTMAN, LAWRENCE B. 1978, 1979.
3 hrs. 101 p. MHS and (R) Restricted.
The project manager for the Minnesota Environmental Quality Board charged with site evaluation for the powerline.

1138. HAYENGA, WALLACE. 1978. 55 min.
32 p. MHS and (R) Restricted.
A staff assistant at Blue Earth-Nicollet-Faribault Cooperative Electric Assn. in Mankato, Blue Earth County.

1139. HEDNER, GORDON AND HELEN B. HEDNER.
1977. 80 min. 51 p. MHS and (R) Restricted.
Farmers from Pope County and members of Families Are Concerned Too.

1140. HIRSCH, MERLE N. 1979. 45 min.
26 p. MHS and (R) Restricted.
The professor of physics and chairman of the science and mathematics division, University of Minnesota-Morris, Stevens County.

1141. JACOBSON, DONALD G. 1978. 2 hrs., 35 min. 107 p. MHS and (R) Restricted.
The public relations manager, United Power Assn.

1142. JENKS, SCOTT AND LORRAINE L. JENKS.
1977. 80 min. 55 p. MHS and (R) Restricted.
Farmers from Lowry, Pope County, and members of Families Are Concerned Too and Save Our Countryside.

1143. JOST, PAUL J. 1979. 105 min. 45 p. MHS and (R) Restricted.
A farmer from Alberta, Stevens County, and board member of Agralite Cooperative and the Cooperative Power Assn.

1144. KOUDELA, CAROLYN. 1979. 80 min.
51 p. MHS and (R) Restricted.
A dairy farmer from Alexandria, Douglas County, and president of Save Our Countryside.

1145. LENNICK, TED V. 1978. 2 hrs., 45 min.
94 p. MHS and (R) Restricted.
The general manager of Cooperative Power Assn., Minneapolis.

1146. MARTIN, PHILIP O. 1978. 3 hrs. 92 p. MHS and (R) Restricted.
The general manager of United Power Assn., Elk River.

1147. MILLHONE, JOHN. 1978. 55 min. 27 p. MHS and (R) Restricted.
The director, Minnesota Energy Agency (1975-78), and member, Minnesota Environmental Quality Board.

1148. NELSON, C. DAVID. 1977. 23 min.
12 p. MHS and (R) Restricted.
Pope County attorney and resident of Glenwood.

1149. NELSON, JAMES. 1977. 2 hrs., 20 min.
72 p. MHS and (R) Restricted.
A grain farmer from Elbow Lake, Grant County, and president of No Powerlines.

1150. OLHOFT, WAYNE. 1977. 55 min. 34 p. MHS and (R) Restricted.
Minnesota legislator (1972-   ) from Herman, Grant County.

1151. OLSON, DONALD. 1978. 85 min. 49 p. MHS and (R) Restricted.
A powerline opponent and protest organizer from Minneapolis.

1152. PICK, DEBORAH. 1979. 105 min. 63 p. MHS and (R) Restricted.
A powerline opponent and resident of Lowry, Pope County.

1153. RICHARDSON, HERVEY. 1977. 70 min.
25 p. MHS and (R) Restricted.
A retired farmer and member of the Agralite Cooperative board of directors, Benson, Swift County.

1154. RUTLEDGE, DENNIS AND NINA H. RUTLEDGE.
1978. 105 min. 57 p. MHS and (R) Restricted.
Grain and beef farmers from Lowry, Pope County, and members of several protest organizations.

1155. SCHROM, ED. 1978. 70 min. 35 p. MHS and (R) Restricted.
A Minnesota legislator and farmer from Albany, Stearns County.

1156. SCHUMACHER, WAYNE. 1977. 55 min.
27 p. MHS and (R) Restricted.
A farmer and former Minnesota legislator from Glenwood, Pope County.

1157. SHELDON, ROBERT. 1979. 105 min.
55 p. MHS and (R) Restricted.
The public relations manager for Cooperative Power Assn., Minneapolis.

1158. SIELING, LOUIS. 1977. 50 min. 37 p. MHS and (R) Restricted.
A farmer from Perham, Otter Tail County, and member, board of directors, Lake Region Cooperative Electrical Assn.

1159. STONE, JOHN R. 1979. 90 min. 38 p. MHS and (R) Restricted.
The editor of the Pope County Tribune.

1160. STRAND, ROGER E. 1978. 2 hrs., 20 min. 64 p. MHS and (R) Restricted.
A farmer and Minnesota legislator from Cyrus, Pope County.

1161. TOLLEFSON, PAUL. 1978. 45 min. 23 p. MHS and (R) Restricted.
A farmer and powerline supporter from Northfield, Rice County.

1162. TORBORG, ELMER. 1978. 80 min. 54 p. MHS and (R) Restricted.
A Roman Catholic priest and director, Catholic Rural Life Office in Minnesota.

1163. TRIPP, ALICE R. 1977. 80 min. 44 p. MHS and (R) Restricted.
A dairy farmer, former teacher, candidate for Minnesota governor (1978), and member of Keep Towers Out.

1164. VANDERPOEL, PETER. 1978. 75 min. 38 p. MHS and (R) Restricted.
A journalist and former director of the Minnesota State Planning Agency and Minnesota Environmental Quality Board (1975-79).

1165. WALD, KENNETH. 1978. 25 min. 14 p. MHS and (R) Restricted.
An environmental use planner with Minnesota Department of Natural Resources.

1166. WOIDA, MATH AND GLORIA B. WOIDA. 1979. 2 hrs., 45 min. 91 p. MHS and (R) Restricted.
Farmers and powerline opponents from Sauk Centre, Stearns County.

[[[[[[[[[[[∘]]]]]]]]]]]

PERSPECTIVES: URBAN AND RURAL CHURCHES IN CENTRAL MINNESOTA

These interviews with members of urban and rural congregations provide information on each group's perceptions of the differences and similarities between its own church and its urban or rural counterparts. The interviews include material on church finances, social service functions, use of a foreign language in church services, social activities, church politics, religious schools, the contrasting problems faced by urban and rural clergy, doctrinal differences among and within various church groups, and the histories of the narrators' congregations. John C. LeDoux and Professor Calvin C. Gower, St. Cloud State University, conducted the interviews.

1167. BEAVER, ANGELINE. 1978. 75 min. (C)
A housewife comments on changes in the Protestant Episcopal church and church work during World War II.

1168. BLILIE, PHILLIP. 1978. 75 min. (C)
A Lutheran clergyman from Princeton, Mille Lacs County, comments on his family, his decision to enter the seminary, the congregations he has served in Minnesota and South Dakota, the history of the Glendorado Lutheran Church in Benton County, and changes in the Lutheran church during his years in the ministry.

1169. BRANDER, ANITA. 1979. 60 min. (C)
A minister discusses the history of the First Congregational Church in Princeton, Mille Lacs County, including information on the Princeton community and Congregational church doctrine.

1170. CARLSON, STELLA LARSON. 1978. 45 min. (C)
A member of the Glendorado Lutheran Church in Benton County discusses Sunday school activities, youth and women's groups, Norwegian traditions, and disputes over church doctrine in the 1920s.

1171. CARROLL, ROBERT. 1978. 30 min. (C)
Carroll includes information on the Finlayson Methodist Church, Pine County.

1172. DENERY, JOHN F. 1978. 70 min. (C)
A Roman Catholic priest from Pearl Lake, Stearns County, discusses the 1930s Depression, prohibition, seminary life, and the history of Pearl Lake.

1173. FIRST BAPTIST CHURCH, LONG PRAIRIE. 1979. 75 min. (C)
The members of a church in Todd County discuss its history, radio program, youth activities, and the growth of Long Prairie.
Narrators: Marie Carlson, Grace Sargeant, Rev. Paul Twist

1174. FIRST PRESBYTERIAN CHURCH, PINE CITY. 1979. 100 min. (C)
Ralph Ausmus and James W. Clark discuss the history of the church, the development of Pine County, and the 1894 Hinckley fire.

1175. KOST, HAROLD. 1978. 90 min. (C)
A Roman Catholic priest discusses the community of Belle Prairie, Morrison County, and the history of Holy Family Church.

1176. KOST EVANGELICAL FREE CHURCH, KOST. 1978. 45 min. (C)
The members of a church in Chisago County

discuss its history and the Swedish settlers who founded it.

Narrators: Anna Mae Berglund, Daisy Gustafson, William Gustafson, Esther Johnson

1177. KROLL, PETER J. 1978. 56 min. (C)
A Roman Catholic priest from St. Cloud, Stearns County, discusses his experiences as a chaplain during World War II.

1178. LYNCH, ALDEN. 1979. 95 min. (C)
A minister discusses the history of the First Baptist Church of Cambridge, Isanti County, including information on Swedish settlement.

1179. MARTIN, CHARLES. 1979. 90 min. (C)
Martin includes information on St. Mary's Catholic Church in Little Falls, Morrison County, campus life at St. Cloud State University, and his poetry.

1180. NELSON, ERNEST G. 1978. 90 min. (C)
A former minister describes his work as pastor of the South Isanti Baptist Church in Isanti County, church politics, and his decision to leave the ministry.

1181. OWENS, DAVID. 1978. 85 min. (C)
A minister discusses the history of the Reynolds Baptist Church, Long Prairie, Todd County, and differences among various Baptist churches.

1182. PEASE CHRISTIAN REFORMED CHURCH, PEASE. 1978. 80 min. (C)
The members of a Dutch Reformed church in Mille Lacs County discuss its history, doctrines, and former church school.

Narrators: Sam Droogsma, Rev. Roger A. Kok, John F. Vedders

1183. PILLAGER BAPTIST CHURCH, PILLAGER. 1978. 60 min. (C)
The members of a church in Cass County discuss its history, social activities, and a fire that partly destroyed the church.

Narrators: Mrs. Harold Gillson, Lucille Nelson, Rev. Robert Osell

1184. PINE LAKE UNITED METHODIST CHURCH, PINE LAKE. 1978. 100 min. (C)
The members of a church in Pine County discuss its history, problems, and the growth of the town of Pine Lake.

Narrators: Rev. Marvin Andros, Clark D. Howe, Kenneth Price, Isabel Welton

1185. RODRIGUEZ, VIOLET. 1978. 60 min. (C)
Rodriguez includes information on the Dalbo Baptist Church in Isanti County, co-operation between Swedish Lutheran and Baptist churches, and doctrinal differences among various Baptist conferences.

1186. ST. ANDREW'S CHURCH, ELK RIVER. 1979. 100 min. (C)
Rev. Lloyd Haupt and Vina Koehler discuss the history of this Roman Catholic church in Sherburne County, including information on youth ministries and changes in the church.

1187. ST. ANTHONY OF PADUA CHURCH, PADUA. 1978. 90 min. (C)
The members of a Roman Catholic church in Stearns County discuss Irish, German, and Bohemian settlements and the growth of the church.

Narrators: Richard R. Brooten, Helen Fellings, Josephine Rooney, Rev. Vincent J. Santo, Adolph Weiner

1188. ST. PATRICK'S CHURCH, DUELM. 1978. 2 hrs. (C)
The members of a Roman Catholic church in Benton County discuss its history, parish events, and the Polish, German, and Irish settlers who founded it.

Narrators: Pauline Balder, Raymond Corrigan, Rev. Robert C. Harren, Frances G. Jackels, John J. Jackels

1189. SNADER, EARL. 1978. 45 min. (C)
The minister at the United Church of Christ in Sandstone, Pine County, discusses co-operation between his church and the Finlayson Methodist Church.

1190. SOUTH SANTIAGO LUTHERAN CHURCH, BECKER. 1978. 80 min. (C)
The members of a church in Sherburne County discuss its history, the split with Glendorado Lutheran Church, use of the Norwegian language, women's groups, and the Luther League.

Narrators: Bernard E. Graning, Hazel L. Halverson, Rev. Dennis Larson

1191. STEBNER, HERMAN W. 1978. 60 min. (C)
Stebner comments on the growth of the Methodist church in Waite Park, Stearns County.

1192. STEFFEN, GEORGE F. 1979. 110 min. (C)
A minister discusses the First Congregational Church in Brainerd, Crow Wing County, including information on church doctrine, the role of the pastor in civic affairs, and the use of summer drive-in services.

1193. TRINITY LUTHERAN CHURCH, SAUK RAPIDS. 1979. 110 min. (C)
Oscar Krieg and Rev. Victor Ostermann

discuss the church's history, the Lutheran Missouri Synod, and development of the community of Sauk Rapids, Benton County.

1194. UNITED METHODIST CHURCH, MORA. 1979. 80 min. (C)
The members of a church in Kanabec County discuss its history, Methodist doctrine, marriage counseling, and the role of the pastor.
Narrators: Margaret Bronniche, Margaret Ellens, Rev. James Gaugen

1195. WIED, KURT. 1979. 100 min. (C)
A minister discusses the history of Immanuel Lutheran Church in Wadena, Wadena County, including information on the Lutheran Church in America and how it is different from other Lutheran synods.

1196. ZION LUTHERAN CHURCH, BUFFALO. 1979. 90 min. (C)
Rev. John Folkerds and Clifford Peterson discuss church history, Lutheran doctrine, and the church's role in Wright County.

1197. ZYLLA, PAUL. 1978. 2 hrs. (C)
A Roman Catholic priest from Rockville, Stearns County, discusses his family; early work as a shoe shiner in his father's barbershop; life in the seminary during World War II; reminiscences of postwar study in Washington, D.C., and Rome; his duties as vice-chancellor and chancellor of the diocese of St. Cloud (1960-70); his parish in Rockville; and contemporary changes in the Catholic church.

[[[[[[[[[[[o]]]]]]]]]]]

PIONEER AVIATOR: THE MAX A. CONRAD, JR., ORAL HISTORY PROJECT

Max A. Conrad, Jr. (1903-79), was an aviator and barnstormer from Winona. After construction of the Winona Airport in 1928, Conrad formed the Max Conrad Flying School, operated a charter air service, and served in the civilian pilot training program and, later, as a commercial pilot. Among project narrators are many of Conrad's students, including several who became instructors in his school. The interviews were conducted by Professor George Bates, Winona State University.

1198. BIESANZ, CHARLES W., SR. 1975. 60 min. 18 p. (W)
A Winona businessman discusses the Conrad family and barnstorming.

1199. BACKUS, LEROY. 1975. 25 min. 22 p. (W)
A retired businessman from Winona discusses the fire that destroyed the Winona Airport in 1943.

1200. HITTNER, EDWARD L. 1975. 105 min. 52 p. (W)
A retired Winona police officer discusses his work as a police pilot.

1201. ROGGE, HAROLD F. 1975. 45 min. 19 p. (W)
A psychology professor at Winona State University discusses instruction at the Max Conrad Flying School and experiences in the Royal Canadian Air Force and in Europe during World War II.

1202. SPELTZ, ALFRED. 1975. 60 min. 21 p. (W)
A statistics professor at Winona State University discusses his work as an instructor for Conrad and in the U.S. Air Force.

1203. THERN, ROYAL G. 1975. 30 min. 13 p. (W)
A Winona businessman discusses the Thern Co., a machinery manufacturer.

1204. TUSHNER, DANIEL J. 1975. 25 min. 21 p. (W)
A retired businessman from Winona discusses flying for Conrad and participation in the Winona Flying Club.

1205. VENABLES, C. PAUL. 1975. 60 min. 23 p. (W)
A retired businessman from Winona discusses domestic flying during World War II.

1206. VOSE, ROY. 1975. 110 min. 31 p. (W)
A U.S. Army Air Corps pilot discusses flying in the India-China-Burma theater in World War II, barnstorming, crop dusting, and air mail contracts.

1207. WIER, HUBERT M. 1975. 45 min. 11 p. (W)
A retired employee of Bay State Milling Co., Winona, discusses the Conrad family and aviation accidents.

[[[[[[[[[[○]]]]]]]]]]]

THE RED RIVER VALLEY DURING THE 1930S DEPRESSION

In this series of interviews dealing with the impact of the 1930s Depression on urban and rural life in the valley of the Red River of the North, narrators discuss development of welfare programs; the Works Progress Administration; the New Deal; and the effects of the depression on farming, business, schooling, and social life. The interviews were conducted under the direction of Professor I. Kenneth Smemo, Moorhead State University.

1208. BLUMER, MATILDA ENVIK. 1978. 60 min. (M)
A retired farmer discusses emigration from Norway, homesteading near Hazelton, N.Dak., and farming during the depression.

1209. BOETTGER, MAUDE IRWIN. 1974. 50 min. 27 p. (M)
A retired North Dakota farmer comments on farming during the depression.

1210. BRANIGAN, GERTRUDE ALLMAN. 1974. 40 min. 14 p. (M)
Mrs. Clifford Branigan comments on the economic effects of the depression and various U.S. government programs related to rural family life in Clay County.

1211. BROLIN, EDWIN. 1974. 45 min. (M)
A blacksmith from Ortonville, Big Stone County, describes his work and patented ice auger.

1212. COULTER, MILT. 1973. 60 min. 19 p. (M)
A retired laborer and World War II draft resister from Fargo, N.Dak., comments on the effects of the war on family life.

1213. GRONSKEI, ANNIE NESSET. 1974. 20 min. 17 p. (M)
Mrs. Olav Gronskei, who with her husband emigrated from Norway in 1927, recalls the impact of the depression on the Wheaton, Traverse County, area.

1214. HOLT, JULIUS A. 1974. 15 min. 12 p. (M)
A banker from Parkers Prairie, Otter Tail County, discusses the depression economy.

1215. JOHNSON, ARTHUR J. 1974. 30 min. 12 p. (M)
A banker from Miltona, Douglas County, comments on farm mortgage foreclosures.

1216. JOHNSON, MYRTLE ALLEN. 1973. 2 hrs. 58 p. (M)
A farmer from Sabin, Clay County, discusses social and economic changes in farm life, college experiences at North Dakota State University, World War I, and the effects of the depression on farming.

1217. KIEFER, JACOB, SR. 1973. 60 min. (M)
The owner of a Moorhead, Clay County, automobile dealership comments on business during the depression.

1218. MARGET, MANNY. 1973. 45 min. 23 p. (M)
A radio sportscaster from Moorhead, Clay County, recollects athletic events he has covered and his experiences as a traveling salesman during the 1920s.

1219. NELSON, J. WALTER AND HELEN ERICKSON NELSON. 1973. 60 min. 30 p. (M)
Retired farmers from Wheaton, Traverse County, discuss federal policies in the depression.

1220. OGREN, BYRON AND IRENE IVERSON OGREN. 1973. 45 min. 16 p. (M)
Farmers from the Moorhead, Clay County, area discuss farming during the depression.

1221. OLSON, TALLOF. 1974. 25 min. 6 p. (M)
A farmer from Madison, Lac qui Parle County, discusses farming during the depression and activities of the Farm Holiday Assn.

1222. OLSON, TINA AMANDA. 1978. 60 min. (M)
A retired schoolteacher discusses her family's settlement in Prairie View Township, Wilkin County, and the effects of the depression and World Wars I and II on the Red River Valley.

1223. OLSON, OLE A. 1978. 55 min. (M)
A retired insurance agent discusses childhood in Norway, emigration to the U.S., homesteading in South Dakota, and his business during the depression.

1224. SCHUMACHER, SIGRID PETERSEN. 1974. 15 min. (M)
Mrs. August Schumacher discusses the depression years in Miltona, Douglas County, the Works Progress Administration, and rural social life.

1225. THOMPSON, MABEL DAVID. 1974. 50 min. 4 p. (M)
Mrs. Sylvester Thompson, Grey Eagle, Todd County, discusses her family's former mink

ranch in Aitkin, Aitkin County, and her memories of the depression.

[[[[[[[[[[∘]]]]]]]]]]

SCANDINAVIAN HERITAGE ORAL HISTORY PROJECT

This series of interviews documents Scandinavian immigration and acculturation in northwestern Minnesota, with emphasis on degrees of linguistic and cultural retention among second and third generation Scandinavians. The ethnic backgrounds of the narrators are identified in each entry. The interviews were conducted by Dr. Gerald D. Anderson, Moorhead State University.

1226. ALM, FRANK. 1976. 60 min. (M)
    Retired Christine, N.Dak., farmer. Swedish. Includes comments on the Milwaukee Road, World War I, and the 1918 influenza epidemic.

1227. ANDERSEN, LOUISE HANSEN. 1976. 44 min. (M)
    Retired Fargo, N.Dak., secretary. Danish. Includes comments on Westby, Mont., and disputes between cattlemen and farmers.

1228. ANDERSEN, PHILIP. 1976. 60 min. (M)
    Retired Fargo, N.Dak., maintenance man. Danish. Includes comments on his childhood in Westby, Mont.

1229. ANDERSON, CARL AXEL. 1976. 60 min. (M)
    Retired teacher and county commissioner from Erhard, Otter Tail County. Swedish. Includes comments on his teaching career and service in World War I.

1230. ANDERSON, VICTOR. 1976. 60 min. (M)
    Retired milk deliveryman from Moorhead, Clay County. Swedish.

1231. ANDERSON, WILFRED. 1975. 60 min. (M)
    Retired Hitterdal, Clay County, farmer. Norwegian and Swedish. Includes comments on the history of Hitterdal and the impact of World War I on that community.

1232. ARNESON, ARNE. 1976. 30 min. (M)
    Retired janitor and bartender from Fargo, N.Dak. Norwegian.

1233. ASKEGAARD, OSCAR. 1976. 47 min. (M)
    Retired farmer from Moorhead, Clay County. Norwegian. Includes comments on his

service as a county commissioner and in World War I and the early history of Comstock.

1234. AUNE, JOHANNA NELSON AND GERTIE NELSON HOLM. 1976. 54 min. (M)
    Farmers from Moorhead, Clay County. Norwegian.

1235. BARKER, HAZEL MONSON. 1976. 41 min. (M)
    Retired Moorhead, Clay County, teacher and businesswoman. Swedish.

1236. BERG, PETER. 1973. 50 min. (M)
    Includes comments on Franklin D. Roosevelt's New Deal policies by a retired Clay County farmer. Norwegian.

1237. BJORNDAHL, NILMER. 1976. 45 min. (M)
    Carpenter from Moorhead, Clay County. Norwegian.

1238. BJORNSON, FREDA GUDMONSON. 1976. 45 min. (M)
    Gift shop employee from Moorhead, Clay County. Icelandic. Includes comments on homesteading in North Dakota and Saskatchewan and her career as cook for a threshing crew.

1239. BRATLIEN, OSCAR. 1976. 60 min. (M)
    Retired Hawley, Clay County, farmer. Norwegian.

1240. BURGESS, HENRIETTA CHRISTENSEN. 1976. 44 min. (M)
    Retired Moorhead, Clay County, teacher. Swedish and Danish.

1241. CAMPBELL, ROSA McNAB. 1976. 25 min. 1 p. (M)
    Moorhead, Clay County, housewife. Icelandic. Includes comments about her childhood in Gardner, N.Dak.

1242. CARLANDER, ROBERT. 1976. 56 min. (M)
    Retired Moorhead, Clay County, bricklayer and teacher. Swedish. Includes comments on his career and World War I service.

1243. CARLANDER, ROY. 1976. 60 min. (M)
    Retired Moorhead, Clay County, mail carrier. Swedish.

1244. CARLSON, MINNIE. 1975. 37 min. (M)
    Retired department store employee from Fergus Falls, Otter Tail County. Swedish.

1245. DINUSSON, WAYNE E. 1976. 30 min. 1 p. (M)
    Animal science instructor at North Dakota State University, Fargo. Icelandic. Includes comments on the Icelandic naming system.

1246. ENGER, MABEL OPSAHL. 1976. 35 min.
(M)
     Housewife from Oakes, N.Dak. Norwegian.
Includes comments about life in Maiden Rock,
Wis.

1247. ERICKSON, ALLEN. 1976. 70 min. (M)
     Retired Moorhead, Clay County, physician.
Norwegian.

1248. ERICKSON, AMY. 1976. 47 min. (M)
     Retired Lake Park, Becker County, teacher
and dietitian. Swedish.

1249. ERICKSON, RUTH DAHL. 1976. 29 min.
(M)
     Housewife from Moorhead, Clay County.
Norwegian. Includes comments on her childhood
in Crookston, Polk County.

1250. FAUST, DAGNE PETERSON. 1976. 33 min.
(M)
     Retired farmer from Valley City, N.Dak.
Norwegian.

1251. FOSSAY, CATHERINE EDLUND. 1976. 50
min. (M)
     Retired teacher from Moorhead, Clay Coun-
ty. Swedish.

1252. FURCHT, CLARA EUREN. 1976. 25 min.
(M)
     Retired railroad employee from Moorhead,
Clay County. Swedish. Includes comments on
her career.

1253. FYNSKOV, MABEL ERICKSON. 1976. 50
min. (M)
     Retired nurse from Osakis, Todd County.
Norwegian. Includes comments on her childhood
in Turtle Lake, N.Dak.

1254. GALE, ELSIE BERGMAN. 1976. 48 min.
(M)
     Housewife and hospital volunteer from
Moorhead, Clay County. Swedish. Also dis-
cusses her early life in Clearbrook, Polk
County.

1255. GLASRUD, CLARENCE. 1976. 40 min. (M)
     Retired English teacher from Moorhead,
Clay County. Norwegian. Includes comments on
World War I bond sales and Red Cross fund
drives.

1256. GREGERSON, OBERT AND ANNA ULEN GREGER-
SON. 1976. 60 min. (M)
     Retired Ulen, Clay County, farmers. Nor-
wegian. Includes comments on homesteading in
Montana (1910) and the early history of Ulen
and Hitterdal in Clay County and Lake Park in
Becker County.

1257. GRONNER, JOHN. 1976. 60 min. (M)
     Retired Underwood, Otter Tail County,
farmer. Norwegian.

1258. HANSON, ANNA MELIN. 1976. 50 min.
(M)
     Retired Moorhead, Clay County, teacher.
Swedish. Includes comments on her career.

1259. HANSON, CLARA LEE. 1976. 90 min. (M)
     Retired nurse, teacher, and farmer from
Ulen, Clay County. Norwegian.

1260. HANSON, MARIE HUGELEN. 1976. 60 min.
2 p. (M)
     Mrs. Arthur E. Hanson, a housewife from
Moorhead, Clay County. Norwegian. Includes
comments on her childhood near Thompson, Iowa;
her years in Fergus Falls, Otter Tail County;
and her husband's service as president of the
northern Minnesota districts of the Evangelical Lutheran Church (1951-60) and the American
Lutheran Church (1961-64).

1261. HAUGEN, LOUIS. 1976. 58 min. (M)
     Retired Crookston, Polk County, railroad
construction worker and businessman. Norwegian. Includes comments on his military service in Norway (1905-07), his career with the
railroad, and his work with a lumber company
in Fertile, Polk County.

1262. HEGLAND, LELA ERICKSON. 1976. 50 min.
(M)
     Housewife from Moorhead, Clay County.
Norwegian.

1263. HEST, ALVA LETNESS. 1977. 30 min.
(M)
     Retired housekeeper from Perley, Norman
County. Norwegian. Includes comments on her
parents' immigration to the U.S. from Norway
in 1892, her childhood, religion, World War I,
and Norwegian customs in Perley.

1264. HITTERDAL, CLIFFORD. 1976. 60 min.
(M)
     Retired postmaster of Hitterdal, Clay
County. Norwegian. Includes comments on his
World War I experiences in France and the
early history of Hitterdal, which was named
for his grandfather.

1265. HOLLANDS, RALPH. 1976. 60 min. (M)
     Retired dry cleaner and former mayor of
Moorhead, Clay County (1950-51). Swedish.
Includes comments on his business career and
service in Moorhead city government.

1266. HOLMGREN, HENRY. 1976. 65 min. (M)
     Retired blacksmith and mayor of Henning,
Otter Tail County (1935-65). Swedish. In-

cludes comments on his World War I service, his career as a blacksmith, and the history of Henning.

1267. HOLMQUIST, DELSIE. 1976. 55 min. (M)
Retired professor of education at North Dakota State University (NDSU), Fargo. Includes comments on her career at NDSU and at Moorhead State University, Clay County, and Scandinavian influences on those schools as perceived by a non-Scandinavian.

1268. IVERSON, ABIGAIL ANDERSON. 1976. 60 min. (M)
Retired farmer from Hitterdal, Clay County. Swedish and Norwegian.

1269. JACOBSON, GEORGE. 1977. 36 min. (M)
Retired farmer from Perley, Norman County. Norwegian. Includes comments on the extent of Scandinavian influence, customs, and ethnicity in Perley.

1270. JACOBSON, HENRY. 1976. 44 min. (M)
Retired construction worker from Moorhead, Clay County. Norwegian. Includes comments on Norwegian influence in the Ulen and Hitterdal areas of Clay County.

1271. JOHNARD, HARTWIG. 1976. 55 min. (M)
Retired Hawley, Clay County, food retailer. Swedish. Includes comments on his first trip to the U.S. from Sweden, his subsequent immigration to the U.S., later visits to Sweden, and aspects of modern Swedish life.

1272. JOHNSON, CLARA. 1976. 59 min. (M)
Housewife from Duluth, St. Louis County. Norwegian. Includes comments on her childhood in Dakota Territory and near Underwood, Otter Tail County.

1273. JOHNSON, TORA JEPPESEN. 1978. 60 min. (M)
Housewife from Dawson, Clay County. Danish. Includes information on her childhood in Denmark, voyage to America (1905), World Wars I and II, and the 1930s Depression.

1274. KAEDING, HELENE CARLSON. 1976. 60 min. (M)
Housewife from Moorhead, Clay County. Swedish. Includes comments on the Scandinavian community around St. Peter, Nicollet County.

1275. KLUKKEN, JOHN O. 1976. 60 min. (M)
Retired farmer and Lutheran pastor from Osakis, Todd County. Norwegian. Includes comments on his ordination and on the history of Osakis.

1276. LINDGREN, ANNA UDD. 1976. 54 min. (M)
Mrs. Oscar Lindgren, retired cook from Fargo, N.Dak. Swedish. Includes comments on her early life in Sweden; immigration to the U.S. (1914); Scandinavian influence in Glendive, Mont.; World War I; and reunion with her future husband 40 years after each emigrated from the same village in Sweden.

1277. LINDGREN, OSCAR. 1976. 60 min. (M)
Retired farmer from Fargo, N.Dak. Swedish. Includes comments on the Bledon, N.Dak., area.

1278. MELBERG, ANNA OVERLAND. 1977. 20 min. (M)
Housewife from Moorhead, Clay County. Norwegian. Includes comments on the effects of World War I on Moorhead.

1279. MELBY, WILLIAM. 1976. 38 min. (M)
Retired Hitterdal, Clay County, farmer. Norwegian.

1280. MOORE, INGA HOLSEN. 1976. 30 min. (M)
Housewife from Moorhead, Clay County. Norwegian. Includes comments on childhood in Fargo, N.Dak.

1281. NARVESON, CARL. 1976. 58 min. (M)
Retired Moorhead, Clay County, teacher and administrator. Norwegian. Includes comments on his childhood in the Lutheran Children's Home in Twin Valley, Norman County.

1282. NELSON, NORMAN. 1976. 53 min. (M)
Retired Rollag, Clay County, store owner. Norwegian. Includes comments on his career, the manufacture of farm implements, and the founding and development of the Western Minnesota Threshers Reunion.

1283. NELSON, WILLIAM. 1976. 56 min. (M)
Retired farmer from Rollag, Clay County. Norwegian. Includes comments on family history, Norwegian influence in Rollag, World War I, Norwegian newspapers, and the history of the Lutheran churches in Rollag.

1284. OIEN, NINA ANDERSON. 1976. 60 min. (M)
Housewife and registered nurse from Moorhead, Clay County. Swedish. Includes comments on her childhood in Braham, Isanti County.

1285. OLIVER, ALICE LARSON. 1976. 21 min. (M)
Physician from Moorhead, Clay County.

Swedish. Includes comments on her childhood in Johnsburg, Pa.

1286. OLSON, OSCAR. 1976. 60 min. (M)
Retired farmer from Lake Park, Becker County. Swedish.

1287. OVERBY, NELS AND BORGHILD ANDERSON OVERBY. 1976. 45 min. (M)
Retired Moorhead, Clay County, farmers. Norwegian.

1288. RAMSE, ALMA BAKKEN. 1976. 55 min. (M)
Retired teacher from McIntosh, Polk County. Norwegian. Includes comments on her teaching career.

1289. RUNDQUIST, MYRTLE. 1976. 47 min. (M)
Retired Moorhead, Clay County, librarian. Swedish. Includes comments on her childhood in Lancaster, Kittson County.

1290. SCHAEFER, BEATRICE MUNDAHL. 1976. 45 min. (M)
Registered nurse from Osakis, Todd County. Norwegian. Includes comments on her career and Norwegian settlements in Lac qui Parle County.

1291. SHULSTAD, CHRISTIAN. 1978. 80 min. (M)
Dawson, Lac qui Parle County, farmer. Norwegian.

1292. STRANDNESS, LILLIE. 1976. 45 min. (M)
Retired teacher from Fargo, N.Dak. Swedish. Includes comments on her childhood near Parkers Prairie, Otter Tail County, and her career in education.

1293. STRANDNESS, ODIN. 1976. 54 min. (M)
Retired lawyer and judge from Fargo, N.Dak. Norwegian. Includes comments on his career and his father's work as a traveling preacher.

1294. SWEDBERG, DAVID. 1974. 51 min. (M)
Retired Otter Tail County farmer. Swedish. Includes comments on the 1930s Depression.

1295. THORDARSON, KATHRYN OLAFFSON. 1978. 60 min. (M)
Retired teacher from Fargo, N.Dak., recalls her family's emigration from Iceland (1888), settlement in Pembina County, N.Dak., and Icelandic customs and religion.

1296. TVERDAHL, MARIE PETERSON. 1976. 30 min. (M)

Retired farmer from Wahpeton, N.Dak. Norwegian.

1297. TVERDAHL, PALMER. 1976. 50 min. (M)
Wahpeton, N.Dak., farmer. Norwegian.

1298. WALDON, ART, SR. 1976. 38 min. (M)
Retired mail contractor from Detroit Lakes, Becker County. Norwegian. Includes comments about Bertha, Todd County.

1299. WESTERHOLM, CHARLES. 1976. 45 min. (M)
Moorhead, Clay County, construction worker. Swedish. Includes comments on his career, World War I, and the social positions of women and Indians.

1300. WESTERHOLM, PHOEBE. 1976. 47 min. (M)
Housewife from Moorhead, Clay County. Swedish and Danish. Includes comments on the farming area near Audubon, Becker County.

1301. WESTRUM, GLADYS PEERSON. 1976. 41 min. (M)
Housewife from Moorhead, Clay County. Swedish.

1302. WESTRUM, LLOYD. 1976. 58 min. (M)
Building engineer from Moorhead, Clay County. Norwegian. Includes comments on his boyhood in a sod house near Turtle Lake, N.Dak.

[[[[[[[[[[∘]]]]]]]]]]

SOCIAL SERVICE AGENCIES IN CLAY COUNTY

Officials from a variety of social service agencies in a northwestern Minnesota county co-operated in this project. Their interviews provide information on the operations of the agencies, changing social service philosophy, financing, relations among agencies and community organizations, and the impact of social services on rural communities. The interviews were conducted by Kenneth Corey-Edstrom, Moorhead State University.

1303. BUBOLTZ, LAWRENCE. 1978. 46 min. (M)
The director of the Detroit Lakes Concentrated Employment Program discusses the agency's development, impact, and programs for low-income groups.

1304. COLEMAN, ALBERT. 1978. 34 min. (M)
An employee of the Clay County Social

Service Center discusses the agency's history and changes in social programs since 1948.

1305. HEITKAMP, DENNIS. 1978. 40 min. (M)
The executive director of the Clay-Wilkin Opportunity Council discusses the problems of directing a social service program.

1306. HILGERS, EMILY EVANSON. 1978. 45 min. (M)
The director of the Clay County Developmental Achievement Center, Inc., discusses methods of preparing the mentally handicapped for jobs and for life in society.

1307. LEE, KENNETH. 1978. 40 min. (M)
The director of the Family Service Assn. of Fargo-Moorhead discusses changes in the provision of social services to families and children.

1308. LINDBERG, CAROLYNE. 1978. 20 min. (M)
The president of the Barnesville Senior Citizens Council discusses her work and the operation of the Barnesville Senior Citizens Center in Clay County.

1309. LYONS, LYNN CHRISTOFFER. 1978. 54 min. (M)
The director of the Center for Parents and Children in Moorhead, Clay County, discusses child abuse and parental counseling.

1310. OLSTAD, EVELYN LARSON. 1978. 54 min. (M)
The president of the board of the Senior Citizens Center, Inc., of Moorhead, Clay County, discusses the center's relations with area senior citizens' groups.

1311. SHERMAN, LAWRENCE. 1978. 45 min. (M)
A leader in various 4-H organizations discusses their programs and administration.

1312. SNELL, ELOISE PARADIS. 1978. 32 min. (M)
A municipal government employee describes her work with the Housing and Redevelopment Authority of Moorhead, Clay County.

1313. SORLIE, LAUREL. 1978. 45 min. (M)
The director of the Region IV Area Agency on Aging discusses her work and the development of programs for the aged.

1314. TREVINO, ROBERT. 1978. 30 min. (M)
An official of the Minnesota Migrant Council discusses the organization's history and present programs.

[[[[[[[[[[∘]]]]]]]]]]

SOUTHWEST STATE UNIVERSITY

Southwest State University was established in 1963 as part of the Minnesota State University System. Constructed in Marshall, Lyon County, it opened in the fall of 1967. This series of interviews documents the university's first years of operation, and includes information from many of those who shaped its programs.

1315. ANDERSON, EUGENE. 1978. 60 min. (M)
The chairman of the physical education department discusses the university's athletic teams, programs for the handicapped, women's athletic programs, and the Rural Studies Program.

1316. ASHCRAFT, NORMAN. 1976. 75 min. (S)
A member of the first faculty discusses the university's growth and development, technical programs, and relationship to the Marshall community.

1317. BECHTOL, WILLIAM. 1977. 45 min. (S)
The former director of Omega College at the university discusses changes during its first decade, emphasizing programs of the department of education.

1318. BELLOWS, HOWARD. 1973. 90 min. 46 p. (S)
The first president (1965-73) of the university comments on its organization and operation.

1319. FLANAGAN, MICHAEL. 1972. 50 min. (S)
A business instructor comments on development of the university's business program and his service on the budget committee and with the university bookstore.

1320. FRAZIER, RALPH. 1978. 2 hrs. (S)
A member of the first faculty discusses the university's growth and development.

1321. JONES, JAY. 1973. 60 min. 35 p. (S)
Restricted.
The president of the university (1973-75) discusses its development.

1322. KAELKE, MICHAEL. 1972. 50 min. 11 p. (S)
The first dean of students discusses development of the student affairs program and minority student issues.

1323. REZATTO, HELEN GRAHAM. 1973. 45 min. (S)

An assistant professor of literature reflects on Nonpartisan League activity in North Dakota and on William Langer's terms as governor of North Dakota (1933-34, 1937-39).

1324. ROSSILLON, JOSEPH. 1972. 90 min. 58 p. (S)
The administrative assistant to the first president discusses the university's growth and program development.

1325. SCOTT, DONALD. 1972. 35 min. 14 p. (S)
The first chairman of the division of health and physical education discusses development of those programs.

1326. SEYMOUR, PAUL. 1977. 60 min. (S) Restricted.
The dean of faculties discusses changes and innovations at the university and its impact on the surrounding communities.

1327. SHANE, MARION. 1972. 50 min. (S)
The first academic dean recalls planning and organizing the university curricula.

[[[[[[[[[[∘]]]]]]]]]]]

STAR ISLAND ORAL HISTORY PROJECT

Star Island, a resort island in Cass Lake, Cass County, is associated with Ojibway Indian legends and the heyday of the fur trade. In the early 1900s developers turned it into a summer colony. The narrators discuss island history, their island homes, the Star Island Protective League, the newsletter they publish, and their future under the management of the National Forest Service. Carol C. Ryan, Metropolitan State University, St. Paul, conducted the interviews. The tapes are at the North Central Minnesota Historical Center, Bemidji State University, Bemidji.

1328. AMBERG, MARGARET McHUGH. 1976. 25 min.

1329. BATTEN, SUZANNE WOODRUFF. 1976. 40 min.

1330. BENTRUP, VAL McFADDEN. 1976. 30 min.

1331. BLANKENSHIP, ELIZABETH BOHLINSEN. 1976. 30 min.

1332. BURTON, JUDITH FLANSBURG. 1976. 30 min.

1333. BURTON, MARTHA STEVENS. 1976. 60 min.

1334. BUSH, ANNABELLE DIEHL. 1976. 45 min.

1335. CANINE, RALPH. 1976. 20 min.

1336. CASWELL, MARY MARSTELLER. 1976. 50 min.

1337. CASWELL, MIGNON MARSTELLER. 1976. 55 min.

1338. CHILCOTT, BARBARA BRUBAKER. 1976. 60 min.

1339. COEN, GILBERT E. 1976. 50 min.

1340. COEN, WILBUR FRANKLYN, JR. 1976. 45 min.

1341. COWIE, ANNE MOSEDALE AND JOHN MOSEDALE COWIE. 1976. 90 min.

1342. CREEVY, MICHAEL H. 1976. 55 min.

1343. DAVIDSON, NANCY SHERWOOD. 1976. 45 min.

1344. DAVIS, RAYMOND F. 1976. 55 min.

1345. DONKERSGOED, MARY LOUISE WILSON. 1976. 20 min.

1346. DOSTAL, DOROTHY WILLIAMS. 1976. 30 min.

1347. DRAKE, HELEN BUCKNER. 1976. 40 min.

1348. FLANSBURG, HARRY ERNEST. 1976. 30 min.

1349. GARMERS, HERMAN AND PAUL ANTON GARMERS. 1976. 75 min.

1350. GUICE, MARY ELLEN COWLING. 1976. 45 min.

1351. HAECKER, LETITIA FOSTER. 1976. 60 min.

1352. HARSTAD, DONALD W. 1976. 55 min.

1353. HINES, NORMAN WILLIAM, JR. 1976. 20 min.

1354. IDE, NADINE SMITH. 1976. 30 min.

1355. KING, MARY LOU KENWORTHY. 1976. 60 min.

1356. LAMBERT, BEATRICE DAILY. 1976. 50 min.

1357. LAMBERT, RICHARD F. 1976. 50 min.

1358. LARSON, PHYLLIS ANN. 1976. 30 min.

1359. LUND, CURTIS JOSEPH. 1976. 30 min.

1360. McBRIDE, MARY MUNGER. 1976. 40 min.

1361. MARSH, AUDREY OLSON. 1976. 60 min.

1362. MARSTELLER, JAMES LEE. 1976. 45 min.

1363. MARTIN, E. ROSS AND MARY BATES MARTIN.
1976. 55 min.

1364. MARTIN, SHIRLEY WISE. 1976. 30 min.

1365. MATTISON, RAYMOND E. 1976. 30 min.

1366. MILLER, CHARLENE JESSEE. 1976. 40
min.

1367. MUGG, MARY DRAKE. 1976. 55 min.

1368. NIER, ALFRED OTTO CARL. 1976. 45 min.

1369. OBERG, EINAR J. 1976. 35 min.

1370. ORTHWEIN, CHARLES F. 1976. 60 min.

1371. RECHT, THOMAS. 1976. 25 min.

1372. RICE, JANE NEWMYER. 1976. 30 min.

1373. RIST, MARJORIE MARTIN. 1976. 30 min.

1374. RUCKMICK, JOHN CHRISTIAN. 1976. 60
min.

1375. RYAN, CAROL CRAWFORD. 1976. 50 min.

1376. SCHMIDT, PHILIP S. 1976. 35 min.

1377. SCHNEIDER, MARY McBRIDE. 1976. 30
min.

1378. SHIPPEE, BURRELL WARNER. 1976. 80
min.

1379. SMITH, MARION STORY. 1976. 30 min.

1380. STEEFEL, LAWRENCE D. 1976. 75 min.

1381. TAYLOR, F. RONALD. 1976. 35 min.

1382. UTLEY, ROBERT GRANT. 1977. 75 min.

1383. WAGLER, MARY JANE STARR. 1976. 60
min.

1384. WALMSLEY, W. THOMAS. 1976. 45 min.

1385. WHEELOCK, VIRGINIA ORTHWEIN. 1976. 30
min.

1386. WINTERMOTE, BARBARA FLETCHER. 1976.
30 min.

1387. WOLFE, ELIZABETH SMITH. 1976. 25 min.

1388. WOODRUFF, LUCILLE FOSTER. 1976. 40
min.

[[[[[[[[[[∘]]]]]]]]]]]

STUDENT ACTIVISM AT MOORHEAD STATE UNIVERSITY

Student anti-war and related movements at
Moorhead State University, Moorhead, during
the period 1967-76 are documented in this
series of interviews. Many of the narrators
discuss the university administration's suspension of the student newspaper, The Mistic.
The interviews were conducted by Timothy Madi-
gan, Moorhead State University.

1389. BERNICK, JOSEPH. 1976. 85 min. (M)
A factory worker and former student activist comments on the 1969 suspension of publication of The Mistic.

1390. CLARK, JEROME. 1976. 60 min. (M)
A Canby, Yellow Medicine County, author
and former student activist comments on his
involvement with The Mistic during its suspension in 1969.

1391. DICKINSON, JAMES. 1976. 60 min. (M)
The Moorhead police chief comments on
drug-law enforcement and general police work
(1965-76).

1392. DILLE, ROLAND. 1976. 3 hrs. (M)
The Moorhead State University president
(1967-   ) comments on his handling of student activism and the future of the university.

1393. ESTES, EDWARD. 1976. 80 min. (M)
A Moorhead State University professor of
political science comments on his early life
in the South and the condition of blacks in
that area.

1394. GRIFFIN, CARL H., JR. 1976. 80 min.
(M)
A Minneapolis Tribune reporter comments
on his experiences as a black student at Moorhead State University in the late 1960s and
his involvement with The Mistic.

1395. HAMILTON, STEVEN. 1976. 50 min. (M)
A former student comments on his involvement in the Youth for DFL (Democratic-Farmer-Labor party), Students for a Democratic Society, and The Mistic.

1396. HANSON, ROBERT. 1976. 55 min. (M)
The Moorhead State University vice-president (1971-77) and dean of academic affairs (1968-71) comments on curriculum changes and gives a historical overview of student activism (1850s-1970s).

1397. HUME, EILEEN. 1976. 55 min. (M)
Moorhead State University dean of women (1963-67) and associate dean of students (1967-   ).

1398. ROWELL, JOHN. 1976. 60 min. (M)
Moorhead lawyer and president of the Moorhead State University Student Senate in the early 1970s.

1399. SELBERG, LOIS CORNELL. 1976. 60 min. (M)
A Moorhead State University administrator comments on her leadership of Project E-Quality in the late 1960s.

1400. SHERMAN, JOHN. 1976. 90 min. (M)
A Moorhead State University English professor comments on the growth of the faculty and the future of liberal arts.

1401. SEVENSON, KENNETH. 1976. 90 min. (M)
Minnesota state government employee and former student activist.

1402. STRAUSS, DAVID AND DEBORAH ZITSOW STRAUSS. 1976. 2 hrs. (M)
North Dakota commissioner of agriculture and wife. Each was a Moorhead State University Student Senate president during the early 1970s.

1403. BRUNGARDT, LAURINDA REILAND. 1979. 60 min. (W)

1404. CURRY, HELEN FITZPATRICK. 1979. 32 min. (W)

1405. DIBLEY, LOLA LAPHAM. 1979. 60 min. (W)

1406. EANS, ELSIE GILOW. 1979. 55 min. (W)

1407. GOLDBERG, MARJORIE CORNELISON. 1979. 30 min. (W)

1408. HOWE, FLORENCE KINNE. 1979. 45 min. (W)

1409. KING, BERTHA E. 1979. 30 min. (W)

1410. KINNE, HARRIET MAY. 1979. 40 min. (W)

1411. LACHER, MYRTLE JOHNSON. 1979. 40 min. (W)

1412. MANN, RUTH HANKENSON. 1979. 60 min. (W)

1413. SCHWARTZ, NICHOLAS E. 1979. 60 min. (W)

1414. SIMON, ELLEN RAFOTH. 1979. 35 min. (W)

1415. STEEGE, MYRTLE Y. 1979. 62 min. (W)

1416. VATER, ROSEMA RISSER. 1979. 30 min. (W)

1417. WILLFORD, GERTRUDE JOHNSON. 1979. 60 min. (W)

1418. WILSON, HILDRED THUROW. 1979. 60 min. (W)

[[[[[[[[[[[∘]]]]]]]]]]]   [[[[[[[[[[[∘]]]]]]]]]]]

WINONA STATE NORMAL SCHOOL

Winona State Normal School, now Winona State University, opened in 1860, the first normal school west of the Mississippi River. A series of interviews with former students provided information on curriculum, student life-styles, faculty, social events, and the narrators' subsequent careers. The interviews were conducted by Barbara A. Williams, Winona State University.

WOMEN IN POLITICS AND BUSINESS IN DULUTH

The involvement of women in the business and political affairs of Duluth, St. Louis County, is documented in this series of interviews. The narrators discuss the motivation behind their political and business activities, their priorities and goals, the discrimination they have encountered, the impact of their careers on family life, methods of coping with the stress of publicity and competi-

tion, and perceptions of women's future in
public life. Barbara J. Sommer, Northeast
Minnesota Historical Center, University of
Minnesota-Duluth, conducted the interviews.

1419. ANDERSON, VICKI LARSEN. 1979. 90 min.
(D)
A physician in Cloquet, Carlton County,
comments on women in medical school and the
problems faced by women as physicians.

1420. BAKER, LURLINE CHAMBERS. 1978.
2 hrs., 15 min. (D)
A job development specialist with the
Area Regional Corrections Office, Duluth, discusses her personal philosophy regarding work
and politics, problems of a black woman in
Duluth and in politics, and her successful
campaign for a seat on the school board.

1421. BYE, MAUREEN ERKENBRACK. 1979.
3 hrs., 30 min. (D)
A Duluth city council member discusses
her work as councilor and for the Democratic-
Farmer-Labor party, the important issues in
her campaign, her association with the League
of Minnesota Cities, her changes in outlook
since joining the council, and the attitude of
her family toward her political activities.

1422. CHURCHILL, DONNA GRIMM. 1978. 2 hrs.
55 p. (D)
A nursing school instructor discusses her
work with the National Organization for Women
(NOW), including information on NOW objectives, organizational structure, strategies
for achieving change, relations with the
media, and her family's attitude toward her
political activities.

1423. CREPS, DONNA ANGUS. 1979. 92 min.
(D)
The founder of a children's specialty
store in Duluth discusses the difficulties
faced by women in business and by small businesses in general.

1424. DODGE, DEIDRE TOMSICH. 1979. 2 hrs.,
30 min. (D)
A St. Louis County commissioner comments
on her campaign, her work with the commission,
the reactions of male colleagues, and the role
of women on the commission.

1425. ELLEFSON, JUNE GRAHAM. 1979. 75 min.
(D)
The assistant vice-president of the Pioneer National Bank, Duluth, discusses women in
banking, salary structures, and education.

1426. EVANS, MARY MINOR. 1978. 105 min.
45 p. (D)

The president of the Duluth chapter of
the League of Women Voters discusses the
league's objectives; her work as a civic leader, volunteer, and director of cultural organizations; and women's networks.

1427. FISHER, JUDITH LAMBERT. 1978. 105
min. 49 p. (D)
The communications and media co-ordinator
of the Institute for Afro-American Awareness
and chair of the South St. Louis County chapter of the Women's Political Caucus discusses
her work.

1428. GRIFFITHS, VIOLET WILLIAMS. 1978. 105
min. 48 p. (D)
A union organizer and president of United
West End-Citizens Organizations Acting Together, Duluth, comments on her work.

1429. HUTCHENS, RITA DONDINEAU. 1979. 91
min. (D)
A lawyer in Duluth discusses the status
of women in law school and the difficulties
encountered by women as attorneys.

1430. JOSEPH, NANCY STUBENVOLL. 1979. 80
min. (D)
A marketing and public-relations officer
for Northern City National Bank, Duluth, comments on goal-definition for women.

1431. KUNDEL, LOIS CHAUSSEE. 1978. 2 hrs.,
30 min. (D)
An insurance agent and member of the
board of the Duluth Port Authority comments on
her campaign for the Minnesota legislature.

1432. LEHTO, ARLENE LIND. 1978. 2 hrs., 30
min. 52 p. (D)
A Minnesota state legislator and officer
of the Save Lake Superior Assn. comments on
her work.

1433. MARSHALL, JULIA N. 1978. 23 p. (D)
A civic leader and first woman director
of the Duluth Chamber of Commerce discusses
the Model City Project, city beautification,
the St. Louis County Heritage and Arts Center,
and a freeway-extension controversy.

1434. MITCHELL, MARY E. 1979. 2 hrs. (D)
A staff assistant at the Duluth, Missabe
and Iron Range Railway Co., Duluth, discusses
women in the marketplace, formation of a business women's support group, and the pressures
of society on women who work outside the home.

1435. PEARSON, MANEY M. 1978. 60 min.
28 p. (D)
A political activist discusses the Farmer-Labor party and its merger with the Demo-

cratic party, the CIO Congress of Women's Auxiliaries, and the AFL-CIO merger.

1436. ROWE, PAMELA M. 1979. 86 min. (D)
The assistant to the president of Maurices, Inc., Duluth, discusses the clothing business.

1437. RYLAND, MARY NELSON. 1978. 2 hrs. 28 p. (D)
An officer of Ryland Ford, Inc., a director of the Duluth National Bank and of the Chamber of Commerce, and the former president of the Duluth school board discusses current women's issues.

1438. SCHROEDER, JANET KNOPE. 1979. 2 hrs. (D)
The director of libraries, Duluth, discusses the changing role of public libraries, the position of women in public administration, and the controversy surrounding the construction of a new public library in Duluth.

1439. SWAIN, SHIRLEY H. 1979. 2 hrs. (D)
The executive director of the St. Louis County Heritage and Arts Center, Duluth, discusses the development of a cultural center.

1440. VAN EVERA, MARY CONGDON. 1978. 2 hrs. (D)
A civic leader discusses the controversy surrounding construction of the new Duluth Public Library.

1441. WATTERS, KATHERINE PIERCE. 1978. 2 hrs., 15 min. (D)
A community leader discusses her work with the Democratic-Farmer-Labor party and the women's liberation movement.

1442. WELLS, INGRID KAINU. 1978. 105 min. 55 p. (D)
A former Duluth postmistress (1963-65) discusses the Democratic-Farmer-Labor party, the Duluth DFL CAmpaign Coordinating Committee, and the Arrowhead Council on the Status of Women.

[[[[[[[[[[[∘]]]]]]]]]]]

WORLD WAR II: THE HOME FRONT IN WESTERN MINNESOTA

The politics and social dynamics of war mobilization and life on the home front during World War II form the basis of these interviews. Local residents comment on the experi-

ences, activities, and attitudes of people involved in service on draft and ration boards, civil defense committees, and other national, state, and local organizations. Several interviews contain information on the use of German prisoners of war as laborers on area farms. Daniel Holen, Moorhead State University, and David Ripley and Charles Bollinger, University of Minnesota-Morris, conducted the interviews.

1443. ASP, BJARNE. 1977. 46 min. (M)
Moorhead, Clay County, teacher.

1444. BAUER, JACOB. 1980. 105 min. (R)
Bauer discusses the effects of the war on Traverse County, fuel-oil rationing, the scrap-iron salvage program, and the programs of the Rural Electrification Administration.

1445. BERGLAND, ALLARD. 1977. 40 min. (M)
A retired Moorhead, Clay County, gasoline and oil salesman discusses the problems of operating his business during the war.

1446. CLARK, LOREN. 1973. 45 min. 18 p. (M)
An Ortonville farmer discusses the use of German prisoners of war on Big Stone County farms during World War II.

1447. EASTLUND, HAROLD. 1979. 70 min. (R)
A school-textbook salesman during the war discusses anti-war sentiment in Glenwood, Pope County, black-market operations, tire and gas rationing, women in the labor force, income controls, conscientious objectors, and the quality of medical service in Glenwood during the war.

1448. ERENBERG, BETTY JANE HANSON. 1979. 75 min. (R)
A pilot discusses the Women's Air Service Pilots Program, the Civilian Pilots Training Program, and her work flying transport planes during the war.

1449. ERNEST, WILLIAM H. 1980. 90 min. (R)
A retired farmer from Alberta, Stevens County, discusses the effects of the war on farming, price controls, rationing, black markets, and labor shortages.

1450. HALVORSON, ANNA. 1980. 42 min. (R)
A retired Red Cross worker discusses her war work and the role of women during the war.

1451. HOLEN, CARL. 1977. 60 min. (M)
A retired farmer from Fertile, Polk County, comments on the early settlement of Fertile and the Norwegian influence in the area.

1452. HOLEN, JAMES. 1977. 45 min. (M)
Holen was the manager of the Agricultural Stabilization and Conservation Service in Red Lake Falls, Red Lake County.

1453. JOHNSON, EDGAR. 1974. 40 min. 17 p. (M)
A Wheaton farmer who used German prisoners of war on his farm during the war discusses the prisoners and related federal programs in Traverse County.

1454. JOHNSON, VERN. 1980. 2 hrs. (R)
The president of the Coca-Cola Bottling Co. of Alexandria, Douglas County, discusses the effects of the war on business, including information on sugar rationing and on the development and growth of the beverage industry.

1455. JORDAHL, ERNEST A. 1977. 20 min. (M)
A retired Lake Park, Becker County, store owner.

1456. KIEF, MINNA SCHULTZ. 1980. 40 min. (R)
A housewife discusses Red Cross volunteer work, home canning, and rationing in Montevideo, Chippewa County, during the war.

1457. KIRKEVOLD, MARIE JOHNSON. 1977. 46 min. (M)
A retired Moorhead, Clay County, farmer discusses her service on the Clay County Ration Board and the 1918 influenza epidemic.

1458. LONGTIN, LUDGER P. 1977. 71 min. (M)
A Crookston, Polk County, teacher discusses his experiences in the Pacific Theater in World War II and his capture during the Korean War.

1459. MAGLOUGHLIN, NANCY MOLANDER. 1977. 51 min. (M)
A retired businesswoman from Moorhead, Clay County, discusses the use of German prisoners of war as farm laborers.

1460. MALLARD, MANLEY. 1977. 43 min. (M)
A resident of Crookston, Polk County, comments on his move from Iowa to the Red River Valley.

1461. MOEN, NORMAN. 1977. 80 min. (M)
A meatcutter from Crookston, Polk County, discusses selling his farm after he was drafted and his training and service in Europe as a tank driver.

1462. NOLTE, ORVIS. 1977. 40 min. (M)
A farmer from Fertile, Polk County, comments on the prejudice he encountered in the job market as a German American.

1463. PETERSON, JUDITH ERICKSON. 1977. 24 min. (M)
A retired teacher from Audubon, Becker County, describes children's activities for the war cause.

1464. RICHARDSON, HERVEY. 1979. 2 hrs. (R)
Richardson discusses farm policy during the war and the effects of the war on farm prices.

1465. ROSTEN, RUTH STORLIE. 1980. 60 min. (R)
A retired farmer discusses the effects of the 1930s Depression and the war on her farming operation and her experiences in farming alone during her sons' war service.

1466. SCHULTZ, MILDRED SHAVE. 1979. 60 min. (M)
A retired farmer discusses the First Congregational Church of Glyndon, Clay County, and the English Yeovil colony settlers who briefly farmed Northern Pacific Railway Co. lands near Glyndon.

1467. SHERVEY, GEORGE M. 1980. 2 hrs., 55 min. (R)
A farm-implement dealer discusses the effects of the war, rationing, black-market operations, and the Civil Defense program in Elbow Lake, Grant County.

1468. SLETTO, JOSEPHINE SKAVANGER. 1980. 85 min. (R)
A retired farmer discusses work with the Douglas County Selective Service Office and effects of the war on Alexandria.

1469. SOBERG, ELVIRA LARSON. 1979. 90 min. (R)
A retired farmer and teacher discusses her work in rural education programs and later activities in the Minnesota Seniors Federation.

1470. SPRUNG, WILLIAM AND FAITH EVERS SPRUNG. 1973. 45 min. (M)
Farmers discuss the use of German prisoners of war on their Ortonville, Big Stone County, farm during the war and the effects of rationing.

1471. STROM, HATTIE NYLANDER. 1977. 37 min. (M)
A farmer from Lake Park, Becker County, comments on the Victory Tax and the Big Band era.

1472. TROST, WALTER. 1979. 30 min. (R)
A retired businessman discusses the effects of the war on his meat market in Donnel-

ly, Stevens County, and the role of women during the war.

1473. WARREN, MURRAY. 1977. 2 hrs., 6 min. (M)
A Crookston, Polk County, teacher discusses his service as a signal corpsman in Burma, China, and India and compares the 1970s with the World War II era.

1474. ZECK, OTTO. 1977. 50 min. (M)
A Detroit Lakes, Becker County, museum employee comments on the Detroit Lakes region during the war.

Index of Interviewers

Index of Names, Places, and Subjects

NOTE: For information about specific localities, see both the county
and the community name

AANESTAD, REV. OTTO HERBERT, 643
Abel, Walter C., actor, 1
Accidents, 23, 100, 900, 1207
Ackman, Zina, bookkeeper, 644
Adams, Cyrus Field, editor, 265
Adams, John Q., publisher, 265, 266
Advertising, 741
AFL-CIO, 47, 168, 169, 216, 451,
452, 457, 463, 465; history, 462.
See also American Federation of
Labor, Congress of Industrial Organizations
Afro-American League, 266
Agency for International Development, 226
Agency on Aging, 1313
Agralite Cooperative, Benson, 660,
1143, 1153
Agriculture, 41, 97, 108, 440, 484,
662, 769, 832, 889, 896, 970,
1079, 1086, 1216; farm life described, 6, 7, 26, 29, 36, 268,
351, 371, 384, 397, 501, 506, 672,
673, 679, 681, 688, 693, 698, 712,
714, 720, 721, 729, 730, 758, 766,
767, 770, 771, 776, 812, 828, 829,
836, 841, 852, 860, 867, 871, 874,
882, 885-887, 889, 890, 896, 941,
946-948, 952, 957, 969, 975, 980,
988, 1000, 1017, 1120; co-operatives, 20, 45, 464, 618, 720, 964,
989, 1006, 1035; threshing, 26,
378, 1239; North Dakota, 26, 401;
itinerant labor, 29, 74, 482, 513,
514, 519, 527; organizations, 45,
464, 654, 717, 732, 743, 770, 798,
878, 885, 890, 891, 898, 932, 952,
985, 988, 1009, 1032, 1074, 1078,
1080, 1081, 1086, 1088, 1089,
1093, 1094, 1097, 1102, 1221;
dairy farming, 99, 830; farming
technology, 108, 657, 741, 766,
767, 961, 1282; sugar-beet fields,
474, 480, 483, 488, 501, 503, 508,
513, 522, 539; aerial crop spraying, 698, 1206; prisoners of war
used, 701, 898, 1446, 1453, 1459,

1470; extension service, 708, 890;
1930s Depression, 722, 729, 829,
841, 889, 896, 1075, 1097, 1208,
1209, 1216, 1220, 1221, 1465; in
World War II, 722, 1075, 1449,
1464, 1465; use of horses, 729,
886; role of government, 798, 841,
843, 867, 891, 1026, 1038, 1096,
1210, 1464; farm foreclosures,
957, 1086, 1101, 1215
Aguilar, Rev. Dagoberto, 467
Ahlgren, Clifford E., forester, 351
Ahonen, Anna M., reminiscences, 342
Aitken, Conrad, author, 83
Aitkin County, agriculture, 672
Akeley, growth, 849
Alberta, growth, 734
Albrecht, Clara Timm (Mrs. Henry),
teacher, 645
Alcoholism, Stevens County, 646
Alderink, George, state legislator,
977
Alexandria, 263, 739, 904
Allanson, George G., 690
Allen, Byron G. (Barney), politi-
cian, 159, 978
Allen, Gordon, counselor, 646
Allen, Myron R., businessman, 647
Allen, R. P., Co., McGregor, 647
Alm, Frank, farmer, 1226
Alsop, Wayne, auditor, 648
Alvarado, María Antonia (Sister En-
gracia), 468
Alvo, Stella, day-care worker, 469
Amalgamated Clothing Workers of
America International, 450
Amberg, Margaret McHugh, Star Island
resident, 1328
American Agriculture movement, 798,
891
American Cedar Co., 394
American Civil Liberties Union, 271
American Committee for the Foreign
Born, 612
American Federation of Labor, 209,
448, 1435. See also AFL-CIO
American Federation of State, Coun-
ty, and Municipal Employees, 942,
1063
American Federation of Teachers,
Local 561, 446

American G.I. Forum, St. Paul chap-
ter, 470
American Immigration Co., 79
American Legion Auxiliary, 719
American Lutheran Church, 605, 1260.
See also Lutheran church
American Political Science Assn.,
162, 179, 223
American Red Cross, 44, 703, 1255,
1456
American Society of Public Adminis-
trators, 190
Americans for a Democratic Society,
206
Americans for Democratic Action, 213
Amundson, Tobias, sheriff, 649
Anahuac Society, 487, 499, 529
Anaya, Joseph E., businessman, 470
Andersen, Elmer L., governor, 129,
147, 247
Andersen, Louise Hansen, secretary,
1227
Andersen, Philip, maintenance man,
1228
Anderson, Adolph, conservationist,
412
Anderson, Alberta Ihm (Mrs. Errol),
farmer, 654
Anderson, Andrew M., fisherman, 550
Anderson, Anna, reminiscences, 650
Anderson, Bergit I., teacher, 352,
391
Anderson, Carl, reminiscences, 651
Anderson, Carl Axel, teacher, 1229
Anderson, Charles L., farmer, 1123
Anderson, Clyde Elmer, governor,
127, 129, 248, 979
Anderson, Edith Seger, Westbrook
resident, 652
Anderson, Emil, county commissioner,
653
Anderson, Ernest J., state legisla-
tor, 980
Anderson, Errol, farmer, 654
Anderson, Eugene, educator, 1315
Anderson, Eugenie Moore (Mrs. John
Pierce), ambassador, 122, 160
Anderson, Helen Anderson (Mrs. Har-
vey), teacher, 655
Anderson, Irvin N., state legisla-
tor, 233

GAARENSTROOM, CHRISTIAN FREDERICK, attorney, 999
Gaarenstroom, Conrad F., attorney, 999
Gade, Florence, housewife, 744
Gaida, Larry, service station operator, 745
Gale, Elsie Bergman, housewife, 1254
Gallagher, Justice Henry M., 228, 231
Gallagher, Justice Thomas F., 228
Galván, Alfonso, reminiscences, 487
Galvin, Sister Eucharista, educator, 597
Galvín, George, labor organizer, 488
Gammons, Earl H., radio station manager, 33
García, Angel, businessman, 489
García, María (Mrs. Angel), businesswoman, 489
Garmers, Herman, Star Island resident, 1349
Garmers, Paul Anton, Star Island resident, 1349
Garrity, James A., judge, 746
Garrity, James E., judge, 746
Gartner, David, political aide, 180
Gary, steel plant, 260, 264
Gates, Frederic, political aide, 181
Gaugen, Rev. James, 1194
Gavin, Emmet J., packinghouse employee, 747
Gawboy, Helmi Jarvinen, teacher, 345
Gawboy, Robert, Ojibway medicine man, 748
Gawlick, John A., Sr., printer, 587
Gaylord, Margaret Grannis, Duluth resident, 749
Gaylord, Paul, photographer, 749
Gelbman, James, adminstrator, 1134
Geldman, Max, political activist, 34
Gemmell, agriculture, 371
General Minnesota Utilities Co., 647
Genis, Sander D., labor leader, 450
Geraghty, H. J., grocer, 309
German Presbyterian Synod of the West, 668, 687, 693, 721, 729, 730, 781, 784, 794, 861, 955
Germans, immigrants, 1, 81, 463, 686, 687, 710, 808, 809, 874, 885, 955; settlements, 1187, 1188
Gesell, Raymond L., state legislator, 1000
Ghent, ethnic groups, 97, 111
Gibbs, Adina Adams, reminiscences, 265
Giddens, Paul H., educator, 598
Gilbertson, Addie Daniels, businesswoman, 1106
Gilbertson, Selma Falla (Mrs. Gerhard), Montevideo resident, 750
Gillson, Mrs. Harold, reminiscences, 1183
Glasrud, Clarence, professor, 751, 1255
Glass Block Department Store, Duluth, 1055
Glendive, Mont., Scandinavians, 1276
Glendorado Lutheran Church, 1168, 1190
Glyndon, 1466
Godfrey, Charles H., land commissioner, 35, 752
Godfrey Boat Co., 35
Godin, Lars A., reminiscences, 554

Goede, William C., reminiscences, 1078
Goetz, James B., lieutenant-governor, 238
Goff, Robert E., political aide, 128
Gold, Donald W., insurance broker, 1079
Goldberg, Blanche Halpern (Mrs. Isadore), reminiscences, 429
Goldberg, Isadore, physician, 430
Goldberg, Marjorie Cornelison, reminiscences, 1407
Golden Cream Dairy, Morris, 846
Goldish, Harry, businessman, 555
Gómez, Casimira (Mrs. Francisco), reminiscences, 490
Gómez, Francisco, reminiscences, 490
Gonsález, Ben P., businessman, 491
González, Gregory L., accountant, 492
Goodhue, Horace, teacher, 36
Goodhue, James M., journalist, 36
Goodyear, Walter H., railroad, manager, 580
Gopher Ordnance Plant, Rosemount, land taken, 295, 297, 311, 313, 321, 323, 332; employees, 299, 320, 335; appeal of settlement, 314, 317
Gorman, Alberta Engebretson, restaurant operator, 753
Goulet, Maria Boutain, housewife, 1107
Graham, Charles A., governor's aide, 129
Gramm, Margaret, Stevens County resident, 754
Gran, Frank Walter, farmer, 37, 38
Gran-A-Stone, Inc., Waite Park, 809
Grand Opera House, Minneapolis, 87
Grand Portage Indian Reservation, 61, 94
Grand Rapids, homesteading, 353
Granger, Stephen, educator, 755
Graning, Bernard E., reminiscences, 1190
Granskou, Clemens M., educator, 599
Grant County, law enforcement, 649
Graphic Arts International Union, Local 229, 592
Grass Roots Fund for Farmers, 985
Graven, David L., attorney, 149
Graves, Peter, Indian leader, 39
Great Northern Railway Co., 361, 372, 856
Greeks, immigrants, 931
Green, Maude Little, teacher, 756
Green, William, conservationist, 417
Greenberg, Morris, attorney, 613
Greene, Florence Glick, reminiscences, 431
Greenman, Frances Cranmer, artist, 40
Gregerson, Anna Ulen (Mrs. Obert), farmer, 1256
Gregerson, Obert, farmer, 1256
Grengs, Aloysius, carpenter, 41
Griffin, Carl H., Jr., reporter, 1394
Griffiths, Violet Williams, labor leader, 1428
Grittner, Karl F., state legislator, 239
Gronner, John, farmer, 1257

Gronskei, Annie Nesset (Mrs. Olav), reminiscences, 1213
Grove Lake Academy, Sauk Centre, 17
Grover, Donovan, mail carrier, 757
Gruber, Max, 51
Gruenes, David, state legislator, 1001
Grussing, George P., state legislator, 1002
Guckeen, Pentecostal church, 491
Guerrero, Manuel P., professor, 493
Guice, Mary Ellen Cowling, Star Island resident, 1350
Gull River Lumber Co., 966
Gunderson, Emma Bakken (Mrs. George), Minneota resident, 758
Gustafson, Daisy, reminiscences, 1176
Gustafson, Earl B., state legislator, 240
Gustafson, William, reminiscences, 1176
Gustavus Adolphus College, St. Peter, 596, 1128
Gutaw, Warren, businessman, 1003
Guthrie, Mike, forester, 42
Guttarnsson, Rev. Stephen, 759
Guzmán, Dolores Rodríguez (Mrs. Francisco), reminiscences, 494
Guzmán, Francisco, reminiscences, 494
Guzmán, Frank C., migrant organizer, 495

HAALA, RAYMOND S., printer, 760
Haecker, Letitia Foster, Star Island resident, 1351
Hafeman, William, canoe builder, 43
Hagen, Harold, farmer, 1135
Hagg, Harold T., professor, 761
Haik, Raymond, conservationist, 418
Haines, Richard, artist, 544
Hall, Gus, Communist party leader, 609
Hall, S. Edward, barber, 266
Hallie Q. Brown Community Center, St. Paul, 266, 287
Halverson, Hazel L., reminiscences, 1190
Halverson, Leila, nurse, 44
Halvorson, Anna, Red Cross worker, 1450
Hamilton, Arthur, businessman, 762
Hamilton, Mildred Engen (Mrs. Arthur), organist, 763
Hamilton, Steven, student, 1395
Hamline University, St. Paul, 114, 458, 598
Hammett, Anne G., teacher, 764
Hansen, Ernie H., mail carrier, 765
Hansen, Pierre T., farmer, 766
Hanson, Anna Melin, teacher, 1258
Hanson, Arthur E., 1260
Hanson, Bert, farmer, 767
Hanson, Clara Lee, nurse, 1259
Hanson, Ethel Ellingson, farmer, 768
Hanson, Herbert M., store owner, 769
Hanson, Laura Wolfe, farmer, 770
Hanson, Marie Hugelen (Mrs. Arthur), housewife, 1260
Hanson, Maybelle (Mrs. Allen), reminiscences, 364
Hanson, N. P., county agent, 1080

966, 1120, 1261; on Indian lands, 39; logging camps, 60, 362, 393. See also individual companies

Lumberjacks, life described, 68, 74, 359

Lund, Clarence, farmer, 1087

Lund, Curtis Joseph, Star Island resident, 1359

Lund, Guy H., salesman, 1088

Luther, Sara L. F. (Sally), state legislator, 139

Luther Hospital Training School, St. Paul, 44

Luther League, 1190

Luther Theological Seminary, St. Paul, 338, 593, 599, 605

Lutheran Children's Home, Twin Valley, 1281

Lutheran church, 605, 828, 1260, 1275; changes, 667, 1168; congregations, 719, 763, 807, 862, 887, 925, 1028, 1190, 1193, 1195, 1196, 1283. See also individual communities

Lutsen, homesteading, 269

Lutsen Resort, Lutsen, 80

Lyght, Norman Paul, reminiscences, 269

Lynch, Rev. Alden, 1178

Lynd, businesses, 858

Lynn, James Richard, janitor, 270

Lyon, Mabel Esther, Dakota County resident, 316

Lyon County, agriculture, 688, 889; rural life described, 758, 844, 1095

Lyons, Lynn Christoffer, administrator, 1309

Lyons, Vera Nissenson, teacher, 433

Lysfjord, Charles, farm manager, 832

MACALESTER COLLEGE, St. Paul, student life, 5, 30, 507; faculty, 203, 603; president, 607

McBride, Mary Munger, Star Island resident, 1360

McBrien, John J., attorney, 317

McBrien, Ruth (Mrs. John), Farmington resident, 317

McCann, Rev. Edward, 72

McCarthyism, 635-642, 1003. See also Communist party

McClure, Marilyn E., social worker, 507

MacDonald, Harriet, teacher, 833

McDonough, Andrew, Rosemount resident, 318

McEvoy, James, co-op employee, 73

McGee, Billy, guide, 83

McGinn, George, lumberjack, 74

McGough, Mary, teacher, 75

McGovern, George S., Senator, 182, 200, 225

McGrath, Thomas, reminiscences, 1013

Mack, John, attorney, 834

McLaughlin, Michael, political aide, 154

McMillen, Patrick, cook, 1062

McPherson, Harry C., Jr., attorney, 201

Magloughlin, Nancy Molander, businesswoman, 1459

Mahnomen High School, Mahnomen, 897

Mahowald, Robert A., state legislator, 1014

Mail service, rural, 765, 884, 941; air-mail contracts, 1206

Maki, Emily Starkman, reminiscences, 348

Maki, Martin, labor leader, 621

Maki, Toini (Mrs. Martin), reminiscences, 621

Mallard, Manley, Crookston resident, 1460

Malm, Winifred Walsh, reminiscences, 327

Manfred, Frederick F., author, 199

Mankato, 706, 833, 963

Mankato Normal School, 963

Mankato State University, 831, 963

Mann, Ruth Hankenson, reminiscences, 1412

Mannausau, Joseph, farmer and logger, 385

Mannausau, Louis, farmer, 386

Manthey, Dolores, printer, 835

Marc, John, logger, 836

Marc, Peder, logger, 836

Marget, Manny, radio announcer, 1218

Marks, Tina Leonard, farmer, 837

Marsh, Audrey Olson, Star Island resident, 1361

Marshall, Fred, Congressman, 140

Marshall, Julia N., civic leader, 1433

Marshall, 643, 1316

Marsteller, James Lee, Star Island resident, 1362

Martin, Charles, reminiscences, 1179

Martin, E. Ross, Star Island resident, 1363

Martin, Florence Ebeling (Mrs. C. Paul), reminiscences, 838

Martin, Jerry, Ojibway Indian, 69

Martin, Katherine, Ojibway Indian, 69

Martin, Mary Bates, Star Island resident, 1363

Martin, Philip O., company manager, 1146

Martin, Richard, school board member, 839

Martin, Rosemary, reminiscences, 579

Martin, Shirley Wise, Star Island resident, 1364

Martínez, Angelita Reyes (Mrs. Roman), reminiscences, 504

Martínez, Luis, automobile dealer, 505

Martínez, Tony, businessman, 506

Martinson, Henry R., reminiscences, 1015

Marvin, Margaret, housewife, 1016

Masnari, Beatrice Massari, reminiscences, 70

Mathisen, Sverre, fisherman, 566

Matson, George A., farmer, 840

Mattala, Emma, reminiscences, 71

Mattice, Anne Anderson (Peggy), tavern owner, 387

Mattison, Raymond E., Star Island resident, 1365

Mattson, Axel, farmer, 841

Mattson, Hjalmer, fisherman, 1117

Mattson, Milton, East Beaver Bay resident, 567

Maughan, William E., Morris resident, 842

Maupins, William F., Jr., laboratory supervisor, 271

Maurices, Inc., Duluth, 1436

Maxwell, Stephen L., judge, 272

Mayberg, William, grocer, 434

Meade, F. J., agricultural agent, 843

Meat-packing industry, 449, 480. See also individual firms

Medicine, nursing, 44, 50, 845, 897, 922, 972, 1290; history, 344, 913, 1447; home remedies, 349, 485, 502, 782; training and practice, 424, 430, 685, 876, 883, 913, 1419; Indian, 680, 748; in rural areas, 685, 723, 816, 907, 908, 922, 938, 968

Medina, Louis G., reminiscences, 508

Meehl, Percy, judge, 1089

Meili, Olive, reminiscences, 637

Mejía, Matilde (Sister Marta), 509

Melberg, Anna Overland, housewife, 1278

Melby, William, farmer, 1279

Melby, history, 655

Méndez, Jesús A., educator, 510

Méndez, Ramona (Mrs. Jesús), reminiscences, 510

Mercado, Jesús (John), police officer, 511

Merrill, Joseph, farmer, 76

Merritt, Glen, reminiscences, 555

Methodist church, 72, 283, 1171, 1184, 1194. See also individual communities

Metropolitan State University, St. Paul, 78

Mexican Americans, acculturation, 469, 486, 496, 498, 520, 522, 531; religion, 471, 472, 497, 518, 522; immigrants, 471, 473, 474, 480-483, 485-487, 490, 494, 497-499, 501, 502, 508, 510-513, 518-520, 522, 525, 529, 533; customs, 472, 485, 487, 489, 490, 494, 497, 504, 510, 515, 516, 518, 522, 526, 530, 539; businesses, 476, 506, 523, 531; celebrations, 497, 498, 515, 518, 522; sports, 528

Meyer, Ulrich, farmer, 844

Meyers, Mildred Young, nurse, 845

Mi Cultura, St. Paul, day-care center, 469

Mickelsen, (Wilhelm) Herman, fisherman, 568

Mickelsen, Mickel, fisherman, 568

Micklish, Willard, dairy manager, 846

Midland Cooperative Wholesale, 20, 73

Mies, Santa, reminiscences, 512

Migrant Education Program, Crookston, 510

Migrant Health Services, Inc., 527, 540

Migrant labor, see Agriculture

Migrants in Action, Inc., St. Paul, 495

Mihelcic, Father Frank, 77

Mikulewicz, Ruth Velzora Benson, teacher, 319

Milaca, history, 709, 860

Miletich, Eli J., labor leader, 1063

Miller, Charlene Jessee, Star Island resident, 1366

Neal, Eva Bell, St. Paul resident, 275

Nehotte, Stephen, labor leader, 207

Nelsen, Marlin B., state legislator, 1019

Nelson, Agnes, teacher, 853

Nelson, Alfred E., Bemidji resident, 854

Nelson, C. David, attorney, 1148

Nelson, Donald, farmer, 855

Nelson, Edward, railroad worker, 856

Nelson, Rev. Ernest G., 1180

Nelson, George U., resort operator, 80

Nelson, Helen Erickson (Mrs. J. Walter), farmer, 1219

Nelson, Herman, farmer, 860

Nelson, J. Walter, farmer, 1219

Nelson, James, farmer, 1149

Nelson, John, resort operator, 388

Nelson, Knute, governor, 138

Nelson, Lucille, reminiscences, 1183

Nelson, Norman, store owner, 1282

Nelson, William, farmer, 1283

Nemzek, John P., police officer, 857

Ness, Ed, reminiscences, 569

Nett Lake, homesteading, 376

Neumaier, John, educator, 81

Nevins, Richard, campaign worker, 209

New Deal, 865, 1003, 1024, 1086, 1096, 1236; legislation, 1025, 1083, 1091, 1092

New Riverside Cafe Collective, 633

New York Mills, 79, 881; homesteading, 71

Newman, Cecil, editor, 274

Newspapers, 36, 45, 125, 265-267, 274, 277, 459, 591, 760, 984, 1085; labor, 110, 585, 588, 1064; ethnic, 877, 1283; student, 1389, 1390, 1394, 1395. See also individual papers

Nicholl, David T., railroad manager, 581

Nichols, Edward, reminiscences, 276

Nicholson, Richard W., businessman, 858

Nicollet County, agriculture, 961

Niehaus, Joseph T., state legislator, 1020

Nier, Alfred Otto Carl, Star Island resident, 1368

Nininger, 13, 62

Nisswa, mayor, 979

Nixon, Richard M., President, 131

No Powerlines, 1149

Nobles County, 838, 861

Noblitt, Harding, professor, 1021

Nolan, Richard M., Congressman, 994, 1022

Nolte, Fred A., reminiscences, 861

Nolte, Orvis, farmer, 1462

Nonpartisan League, 28, 45, 91, 126, 134, 138, 739, 757, 769, 820, 885, 956, 984, 1015, 1032, 1039, 1040, 1078, 1093, 1098; North Dakota, 635, 1323. See also Farmer-Labor party

Nora Lutheran Church, 807

Norgant, Ansel, businessman, 862

Norha, Eino M., reminiscences, 349

Norman, Gertrude Branum (Mrs. Rowland), farmer, 859

Norman, John P., reminiscences, 863

Norman, Rowland, farmer, 859

Norman County, education, 799

North Central Publishing Co., St. Paul, 589

North Dakota, homesteading, 50, 91, 1208, 1238

North Dakota State University, Fargo, 1267

North Shore Freight Lines, Duluth, 568, 575

Northeast Minnesota Historical Center, 967

Northern City National Bank, Duluth, 1430

Northern Natural Gas Co., 309

Northern Pacific Railway Co., 508, 579-584

Northfield, black community, 259

Northwest Airlines, 56

Northwest Bancorporation, 25

Northwest Monitor, black newspaper, 267

Norwegian-American League, 559

Norwegian Bible school, 887

Norwegians, immigrants, 7, 46, 49, 50, 117, 362, 458, 550, 559, 564-566, 568, 570, 574, 577, 649, 663, 773, 788, 792, 972, 1121, 1208, 1223; customs, 764, 771, 780, 807, 811, 828, 869, 880, 895, 951, 1028, 1046, 1170, 1263; settlements, 780, 1290, 1451; language, 887, 950

Nu-Ply Corp., Bemidji, 727, 888

Nursing, see Medicine

Nute, Grace Lee, author, 82

Nyberg, Leonora McCracken (Mrs. Carlton), reminiscences, 864

Nycklemoe, Henry, state legislator, 1023

Nygaard, Karl E., mayor, 1024

Nystrom, William, state legislator, 865, 1025, 1091

OBERG, EINAR J., Star Island resident, 1369

Oberg, Roy, boat captain, 1118

Oberholtzer, Ernest C., conservationist, 83

O'Brien, Sister Antonine, educator, 597

O'Donnell, Gerald J., labor leader, 453

Office of Economic Opportunity, 169

Ogren, Byron, farmer, 1220

Ogren, Irene Iverson (Mrs. Byron), farmer, 1220

Ohman, Edward, reminiscences, 84

Ohman, Olof, discoverer of Kensington rune stone, 37, 38, 84, 121

Oien, Nina Anderson, nurse, 1284

Ojibway (Chippewa) Indians, 29, 39, 61, 94, 105, 343, 675, 953, 974; stories and legends, 52, 69, 83, 748

Okabena, pioneer life, 956

O'Konek, Hazel Johnson (Mrs. Jack), Aitkin County resident, 389

O'Konek, Jack, reminiscences, 389

Old Wonderland Theater, Mankato, 706

Olhoft, Wayne, state legislator, 1150

Oliver, Alice Larson, physician, 1285

Ollila, John, logger, 390

Olsen, Harold J., butcher, 866

Olsen, Wesley, farmer, 867

Olson, Alice Guthrie, teacher, 391

Olson, David E., farmer, 1092

Olson, Donald, powerline opponent, 1151

Olson, Florence Peterson (Mrs. Joseph), reminiscences, 868

Olson, Floyd B., governor, 120, 126, 127, 133, 135, 141, 143, 144, 146, 450, 458, 785, 999, 1034

Olson, Myrtle, teacher, 869

Olson, Ole A., insurance agent, 1223

Olson, Oscar, farmer, 1286

Olson, Peter, architect, 870

Olson, Sigurd F., conservationist, 85

Olson, Tallof, farmer, 1221

Olson, Tina Amanda, teacher, 1222

Olson, William M., farmer, 871

Olstad, Evelyn Larson, administrator, 1310

O'Meara, Walter, author, 358

Onamia, Methodist church, 72

Onnen, Tony, state legislator, 1026

Order of Railway Conductors and Brakemen, 1072

Orendain, Juan C., reminiscences, 86

Orr, homesteading, 361

Orthwein, Charles F., Star Island resident, 1370

Ortonville, agriculture, 701, 1446, 1470; growth, 921

Osakis, history, 1275

Osell, Rev. Robert, 1183

Ostermann, Rev. Victor, 1193

Otterness, Eleanor, social worker, 638

Otterstad, Carl J., railroad worker, 872

Our Lady of Guadalupe Church, St. Paul, 515, 526; parish credit union, 470, 492

Our Lady of Guadalupe Society, St. Paul, 482, 483, 525

Overby, Borghild Anderson (Mrs. Nels), farmer, 1287

Overby, Nels, farmer, 1287

Owens, Rev. David, 1181

PADUA, Catholic church, 1187

Palm, James, school superintendent, 873

Palmer, Benjamin, physician, 51

Palomo, María G. (Mrs. Francisco), factory worker, 519

Pamel, George C., administrator, 590

Pankonin, Minnie Schwanke (Mrs. Charles), farmer, 874

Parker, Charles Asa, theater owner, 87

Parker, Frederick Douglass, editor, 277

Parker, Frederick L., reminiscences, 277

Parks, 3, 136

Parliament, Steve, Cedar-Riverside opponent, 629

Parsons, Edith Burmeister, Redwood Falls resident, 875

Sanderson, Arnold, school principal, 912

Sandstone, prison, 34; Church of Christ, 1189

Santo, Father Vincent J., 1187

Sargeant, Grace, reminiscences, 1173

Satersmoen, Alma, nurse, 913

Saucedo, Catalina (Mrs. Ramedo), accountant, 531

Saucedo, Federico, meat packer, 529

Saucedo, Frederico, reminiscences, 530

Saucedo, Ramedo J., teacher, 531

Saucedo, Rudolph, Jr., reminiscences, 532

Sauer, Philip R., professor, 914

Sauk Centre, 17, 28, 51

Sauk Rapids, 230, 689, 814, 1193

Saunders, Albert C., legislative assistant, 218

Save Lake Superior Assn., 1432

Save Our Countryside, 1142, 1144

Savelkoul, Henry J., state legislator, 246

Schaefer, Beatrice Mundahl, nurse, 1290

Schaeffer, Elaine C., educator, 915

Schanfield, Maurice J., reminiscences, 439

Scharf, John A., administrator, 916

Schmid, George, clerk, 583

Schmidgall, Dora Zeltwanger (Mrs. Floyd), businesswoman, 917

Schmidgall, Floyd, businessman, 917

Schmidt, Irene Powers, farmer, 918

Schmidt, Jerry, fire fighter, 919

Schmidt, Philip S., Star Island resident, 1376

Schneider, Mary McBride, Star Island resident, 1377

Schoen, Gilbert Harry, musician, 325

Schoff, Florence Karp Kunian, reminiscences, 440

Scholta, Veda (Mrs. Norman), Loman resident, 400

Schonberger, George, farmer, 1040

Schools, see Education

Schroeder, Janet Knope, library director, 1438

Schroeder Lumber Co., 572

Schrom, Ed, state legislator, 1041, 1155

Schuiling, John, school superintendent, 920

Schulstad, Christian, farmer, 1291

Schultz, Frank W., labor leader, 456

Schultz, Mildred Shave, farmer, 1466

Schumacher, Sigrid Petersen (Mrs. August), reminiscences, 1224

Schumacher, Wayne, state legislator, 1156

Schumaker, Mary, teacher, 921

Schumann, Marvin C., state legislator, 1042

Schwartz, Edward P., printer, 219, 441

Schwartz, Nicholas E., reminiscences, 1413

Scots, immigrants, 864

Scott, Donald, educator, 1325

Scott, Kathryn Fruegell, nurse, 922

Sears, Roebuck and Co., Redwood Falls, 1079

Security Bank and Trust Co., Owatonna, 145

Selberg, Lois Cornell, administrator, 1399

Senior Citizens Center, Inc., Moorhead, 1310

Senior Citizens Federation, 461

Sentinel Printing Co., Sauk Rapids, 835

Sevareid, Eric, author, 83

Sevenson, Kenneth, government employee, 1401

Seymour, Paul, educator, 1326

Shane, Marion, educator, 1327

Shannon, Bishop James P., 608

Shapiro, Nathan M., businessman, 442

Sheffield-King Milling Co., Faribault, 893

Sheldon, Robert, manager, 1157

Sheran, Justice Robert J., 230, 231

Sherburne, Neil C., labor leader, 457

Sherman, John, professor, 1400

Sherman, Lawrence, 4-H leader, 1311

Sherman, Nettie Hayes, entertainer, 101

Shervey, George M., farm-implement dealer, 1467

Shew, Fern M. Gibbs (Mrs. Adelbert), reminiscences, 923

Shields, James M., government employee, 102

Shieldsville, 72

Shinnick, Anne, teacher, 1111

Shippee, Burrell Warner, Star Island resident, 1378

Ships and shipping, accidents, 900; Great Lakes, 1054

Shore, William B., labor leader, 220

Short, Robert E., politician, 155

Sibley, Marjorie, librarian, 639

Sibley County, agriculture, 1017

Sieling, Louis, farmer, 1158

Silha, Otto A., publisher, 591

Sillers, Douglas H., state legislator, 1043

Silver Line, Inc., Moorhead, 939

Simmons, Maceo, reminiscences, 282

Simms, William, administrator, 221

Simon, Ellen Rafoth, reminiscences, 1414

Simon, Paul, Senator, 222

Simon, William J., teacher, 326

Sinner, Father Richard, 924

Sioux Indians, see Dakota Indians

Sirotiak, John, dairy farmer, 401

Sivertson, Arthur, fisherman, 571, 1119

620 Club, Minneapolis, restaurant, 428, 441

Skoglund, Carl, labor leader, 27

Skov, Helen (Mrs. Ray), Loman resident, 402

Skov, Ray, Loman resident, 402

Skrien, Charlotte Skallet, reminiscences, 925

Slaughter, Edward L., union worker, 1067

Slavs, see Yugoslavs

Sleepy Eye, agriculture, 1028

Slen, Theodor S., state legislator, 144, 1044

Sletto, Josephine Skavanger, farmer, 1468

Sligh, Rev. Tommy, 283

Slovaks, immigrants, 401

Smart, Jesse, logger, 403

Smedley, Walter L., veterinarian, 926

Smith, Clarence M., reminiscences, 572

Smith, Elmer, student, 30

Smith, Glanville, architect, 927

Smith, Marion Story, Star Island resident, 1379

Smith, Nora Walsh, reminiscences, 327

Smith, Ralph, teacher, 928

Smith, Tena Macmillan, reminiscences, 404

Smith, Walter F., logger, 405

Smith, William G. M., Redwood Falls resident, 929

Snader, Rev. Earl, 1189

Snell, Eloise Paradis, government employee, 1312

Soberg, Elvira Larson, teacher, 1469

Soccer, 528

Social life, Twin Cities, 32, 93; church-centered, 576, 645, 955, 1190; southwest Minnesota, 652, 744, 750, 909; rural, 665, 695, 723, 734, 769, 775, 813, 828, 929, 970, 1104-1106, 1108, 1109, 1224

Social welfare, see Welfare

Socialist Workers' party, 27, 29, 46; union activity, 445, 448; North Dakota, 1015

Sokol, Czech organization, 90

Sollie, Allen, labor leader, 458

Sollie, Violet Johnson (Mrs. Allen), attorney, 458

Sommer, Clifford C., banker, 145

Sorby, Oscar, railroad worker, 930

Sorlie, Laurel, administrator, 1313

South Dakota, homesteading, 45, 1223

South Isanti Baptist Church, 1180

South Santiago Lutheran Church, Becker, 1190

Southwest State University, Marshall, 1012, 1315-1327

Spaeth, Eva L. C., 67

Spanish Speaking Cultural Club, 537

Spannaus, Warren R., politician, 156

Spanos, Gust, businessman, 931

Speltz, Alfred, professor, 1202

Spicer, Mary Gravley, reminiscences, 932

Sprint, W. Donald, educator, 933

Sprung, Faith Evers (Mrs. William), farmer, 1470

Sprung, William, farmer, 1470

Stalling, Charles M., reminiscences, 284

Stalling, Geraldine H. (Mrs. Charles), reminiscences, 284

Staples, Hazel E. (Mrs. Kenneth), cook, 406

Stapleton, C. L. (Pat), school superintendent, 934

Star Island, Cass Lake, history, 1328-1388

Starbuck, 737, 792, 968

Stassen, Harold E., governor, 131, 137, 256

State Bank of Slayton, 1101

Steamboats and steamboating, 35, 752

Steamfitters Union, Local 455, 453

Stearns County, history, 964

Stebner, Herman W., salesman, 935, 1191

Twin City Rapid Transit Co., 508, 533
Twist, Rev. Paul, 1173

UHDEN, MARTHA, minister's wife, 955
Ulbrich, Della Jancoski, farmer, 331
Ulen, 801, 1256, 1270
Unique Theater, Mankato, 706
Unitarians, Minneapolis, 336–341, 442
United Boom Workers of America, 465
United Church of Christ, Sandstone, 1189
United Garment Workers Union, 451
United Methodist Church, Mora, 1194
United Packinghouse Workers of America, Local 9, 449, 456, 728
United Power Assn., Elk River, 1141, 1146
U.S. Air Force, 1202
U.S. Army Air Corps, 1206
U.S. Congress, 168, 200; Minnesota members, 139, 140, 164, 177, 249, 257
U.S. Dept. of Agriculture, 164, 178, 179, 226, 250
U.S. Dept. of Health, Education, and Welfare, 202
U.S. Dept. of the Interior, 103
U.S. Dept. of State, secretary, 205
U.S. Marine Corps, military service, 511
U.S. Small Business Administration, 176, 227
United States Steel Corp., 1054; Gary plant, 260, 264, 445, 452, 576
United Transportation Union, 1072
United West End–Citizens Organizations Acting Together, 1428
University of Minnesota, 18, 47, 493, 549, 822, 890; faculty, 11, 162, 179, 185, 197, 493, 850; student life, 86, 145, 440, 458, 600, 601, 608; law school, 144, 161, 229–232; medical school, 195, 424
University of Minnesota–Morris, 678, 755, 793, 816, 846, 933, 965, 1134; faculty, 965, 1140
University of Minnesota Technical College, Crookston, 988
Upham, Warren, 82
Urban League, St. Paul, 266
Urvina, Carlos, metal worker, 533
Urvina, Marcelina R. (Mrs. Carlos), nurse's aide, 533
Utecht, Leo F., prison warden, 109
Utley, Robert Grant, Star Island resident, 1382
Uzzolo, Arthur, businessman, 575

VALDEZ, JOSE A., administrator, 534
Van Dam, Silva, Okabena resident, 956
Vanderpoel, Peter, journalist, 1164
Vandersluis, Charles, author, 911
Van Dyke, Frederick T. (Ted), political aide, 225
Van Evera, Mary Congdon, civic leader, 1440

Van Nevel, Deborah Bot (Mrs. Edward), reminiscences, 957
Van Uden, Beatrice Bot (Mrs. Hubert), reminiscences, 957
Vapaa, Ivor, editor, 110
Variety Club Heart Hospital, Minneapolis, 441
Variety Supply Co., see VSC, Inc.
Vater, Rosema Risser, reminiscences, 1416
Vedders, John F., reminiscences, 1182
Velde, Le Grant, farmer, 700
Venable, C. Paul, businessman, 1205
Vermeersch, Arthur, reminiscences, 111
Vermilion Lake Indian Reservation, 345
Vesta, agriculture, 732
Veterinarians, work described, 681, 926
Victory Tax, 1471
Vietnam War, military service, 790
Vigren, Mary Litchke, reminiscences, 408
Villarreal, Alberto, police officer, 535
Villarreal, Bill, reminiscences, 536
Villarreal, Diana, reminiscences, 537
Virginia and Rainy Lake Lumber Co., 361, 363, 369, 390
Virnala, Rudolph, farmer, 958
Visscher, Gertrude, teacher, 642
Voigt, Emma (Mrs. Gus), cook, 409
Vose, Roy, pilot, 1206
Voyageur's National Park, 83, 136
VSC, Inc., Clara City, 973, 1109

WABA-BOSHO, legendary figure, 69
Wachsman, Lempi Matilda B. B., reminiscences, 350
Wachter, Anna Volkert, farmer, 332
Wadena, Lutheran church, 1195
Wagler, Mary Jane Starr, Star Island resident, 1383
Wagner, Lewis J., union worker, 1072
Wahpeton, N.Dak., growth, 821
Waite Park, history, 935
Waite Park Methodist Church, 935, 1191
Wald, Kenneth, planner, 1165
Waldon, Art, Sr., mail contractor, 1298
Waldow, George A., farmer, 333
Waldow, Ruby Strathern (Mrs. George), farmer, 333
Walker, Archie D., reminiscences, 112
Walker, Harriet Christensen, teacher, 410
Walker, Thomas B., lumberman, 112
Walker, 74, 849
Wallace, DeWitt, publisher, 3
Wallace, W. Glen, alderman, 212
Wallin, Irene Peterson, bank employee, 959
Walmsley, W. Thomas, Star Island resident, 1384
Warfield, Herbert C., Bemidji resident, 960
Warner, Charles, government employee, 632

Waroe, John, ore-boat capatin, 576
Waroe, Lillie Johanna (Mrs. John), reminiscences, 576
Warren, Murray, teacher, 1473
Washburn-Crosby Co., WCCO ownership, 33
Washkish, logging camp, 362
Watergate, political scandal, 732, 844
Waters, Herbert J., administrator, 226
Watkins, Gail, union steward, 942
Watson, Betty Ferguson (Mrs. Chester), reminiscences, 623
Watson, Chester, social worker, 623
Watters, Katherine Pierce, community leader, 1441
WCCO, Minneapolis, radio station, 33, 101
Webster, Polletta Vera Leonard, reminiscences, 288
Weck, A. D., real-estate broker, 1101
Wedin, Elof, artist, 549
Wefald, Knud, Congressman, 1049
Wefald, Magnus, state legislator, 1049
Weiner, Adolph, reminiscences, 1187
Welch, Richard, state legislator, 1050
Welfare, agencies, 1303–1314. See also individual agencies
Wells, Ingrid Kainu, postmistress, 1442
Wells, Thornley, businessman, 1051
Welsh, settlements, 774
Welter, Anna, WCTU officer, 795
Welton, Isabel, reminiscences, 1184
Werthner, Frank, logger, 411
West, Michael, trapper, 113
West Central Education Development Assn., 816, 846
West Central School of Agriculture, Morris, 678, 755, 846
Westby, Mont., ranching, 1227, 1228
Westerholm, Charles, construction worker, 1299
Westerholm, Phoebe, housewife, 1300
Western Appeal (St. Paul), 265, 277
Western Minnesota Threshers Reunion, 1282
Western Union, 950
Westrum, Gladys Peerson, housewife, 1301
Westrum, Lloyd, building engineer, 1302
Wetherill, Fred E., agricultural advisor, 961
Wheaton, 777, 1213
Wheelock, Virginia Orthwein, Star Island resident, 1385
White Earth Indian Reservation, 897, 974
White Iron, homesteading, 348
White Spider, Dakota Indian, 63
Whitefield, Edwin, artist, 51
Whitefish, Johnnie, Ojibway Indian, 83
Whittemore, D. D., physician, 962
Wick, Albin, reminiscences, 577
Wick, Mrs. Albin, reminiscences, 577
Wiecking, Emma, librarian, 963
Wied, Rev. Kurt, 1195
Wier, Hubert M., milling company employee, 1207

Wiesinger, Joseph F., machinist, 463
Wigfield, Robert M., railroad clerk, 584
Wilde, Oscar, actor, 87
Wilhelmy, Rudolph, reminiscences, 334
Wilkes, Donnal, reminiscences, 709
Wilkins, Marjorie, nurse, 289
Willenbring, John Alois, labor organizer, 464, 964
Willford, Gertrude Johnson, reminiscences, 1417
William Mitchell College of Law, St. Paul, 458
Williams, Ralph, professor, 965
Williamson, Arthur S., teacher, 114
Willmar Bank Employees Assn., 834, 942, 959
Willmar State Hospital, 646, 942
Wilsey, Lester A., Sr., businessman, 115
Wilson, Chester S., conservationist, 116
Wilson, George, logger, 966
Wilson, H. Watson, Jr., accountant, 967
Wilson, Hildred Thurow, reminiscences, 1418
Wilson, Sanford, physician, 968
Wilson Co., Albert Lea, strikes, 47, 456
Windey, Henry, farmer, 969
Winn, Carl, labor leader, 465
Winona Airport, fire, 1199
Winona Flying Club, 1204
Winona State College, women's athletic programs, 822
Winona State Normal School, 1403-1418
Wintermote, Barbara Fletcher, Star Island resident, 1386
Winton, 342, 346, 347
Wisener, Sam, school bus driver, 578
Wisocki, Stephen, restaurant owner, 1073
Witcoff, Ralph, Cedar-Riverside opponent, 633
WLAG, Minneapolis, radio station, 33, 101
Woida, Gloria B. (Mrs. Math), farmer, 1166
Woida, Math, farmer, 1166
Wolfe, Elizabeth Smith, Star Island resident, 1387
Wolff, Anna Lee (Mrs. Maurice), Jewish activist, 443
Wolff, Maurice, reminiscences, 443
Wollman, Samuel, Hutterite, 970
Woltman, Marian H. D., journalist, 117
Woman suffrage, 892, 936

Women, 576, 754, 882, 897, 909, 936, 1113; domestic life, 6, 8, 19, 50, 344, 384, 429, 432, 438, 518, 652, 656, 688, 874, 895; artists, 40, 546, 670; in public education, 75, 345, 655, 667, 694, 707, 725, 756, 775, 799, 824, 852, 853, 915, 921, 947, 1104, 1111, 1285, 1292; authors, 82, 89, 677; in higher education, 82, 595, 597, 600, 601, 704, 786, 822; politicians, 122, 131, 139, 152, 192, 209, 440, 458, 1420, 1421, 1424, 1428, 1431-1433, 1435, 1441, 1442; in rural society, 652, 656, 744; status and role, 725, 838, 1299, 1450, 1472; in southwest Minnesota, 750, 903, 923; physicians, 800, 876, 1285, 1419; organizations, 1422, 1426, 1427; in business, 1423, 1425, 1429, 1430, 1434, 1436, 1437; civic leaders, 1438-1440
Women's Air Service Pilots Program, 1448
Women's Christian Temperance Union, Milroy, 795
Women's International League for Peace and Freedom, 635-642
Women's Political Caucus, 1427
Woodruff, Lucille Foster, Star Island resident, 1388
Woodstock, settled, 669
Woolridge, Leroy, pilot, 971
Woolson, Albert, Civil War veteran, 118
Workers Alliance, 623
Works Progress Administration (Work Projects Administration), 34, 102, 653, 661, 682, 987, 1224. See also Federal Emergency Relief Administration, Federal Arts Project
World War I, 44, 720, 861, 905, 945, 1067, 1216, 1226, 1231, 1255, 1263, 1273, 1276, 1278, 1283, 1299; military service, 16, 57, 135, 682, 720, 904, 1229, 1233, 1242, 1264, 1266; anti-German sentiment, 781, 848, 898, 921; agriculture, 889
World War II, 13, 659, 787, 806, 823, 910, 958, 1024, 1177, 1206, 1212, 1273, 1463, 1468, 1471, 1474; role of women, 131, 909, 972, 1450; military service, 429, 430, 502, 826, 827, 935, 1201, 1448, 1458, 1461, 1473; German prisoners, 701, 898, 1446, 1453, 1459, 1470; and agriculture, 722, 1075, 1449, 1464, 1465; and business, 762, 825, 1445, 1454, 1472;

anti-German sentiment, 848, 1462; opposed, 1023, 1447; rationing and black market, 1444, 1445, 1447, 1449, 1454, 1456, 1457, 1467, 1470
World's Fair, 1915, 734
Worthington, growth, 949
Worthington High School, 912
Wright, Boyd A., reminiscences, 290
Wright, Donald Orr, state legislator, 146
Wright, Frank, journalist, 158
Wright, Hanny Lund, nurse, 972
Wright, Helen Dix (Mrs. Kenneth), reminiscences, 119
Wright, Kenneth M., photographer, 119
Wright, Raymond R., labor leader, 466
Writers' Union, 45

YELLOW MEDICINE COUNTY, 645, 700, 733
Yellowstone National Park, 950
Yeovil Colony, 1466
Yock, Gordon A., businessman, 973
Young Communist League, 34, 58. See also Communist party
Young Workers League, 45. See also Communist party
Youngdahl, Luther W., governor, 129, 137, 258
Youngdale, James M., author, 1052
Youngquist, Walter R., banker, 120
Yount, Alby Chadima, Inver Grove Heights resident, 302
Yu, Joyce, Minneapolis resident, 634
Yugoslavs, immigrants, 77, 95, 252

ZALK-JOSEPHS CO., Duluth, 1058
Zamora, Arturo, restaurant owner, 538
Zeck, Otto, curator, 121, 974, 1474
Zeidman, Philip F., attorney, 227
Zellmer, Mildred Knebel (Mrs. Roy), farmer, 335
Zellmer, Roy, Sr., farmer, 335
Zepeda, Antonio, reminiscences, 539
Zepeda, Petra T. (Mrs. Antonio), reminiscences, 539
Zion Lutheran Church, Buffalo, 1196
Zionist movement, 434
Zuehlsdorf, Otto, railroad worker, 975
Zuvekas, Ann, administrator, 540
Zylla, Father Paul, 1197